P9-CEN-865

JAN BROKKEN, who was born in 1949, is one of Holland's most highly regarded writers. He has published novels and short stories as well as travel narratives and literary journalism. His passion for travel influences his fiction and non-fiction alike. *The Rainbird* is his third book about Africa and the first to be translated into English. Jan Brokken lives in Amsterdam.

THE RAINBIRD

A Central African Journey

JAN BROKKEN

Translated by Sam Garrett

LONELY PLANET PUBLICATIONS
Melbourne • Oakland • London • Paris

The Rainbird: A Central African Journey

Published by Lonely Planet Publications
    Head Office: PO Box 617, Hawthorn, Vic 3122, Australia
    Branches: 155 Filbert St, Suite 251, Oakland, CA 94607, USA
                  10 Barley Mow Passage, Chiswick, London W4 4PH, UK
                  71 bis rue du Cardinal Lemoine, 75005 Paris, France

First published as *De regenvogel: Een reis door Equatoriaal Afrika* (Uitgeverij De Arbeiderspers, Amsterdam, 1991)

Published by Lonely Planet Publications, 1997

The translation of this edition was produced with the financial support of the Foundation for the Production and Translation of Dutch Literature, Amsterdam.

Printed by SNP Printing Pte Ltd, Singapore

Cover photograph by James Carmichael, The Image Bank
Author photograph by Klaas Koppe
Map by Marcel Gaston & Andrew Tudor

National Library of Australia Cataloguing in Publication Data

Brokken, Jan C.
[De regenvogel. English]
The rainbird

ISBN 0 86442 469 8.

1. Explorers – Gabon – Biography. 2. Gabon – Discovery and exploration.
I. Title. II. Title: De regenvogel. English.
(Series: Journeys (Hawthorn, Vic.).)

910.92

Text © 1991 Jan Brokken
English-language translation © Sam Garrett 1997
Map © Lonely Planet 1997

All rights reserved. No part of this publication may be reproduced, stored in a retrieval system or transmitted in any form by any means, electronic, mechanical, photocopying, recording or otherwise, except brief extracts for the purpose of review, without the written permission of the publisher and copyright owner.

This is the real Africa, the big Africa of impenetrable forests, fetid swamps and virgin wilderness, of mighty Negro tyrants flabbily enthroned at the confluence of endless rivers.

Louis-Ferdinand Céline,
Journey to the End of the Night

It is the dead man we are going to bury. We think he walks too slowly; we want him to pick up the pace, for the sun is sinking and it won't be long before it disappears behind the horizon.

bwiti dancing song

CONTENTS

| Chapter 1 | *Madame David from Port-Gentil* | 9 |

| Chapter 2 | *I Don't Believe Gorillas Smile* | 35 |

| Chapter 3 | *The Hidden River & King Omar's Pretty Little Train* | 81 |

| Chapter 4 | *Men and Other Loneliness* | 122 |

| Chapter 5 | *The Count and the Bastard* | 148 |

| Chapter 6 | *Ibinga or the Wind* | 210 |

| Sources | | 280 |

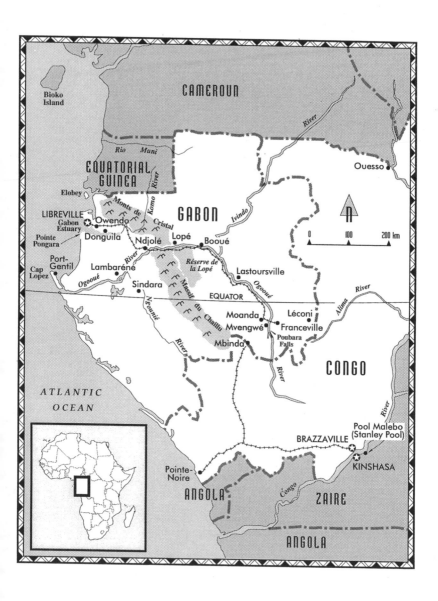

CHAPTER 1

Madame David from Port-Gentil

THE FIRST man I ever knew from Libreville never existed. His name was Joseph Timar. He was young and respectable. Too respectable for a town at the edge of the jungle.

Timar arrived in Africa in the early years of the Depression. The ship that had taken three weeks to bring him to within half a degree of the Equator anchored miles off the coast; a motor launch brought him ashore.

From the sea, Libreville in the early 1930s was little more than a smudge amid steaming greenery. A few houses, a couple of government buildings, a seaside promenade of red cinder lined with palms, a trading post every few hundred meters and, exposed to the wind, a native marketplace. Directly behind this tuft of civilization towered the dull green wall, the visitor's first glimpse of the impregnable jungle.

No one was waiting for Timar, no one inspected his bags. He walked along the concrete pier and flagged down a truck that brought him straight to the Central, the only hotel in town. Its five rooms were empty most of the year. When the lumberjacks came down to the coast on business they ate and drank at the Central. But when bedtime came they would cross the street, stagger into a hut, slip the man of the house a few francs, shoo him away and crawl onto the mat beside his wife. Newcomers stayed at the Central, but only until they adopted the lumberjacks' habits.

Timar was from La Rochelle. At the age of twenty-three he believed what innumerable young Europeans had believed before him: that he could make it in the wilderness by putting his shoulder to the wheel. He wasn't afraid of jungle diseases, and he hoped to find a respectable way to make money out there, hand over fist. That respectability had been pounded into him: he'd been raised by his mother and an older sister, and they had made him so incredibly respectable that it was to be his undoing.

One of his uncles, a politician, a member of the French senate, had arranged a job for him with a colonial firm. Timar was to take charge of a trading post 100 kilometers from the coast.

The first thing he did was report to his new boss, who greeted him with a shrug. The man knew nothing of his appointment. The trading post to which Timar had been assigned was a ten-hour boat trip from Libreville, up where the river ended, "and for starters, the motorized canoe has a hole in it, and second of all, that post is manned by an old nut who's sworn he'll put a bullet in anyone who tries to take his job. You figure it out for yourself, it's none of my business."

Even before his bags were unpacked, Jo Timar had been sacked, with nothing to show for it; in Gabon, the backwoods of Africa, where the Depression had hit every bit as hard as in Europe, where the extreme humidity made it insalubriously hot, 'feverishly hot, the heat of a hospital ward'.

The next morning, Adèle appeared at his bedside.

She had on a black silk dress, and Timar saw right away that she was wearing nothing underneath. He was startled; he had squirmed out of his pajamas in the middle of the night and was lying naked beneath the mosquito netting. But Adèle, the Central's landlady, with her plump arms and taunting eyes, seemed more amused than shocked.

She asked what he wanted with breakfast – coffee, tea or hot chocolate – then, in the same breath, whether he was used to being woken by his mother back in Europe. The sarcasm wasn't lost on him, but her smile had something tender about it.

He figured she was in her mid-thirties.

She pushed the netting aside and said: "Look, you've been hit." Meaning he'd been bitten by a mosquito, on the chest. She sat down on the edge of the bed, scratched at the bump, and Timar did what came naturally – he took her in his arms.

Only when she had put on her dress and was arranging her hair in the mirror did his amazement subside.

Before leaving the room, she said: "Thomas will bring you your coffee."

Thomas was her Negro servant. Four days later he was murdered. In the Central's courtyard. By Adèle.

With this story in the back of my mind, I stepped out of Libreville airport.

"The Central," I told the taxi driver.

He nodded brusquely, and we took off.

What luck. The Central was still here; I'd be able to sleep in the very room where Timar became acquainted with the almost axiomatic sensuality of Equatorial Africa. And who knows, perhaps I would even be woken first thing by a plump, sandy-haired proprietress wearing nothing but a black silk dress. That's the way it goes with travellers, they build upon each other's experiences. After reading du Chaillu, Brazza journeyed to Gabon and picked up where his predecessor had left off, followed in turn by Mary Kingsley, a Victorian spinster who let herself be tickled by jungle spiders as big as a man's fist, and loved it. Jo Timar was a more prosaic traveller; he wasn't looking for the thrill of the unknown, he was looking for work.

The red cinders he'd encountered on the promenade had disappeared beneath asphalt, the palm trees that had lined the way, creating the fleeting illusion of arrival in some kind of paradise, had been chopped down. But directly above the water hung the moon, a baleful full moon, more orange than white.

A moist, tepid wind blew through the window of the taxi; lush gardens, modern villas and two churches with rusty iron roofs went shooting by. Closer to the center of town, apartment buildings had been thrown up willy-nilly: the city had grown quickly, too quickly for any order to be imposed. That was something else I'd read about: just before Gabon gained independence, oil was discovered off the coast. Production entered full swing in the sixties, and ten years later, while we in Europe spoke glumly of 'the oil crisis' and had to leave our cars at the curb each Sunday, the first Rolls-Royces appeared in the potholed streets of Libreville. Buildings began poking through the line of mango trees.

The taxi turned left at the head offices of Elf Gabon and drove up a rather gentle slope. It all added up, I told myself: the Central had been situated halfway up a hill, around a hundred meters from the sea – too far away to feel the breeze, too close to forget the ships bound for France at the quay. A place to get homesick in, and that went for Adèle as much as it did for Timar: her one desire, as soon as she made her fortune, was to move to the Côte d'Azur and live like a real lady, something she'd never been in Libreville.

The taxi stopped.

A white building with a rounded facade facing seaward. Pillars on the top floor. A pleasant building, more pleasant than I'd imagined. But it wasn't a hotel. The big room at the front where the lumberjacks had drunk their *pastis*, where they had eaten their king-sized steaks and grabbed the billiard cues to play a carom or beat each other's brains in, according to the whim of the moment, that room with masks on the walls had become a dentist's office. The rest of the ground floor was divided into a few shops, while the sign hanging from the eaves on the second floor read: Ministry of Economic and Financial Affairs. And beneath that, in smaller letters: Department of Vocational and Study Grants.

The hotel had gone bankrupt two years ago. Because of the crisis, the taxi driver said.

Crisis?

"Yes sir, oil and the dollar."

His hand traced a curve that suddenly dove far below the dashboard.

He shook his head despondently.

"I didn't know you were looking for a hotel. We don't have any street names or house numbers around here, so when you said the Central, I assumed you wanted to be across from the Central or next to it or something. Anyway, you're not missing much, that hotel wasn't so great, there were never any rooms anyway. They'd say: go sleep across the street."

"In a hut. With one of the . . ."

"No, in the hospital garden. But the garden's not there anymore either."

I climbed out, and the taxi driver waited faithfully. Apartment houses blocked my view of the side and rear of the Central, but between them I discovered a narrow path sealed off by a steel gate; I pulled myself up on the bars and saw, in the white light of the moon, what had once been the hotel courtyard. The walls were cream-colored, just like half a century ago.

There, under one of the side galleries, Adèle had shot her Negro servant because he had demanded money, lots of money, enough for a dowry. That's right, he planned to marry, but his fiancée's family wanted a thousand francs, an impossible sum for a poor devil like him. Providence, however, had come to his assistance: he had seen Adèle leaving Timar's room and, unless she paid up, he was going to tell her husband, Eugène.

Eugène had been a lumberjack too, and with the money he'd saved he had bought the only hotel in Libreville. He knew his wife played around, in fact he had profited from it; if Adèle hadn't gone to bed with the public prosecutor and the police commissioner, he would never have had a chance. After all, he had a criminal record – a few minor offences and one conviction for trafficking in women – and his residence permit had been revoked. He was one of those petty criminals in such oversupply in Gabon, yet he had still been allowed to take over the hotel, liquor license and all, thanks to Adèle. But now he was old and sickly; he had hematuria – blood in his urine, a common affliction among whites who kept drinking heavily in the tropics – and his illness had ultimately made a bitter and jealous man of him.

Adèle could see only one way out, a solution that presented no insurmountable conflict with her conscience: after all, she didn't shoot a person, she shot a Negro; for her, as for most colonials in and around the jungle, that was something completely different. She rid herself of him with two shots, and before she even had time to turn around she bumped into Timar, who had innocently strolled into the courtyard.

But down at the police station he kept his mouth shut. No, he hadn't noticed anything out of the ordinary.

How he longed for Adèle, for her strict-but-tender glance that reminded him of his very first teacher at school, for her plump arms and the heavy odor of her perspiration under the mosquito netting. And she, she thought he had manners, nice neat manners, and soft skin, skin like a woman's.

One month later they went into the jungle together.

Georges Simenon was already a famous writer by the time he decided to go abroad. He owed that fame to the first eighteen Maigrets, which had rolled from his typewriter in less than two years. Yet he was not entirely satisfied with those detective novels. He wrote them for his publisher, his pocketbook, sometimes even for fun; after all, it was a challenge to slap together a book like that in two weeks. But he was still too young to rest on his laurels; he wanted to write a few books that would finally cut some ice. Novels that pulled no punches. Quests into the darkest reaches of the human soul. Novels that would not only make him a famous writer, but a great one as well. To write books like that, he had to go out into the world.

15

Life in Paris was too safe for him, too sheltered. He shared Balzac's opinion that a writer is a perfectly normal man who takes things to extremes. He went out looking for the challenge. Not that he wanted to join the ranks of the literati. Literature with a capital 'L', he felt, was rubbish. As a young man he had read Balzac and Gogol, and had left it at that. He cared nothing for a literary career; he wanted to write, and later he would say that writing was a calling, a calling to misfortune.

By the time Simenon took up his typewriter and set out, he had pretty much learned the tricks of the trade. During the twenties he had dashed off two hundred novels under seventeen different pen names, and even though they were titillating trifles with titles like *Une petite très sensuelle* or *Orgies bourgeoises*, there wasn't much you could teach him about developing a plot. He could give a story atmosphere, pace and excitement with mysterious ease, like a master chef who seasons his dishes almost absentmindedly with pinches of salt, pepper and herbs. But his ambition went further than that. Inside every person was someone else, the naked man, and that was the aspect he wanted to home in on. All he needed was material. That one word or certain situation that would let his imagination kick in, because the naked man, in his pettiness, his baseness, or even in his very defiance, had to be a great deal less predictable than anything a writer could conceive of in the stillness of his study.

So he bid farewell to his mistress, Josephine Baker, and climbed aboard the train. In Constantinople he interviewed Trotsky. That was also part of his plan: not to just lean back lazily and travel, no, but to keep his notepad on his knee and ask pointed questions of celebrities, or of drudges sinking into oblivion. To truly become immersed in other characters, and not be led astray by the exotic or the picturesque – swaying palm trees belong on postcards, not in novels or reportage. To talk with revolutionaries and lumberjacks, with engineers building a railroad straight through the jungle, or with greenhorns heading bright-eyed into the wilderness.

From Turkey he sailed to Egypt, and then flew from Cairo to Equatorial Africa in a monoplane with windows you could roll down like in an old bus, even at an altitude of 2000 meters, although the wind hit you in the face like a sledgehammer. In the Belgian Congo he bought a Fiat and hired a black chauffeur, and in the months that followed drove straight through the French Congo to the coast, where he caught a boat to Gabon. And he went back to being what he had been at first: a reporter.

He wrote six reports for *Voilà*, the illustrated weekly published by Gallimard. Not reports in the usual sense. Articles full of rage. Tirades. One long *J'accuse*. His final article ended with: 'Africa is speaking to you! Indeed, Africa says *merde* to you! And Africa is dead right.'

That didn't go down well in Paris. When Simenon wished to return to the French colonies in Africa in 1936, he was denied a visa by the Minister of the Interior, a socialist minister in Léon Blum's Popular Front. In those days, both Left and Right rallied fraternally around the colonial flag.

Yet Georges Simenon had left for Africa as a largely apolitical writer. His father's early death had forced him to leave school at the age of sixteen. He had gone to work as a police reporter for the local daily in his hometown of Liège, and had made the leap to Paris at the age of twenty-two. There he had written like a man possessed, purely and simply to survive. When he stood up from his typewriter in those days it was to dance the Charleston at the

Jockey Club, to pay a visit to Josephine Baker (the undisputed sex symbol of Paris at the time) or to drop in on a hooker; he went through three a day, and he was married at the time. Sex was one thing for which he was willing to take time out – he equated it with food and drink, one of those things you couldn't do without for long – but he really had no time for politics. Left-wing, right-wing, they were all a bunch of bores as far as he was concerned. He made no bones about having once done a stint as secretary to an extreme right-wing politician; it had helped him keep his head above water, and besides, the man was as amiable as could be.

But in Africa the scales fell from his eyes. Simenon was outraged by what he saw in the colonies, and that outrage was reflected in every line of his reports. Upon arrival in Port-Gentil, the second largest town in Gabon, 150 kilometers south of Libreville, he found a hundred Negro men and women herded together like animals in a shed. They were almost all naked. A petite race, with large frightened eyes. Laborers for shipment to Libreville, natives who had simply been rounded up in the jungle and forced to put their mark on something they didn't understand – a four-year labor contract. It had taken ten days to ship them downriver to the coast, like cattle. They were covered in scars. One was missing two teeth, another a hand, and almost all of them had syphilis. They had never seen the sea, never seen a freighter. They called the ship that would take them to Libreville 'the big canoe'.

It was slave labor, plain and simple. The system was kept running by a couple of stooges back in the jungle, totally degenerate whites. Men without hope. 'You tow the line for two or three years. You watch boats leave without getting too homesick. You stop drinking before you're completely shit-faced. You take care of yourself. And then, one day, you flush your quinine down the toilet and throw away your pith helmet! You understand? Because Africa has nothing to do with you. All the baggage you brought along is useless. All your memories of Europe seem like a bad joke. The truths that applied back there are stupidities down here. Nothing is what it was. The formalities are a sham.'

The men Simenon observed in Port-Gentil 'all have bags under their eyes and the same tentative gestures, as though they're afraid of something. Living in this heat is like living in slow motion, conversations drag. Behind pulled blinds they slouch in their chairs and drink in silence, quarrel because they are ill at ease, and fly into a rage at the slightest provocation. Sometimes they get together and play cards. The baby in the cradle shrieks and vomits and is deathly pale; the doctor advises its mother to take the child back to Europe as quickly as possible, but usually it's too late.'

Simenon pitied those men the way one pities the mentally defective. In the middle of the jungle he came across two whites, a resident and a deputy-resident. Both were married. They lived within 300 meters of each other. The only white men in a village weeks from civilization. But did they have a drink together after work, did their wives get together for coffee? The only visits were those paid by the women after one of them had given birth. After all, considerations of rank could not be ignored! Or the two engineers he came across who were building a railroad straight through the jungle without exchanging a single word, all because one of them had gone to a technical university and the other to a technical college. A tech man and a college grad. Didn't even mumble "Morning" to each other at breakfast. And he was told how lumberjacks had hung a disobedient laborer from a tree by his feet, with his head in a tub of water. While blackie was cooling down, the lumberjacks started playing cards, got caught up in the game and forgot where they'd left him.

And all these little potentates came from pleasant French provincial towns, where they'd let themselves be suckered into coming to the colonies by the poster that hung outside the town hall in every village. A clumsily painted coconut palm, a soldier in a natty uniform and a black woman stripped to the waist, proffering the soldier a heavy breast like some tropical fruit. *Young men, come join the colonial army.* At that sight, what red-blooded farmboy would give a damn about malaria or tropical fever? Whether the young men set sail in the service of the colonial army or of a trading firm was really quite irrelevant: the government campaign saw to it that their conception of life in the tropics was that of a brothel where whites could stroll in and out, free of charge. 'That breast on the poster', Simenon contended, 'is true. I have seen a great many such beautiful breasts in passing. What is not true, is that that breast belongs to us.'

This was, however, something like the self-righteousness of the cat that has swallowed the canary. Simenon definitely had more than just a passing acquaintance with such breasts. In Africa he availed himself of at least one girl a day. But they didn't know that back in Paris. At the government ministries they knew only one word for his reports. *Subversive.*

Simenon was no great social analyst. He let himself be carried away by his outrage. He raved. What they failed to pick up on in Paris, livid as they were, was that his campaign was directed every bit as much against native society. For Simenon, the struggle was not between good and evil; the colonials might be bloodsuckers, but the blacks were no angels either.

'The sadness we are so wont to see in the eyes of blacks is not their sadness at all. It is the sadness of all Africa, of the trees, the rivers, the animals, the sadness that wells up even when viewing this monstrous continent on the map. The whites can't do anything about it, or rather, they fall victim to it; for while the blacks learn to live with this bovine languor, Europeans die of it. The boss, the real boss who cracks the whip, over black or white, animal or plant, is Africa itself. The Africa that suddenly snaps on the lights at six in the morning with that burning sun! The Africa that forbids you to move at certain hours of the day, upon pain of death. The Africa that plunges you without warning, at six in the evening, into feverish darkness. The Africa . . . that crushes everything beneath its weight, under its sheer mass, its mathematical regularity, granting you neither a chance to catch your breath, nor the slightest smidgen of control over your own fate.'

Cannibalism? 'After the black man was forbidden to treat other blacks as tender joints of meat, years went by without them devouring a soul. Then suddenly a native hit upon the absolutely irresistible idea of killing a friend who had scolded him twenty years earlier.'

The palavers, the trials by council, the poisonings, the cannibalism were, in Simenon's eyes, a consequence of the 'horrendous guilelessness of children and childlike peoples'.

It wasn't people who were poisoning each other, it was Africa.

Simenon circled the globe twice within a twelve-year period, with the war as his only interruption; after that he never left home again. He visited Asia, and North and South America. He never hated a continent the way he hated Africa. But when he returned to his home in La Rochelle for a few months in 1934, Africa was the continent he missed.

He had gone in search of the naked man. In the hospital heat of Gabon, no one could keep up appearances for long. He had found what he was looking for.

Simenon used his experiences in his novel *Le coup de lune*, moonstroke, the Gabonese term for tropical delirium. A novel about Jo Timar and Adèle. Characters he had invented.

Or had he?

But of course Madame Saint-Jacques had known the landlady at the Central. Was there anyone in Libreville who hadn't known her? At least, anyone in the old Libreville, the way it was when she arrived in the early sixties.

"Libreville was different then. There was no air conditioning. Life was a lot harder, and a lot less boring. Everyone was miserable in the heat, so we all went looking for company."

Madame Saint-Jacques ran a drapery shop on what had once been the ground floor of the Hotel Central. It was no trouble getting her to talk. She talked, and while she talked she went on cutting off lengths of fabric for a customer who was every bit as French as she. Bordeaux-red velours, something you'd expect in a house in La Rochelle, not here, so close to the Equator.

The landlady? She was quite a character! A tough woman, but really very sweet. Like a mother to the lumberjacks, in every way. She coddled the boys from the interior, a bit too much actually, but then chastity was for colder climes, no? Definitely someone with her own little quirks. But if you wanted to fit in here, you had to pass her inspection first. She put you to the test. And if she liked you, all Libreville liked you. *Une meneuse*, that's what she was, a woman who set the tone, who created a mood.

"The first evening you'd dine at the Central, where you'd meet everyone who was anyone in Libreville. It was your baptism of fire, so to speak. The landlady would lean her elbows on the bar, arms crossed . . ."

. . . the varnished mahogany bar with copper fittings, intended to lend the impression of comfort . . .

"She rang up the tabs on the cash register, and when she brought the check she'd talk to you a little bit. She'd ask: 'How are you doing, love?' or 'Where are you from, love?' The atmosphere was like . . ."

. . . light-colored walls in pastel tints reminiscent of Provence . . .

". . . home, I guess you'd say, like being home again. Fans turning on the ceiling, masks on the walls; the interior was definitely tropical, but something about it was also like where we come from, like the countryside in France. When the Central closed down, some people said: now the French era is really over. They were absolutely right. The Novotels and Sheratons are about oil, the Central was about lumberjacks. But anyway, the landlady couldn't keep going. She gave it up about two or three years ago."

"She must still be alive."

"Somewhere in France, probably."

Could the landlady have been the woman who served as inspiration for the character of Adèle? The woman who had gone upriver with Jo Timar? It hardly seemed possible.

Shortly after the murder in the courtyard, Adèle's husband died. She sold the Central and got Timar's uncle working for her. The politician. The senator. Yes indeed, she had judged correctly, a young man with such good manners had to be well connected. With the assistance of Timar's uncle, Adèle was able to obtain a thirty-year ground lease on a stretch of timberland. *Three* years was the legal limit in those days, and no leases, just loan-deeds. With terms like hers, it had to be possible to put together a fortune, and 'fortune' was the word that drove Adèle.

They took the boat upriver. Halfway up they moored at a village. Adèle went into a hut and began negotiating in a whisper with the headman. She was doing business without Timar. That made him uneasy.

As Adèle was walking across the village marketplace, she picked a banana from a bunch and handed it to Timar. Whites could just take a banana without paying. Timar didn't think that was right. In La Rochelle you couldn't just go to the market and grab a banana. So why do it here? It began to bother him. He really wanted to be a colonial – acting the colonial was the manly thing to do – but this was not the way he had been brought up. It wasn't *comme il faut*. It was unseemly.

Simenon put a great deal of himself into the character of Timar. Jo's exasperation at life along the Equator was Simenon's exasperation. Jo's wide-eyed view of things was the view of the young Simmy, who was only twenty-nine years old when he left for Africa. Jo was the epitome of bourgeois mentality: he wasn't a hero or a go-getter, just a perfectly normal man forced by circumstance to take things to extremes.

Adèle's concession lay deep in the interior. It was a huge operation. Two hundred black laborers. A Greek foreman. Dozens of hectares of ebony, mahogany and okoumé, the giant trees used to make the hard outside layer of plywood. The kind of place that could bring in a fortune, especially with those okoumés.

They had barely settled in, Timar had barely recovered from the dengue fever he'd contracted on the trip upriver – one mosquito bite and your teeth chattered for three days – when they heard that a native had been arrested for murder. In his hut in a village along the river they had found the revolver used to kill the servant at the Central. It began to dawn on Timar. Adèle . . . in that hut . . . all that whispering with the headman.

Timar made her confess. That's right, she'd bribed the headman, he and his son-in-law had been on bad terms for years, and it was the son-in-law who'd been arrested with her revolver. Everything had been arranged. They could be happy together. She only had to take care of a few little details in the capital, and then their problems would be over.

She went down to Libreville in the motorized canoe. A few hours later, Timar followed her in a pirogue with twelve rowers. The men sang in unison. Timar stared at them in disbelief. These were people, not animals, not savages; these were people, with voices, with smiling faces. His head was pounding. Adèle had pinned a murder on a black man. That wasn't nice, that wasn't respectable, things like that weren't done, things like that weren't allowed.

By the time he arrived in Libreville, Adèle had disappeared

without a trace. She was probably in bed with the public prosecutor. It was better to be on the safe side; that had always kept her out of trouble before. The lumberjacks supported her to a man, and told Timar so in no uncertain terms. Don't do anything stupid, pal, she's been like a mother to all of us, she deserves a break. Two pistol shots, an accident, not something a white woman has to pay for. And what about all the pleasure she'd given her customers through the years? Behind the bar, in bed?

The next morning Timar burst into the courtroom. And shouted out his revulsion.

The judges weren't white these days; they drank water instead of whisky and no longer wore khaki shorts or put their feet up on the bench. The blacks no longer stood outside during the trial either, but the commotion in the Palace of Justice was as great as it had been in Timar's day. Screaming, shoving and endless pleas. In *At the Edge of the Primeval Forest*, Dr Albert Schweitzer commented on the phenomenon: every black man is a legal scholar. Deliberations concerning a mere chicken may occupy an entire evening, and palavers run for days on end. 'The Negro cannot conceive of a deed remaining unrequited. In this respect, his thinking is utterly Hegelian.'

The defendant was represented by six lawyers who spoke in torrents, drowning themselves in their own imagery. The defendant himself did little more than groan. When he did say something intelligible, it was to contradict himself. He must have borrowed money from at least half his family, for how else could he have afforded *six* lawyers? It took me more than four hours just to figure out what he was accused of. He was a night watchman. One evening he had given a policeman a black eye. The case was dismissed for lack of evidence.

Sitting in the public gallery, watching this stammering watchman dig himself into a legal grave despite the assistance of half a dozen lawyers, I kept seeing the man who had been accused of the murder Adèle had committed. He had spoken of goats. He was old and had absolutely no idea what he was being tried for. He rattled on for hours in his tribal language, with the interpreter occasionally translating a few sentences into French for the judges. "He's talking about goats, your honor. He says it's his father-in-law's fault. They've been fighting about those goats for years. His wife ran away with a man from another village, so he has a right to a couple of goats as compensation for her unfaithfulness . . ."

Timar could no longer contain himself. He forgot his love for Adèle. He forgot her translucent dress. Her forgot her plump arms and maternal solicitude. He forgot that first hot morning at the Central. He forgot, because he found it monstrous that she would let an old black man, for whom the world consisted of a hut, a river and a few goats, take the blame for a murder. So he levelled an accusing finger at her and screamed: "She did it!"

Two days later the police commissioner put Jo Timar on the boat for France. During the entire trip he kept repeating the same sentence, over and over again. "Africa doesn't exist." Dozens of times, hundreds of times, he repeated that sentence. "Africa doesn't exist."

Timar had been struck by the moon.

In the autumn of 1934, shortly after the publication of *Le coup de lune*, a woman boarded the mailboat in Libreville, bound for France.

As far as she was concerned, the trip took three weeks too many.

Once in Paris, she stormed into the offices of a famous lawyer and slammed a book down on his desk.

"I'm the landlady of the Hotel Central, and this is libel."

By the time Georges Simenon began work on his novel in La Rochelle, he had forgotten the name of the only hotel in Libreville. Searching for a fictitious name, he had summoned up the hotel in his mind's eye. It had been on the southernmost edge of town, almost out in the bush. Calling it the Hotel Central should be safe enough.

But when his lawyer handed him the summons, Simenon discovered just how dumb luck can be. A libel suit. The landlady of the Hotel Central was sueing him.

Simenon's jaw dropped even further when he read the charges. She wasn't sueing him because the book had her liquidating a man, or because he'd said she had pinned the murder on a native. And she wasn't denying that she had regularly gone to bed with figures of authority, nor did she protest at the depiction of her husband as a scoundrel of the first water. No, it was that dress. That black silk dress with nothing underneath. She was furious about that.

"How could Mr Simenon possibly know that I was wearing nothing underneath that dress?" she shouted, to the great amusement of the press, who had swarmed to the Paris courtroom. "He writes that you could see that! Who would believe such a thing? The only way he could know that was if he had seen me take off that dress, if we had made love. But if Mr Simenon claims we did that, then I regard it as a smirch on my reputation. It's libel to insinuate that I go to bed with my hotel guests."

Maître Garçon, Simenon's lawyer, literally laughed the whole thing out of court. All the way from Gabon to Paris because of a translucent dress. The writer himself failed to appear in court. Journalists who asked him for details received evasive answers. Only thirty years later did Simenon confide to his English biographer, Fenton Bresler: "No, I never went to bed with her. If I had, I would tell you."

At the table next to mine sat the American ambassador; the one just beyond that was occupied by a Gabonese cabinet minister, drumming his fingers impatiently on a napkin ring. But the chef and owner of Le Pescadou, a stone's throw from the Hotel Central, remained standing at my table. At my table he could talk about the good old days, and who isn't interested in a bit of nostalgia?

"The Central was an institution." He had never read Simenon's book. "They told me it was better not to." But he knew everything about the Hotel Central.

The last landlady had made her getaway just in time. Her creditors missed the boat. That's how things went during an economic crisis. Small businessmen were regularly pulled out of planes with the engines already revved. Pay first, fly later! If you were cunning enough, you took a motorized canoe to Equatorial Guinea, then escaped through Cameroun. Times were tough all round.

Ten years ago the chef was still serving a hundred and twenty meals a night – now it was down to fewer than sixty. Ten years ago there were twenty-five thousand whites living in Libreville, more than ten per cent of the population – now there were only eight thousand.

"In June, when the summer vacation starts, another two thousand whites are going to leave. The honey jar's been licked clean, the wasps have flown."

But the situation also had its advantages. There were no more traffic jams on the seaside boulevard and the city had become as safe as a provincial town before the war. Ten years ago he had to have a guard with a machine gun posted in front of his restaurant.

"There were armed gangs operating in the city; business was good for the riffraff, too."

The landlady at the Hotel Central, the last one, the one who had bolted and run, had taken over the hotel from the father of Jean-Claude Brouille. Brouille was a celebrity, the first husband of the actress Marina Vlady. Jean-Claude was featured regularly in the weekly *Paris-Match*. When he and Marina split up, he set up Air Gabon 'for the darkies'. He knew everyone in town. No wonder: his father had run the Central for years, after he took over from that other woman.

"Adèle."

"That wasn't her real name. Anyway, she sued that writer for libel."

"She lost."

"What a fuss. Over a book! Anyway, like I said, the Central was the heart and soul of Libreville."

"Of white Libreville."

"That's right, but the whites ran things around here until two or three years ago. This country is so incredibly underpopulated. Less than eight hundred thousand inhabitants, and it's half the size of France. No managerial class, no skilled labor, not even retailers. That's why the whites were allowed to stay on. Nothing has really changed in Gabon for the last fifty years. That's why that Simenon book struck such a familiar chord. They're really down on him around here. He made us look like asses."

After my talk with the chef at Le Pescadou, I learned little more in Libreville. My enquiry into Adèle had ground to a halt. A few weeks later I went to Port-Gentil. There I came upon a pier. A concrete pier off the promenade. Half in ruins. But it still seemed familiar. Could this be where Timar came ashore? No, that was impossible, Timar had disembarked at Libreville. Or had the absentminded Simenon mixed up these locations too?

I went back and re-read his reports. Port-Gentil. 'A road through the sand, a broad ribbon of cement so dazzlingly white that it was impossible to look at without sunglasses. Not a smidgin of shade. You walk. You sweat. You feel the sun burning the top of your skull. And, after five minutes, I begin to wonder if I will arrive in one piece. My vision blurs. I pant, my shirt is soaked, and the heat is so intense that at one point it starts feeling cold, the cold that goes with fever.'

After he'd walked for ten minutes, he found himself standing in front of a café. Tables, chairs, a bar. The sheet-iron roof of the café made it burning hot, even inside.

I walked for ten minutes and found myself in front of a café.

Le Wharf. Sheet-iron roof. Old-fashioned interior.

In this café, Simenon met a young man who had been appointed foreman of a trading post while still in France. He had boarded a ship and, while he was crossing the Atlantic, the trading post had gone bankrupt. So much for his career.

That man became Joseph Timar.

The proprietress was pottering around behind the bar when Simenon arrived. He heard that her husband was on his deathbed. He had hematuria, blood in his urine.

That man became Eugène.

And the proprietress herself? A pretty woman, heavy makeup, a *white silk dress*, and when she stood in the light you could see *her long, naked thighs*.

Adèle.

I went in. In one corner of the dining room, a heavily made-up woman in her early sixties was showing her black servant how to set tables. She was smoking a cigarette in an ivory holder. One hand rested loosely on her left hip. High heels.

"Excuse me, ma'am."

"What'll it be, love?"

"I'm looking for information about a woman who ran this café at one time. A woman in a white silk dress. With . . . with nothing on underneath."

"You mean the one who danced the *java* with the lumberjacks and served a hundred bottles of champagne in one night? Madame David. I bought Le Wharf from her in 1952."

So Madame David had served as the model for Adèle. Not the landlady at the Hotel Central in Libreville. The proprietress of Le Wharf in Port-Gentil.

"One of a kind, she was. If you want to find out more about

her, talk to that man at the bar. You see him? The one slouched over a glass of whisky. That's Mr Drouin. And no need to be so shy, love. You're in Gabon now."

His grandfather had become an official resident of Port-Gentil in 1894. His father had spent his whole life there. And he himself, after roaming the globe and fathering a whole slew of children, had ultimately returned to Gabon.

"The link with this damned patch of jungle runs through my family like a thin red line."

He went on to recount the history of his family, starting in the Carolingian era. It took a while before I could swing the conversation around to Simenon.

He knew *Le coup de lune*, of course.

"It's no masterpiece. Lots of atmosphere, little substance. He made Libreville just another French provincial town. A kind of 'Maigret in the Tropics'. Nice, quite readable, but nothing compared to writers like Paul du Chaillu or Mary Kingsley, for example. The British have a rich colonial literature, the French a very meager one. That's because French readers want to identify with fictitious characters. The British don't."

Maybe he was right. After twelve trips abroad, Simenon finally came to the conclusion that, in the long run, the world was the same everywhere you went. Not exactly what you'd call great empathetic power. But I tried to give Mr Drouin a run for his money. After all, in a single passage, the courtroom scene, Simenon was able to depict two cultures passing like ships in the night. Or, in less than half a page of reportage, to summon up the

33

atmosphere of Port-Gentil.

"His description of Port-Gentil was accurate enough," Mr Drouin said. "Except for one little thing."

He smiled mysteriously, as though holding the clue that would definitively unmask the writer of *Le coup de lune*.

"That sweating."

I didn't get it.

"The 300 meters from the pier to Le Wharf; he never walked it."

A handcar ran back and forth from the pier to Le Wharf. A little narrow-gauge car operated by two Negroes pumping a handle.

The year was 1932. Mr Drouin's father sat drinking his apéritif, as he did every afternoon at a quarter past twelve, when the handcar arrived. Behind the pumping Negroes stood a little man in a pith helmet, a pipe clenched between his teeth. Smack in front of Le Wharf, the pipe-smoker hopped off the handcar, plopped down on a chair and ordered a whisky on the rocks, without even taking the pipe out of his mouth.

Mr Drouin's father, who knew every white man in Port-Gentil, called the proprietress over and asked: "Who is that clown?"

And Madame David, who really did walk around all the time in a translucent white silk dress, said: "Hey, keep your voice down! It's some celebrity from Paris, a detective writer or something, real popular stuff. Try to act a bit decent. Next thing you know, he'll be writing about us."

CHAPTER 2

I Don't Believe Gorillas Smile

D IKO WAS going to take me to the woman who watched gorillas. When we left the camp it was still dark, and wonderfully cool. Diko, so short he could only reach the pedals by perching on the edge of the driver's seat, sat as straight as a ramrod behind the wheel of the jeep. He'd spent years watching over the herd with that rigid bearing typical of his people.

A few days earlier, when he had told me he was from Mali, I had casually asked whether he was a Bellah. A little later he consented to take me to the woman who lived near a colony of gorillas.

"Because you know about the Bellah."

It was pure luck on my part. Out of the thousands of African tribes, I knew no more than twenty, but the Bellah was one of them. I had come across them regularly in Burkina Faso and the Ivory Coast, poor souls who never stayed anywhere too long. Wherever they went, these herdsmen of the Sahel were chased away.

Diko had left of his own accord. Both his children died of starvation during the 1977 drought. He left his wife in the lurch and took off on foot, with Allah as his guide and the hope of a better life as his only baggage. He covered more than 3000 kilometers before finally daring to settle down. That was in the heart of Gabon. After that two-year journey, it had taken another year and a half for the soles of his feet to heal. He found a job as general dogsbody in the camp at the edge of the Réserve de la Lopé and, although he was a foreigner, his herdsman's instinct soon made him familiar with the wildlife in his new surroundings. He could eke out a living here, but life didn't mean much to him anymore. He lived alone.

Diko introduced me to rugged central Gabon. He took me to places where human hands had left no trace, and threw open the door to an Africa I had thought existed only in the yellowed pages of explorers' accounts. He did his best for me, but I wouldn't be content until he'd taken me to that woman. He thought it was a terrible idea; he wanted to protect me from all hardships. I was aware of those hardships, underestimated them perhaps, but believed in any case that we could overcome them together. He took a more pessimistic view, and he felt responsible for me. I couldn't talk him out of that. No one in Gabon had ever recognized him as a Bellah, let alone spoken with any understanding of his people's diaspora; I was the friend sent to him by fate, and he would incur the wrath of both Allah and his forefathers if he failed to protect me. Hence his worried expression as we pulled away from the camp before dawn.

We came to a little river, our first obstacle. It had rained heavily during the night and the current was running fast. Diko examined the riverbed in the glow of the headlights, then hit the gas. The chassis slammed against a flat rock in the middle of the swirling water, the jeep listed over and I got ready to jump out. "Sit down," Diko said. The jeep leaned over even further, then the left wheels touched gravel, Diko punched the gas pedal and the jeep shot up out of the water. Only our feet had got wet.

It wasn't the first time that Diko had demonstrated his skill at the wheel, and as always he remained sitting as stiff as a ramrod on the edge of his seat. As a herdsman, he had learned to keep nature in its place; he peered over the wheel as high as he could to detect the slightest movement in the landscape, and hissed softly when he saw anything unusual.

Just beyond the river a herd of buffalo suddenly appeared in front of us. Blinded by the headlights, the animals remained standing in our path. Light brown buffalo or, as Diko said, yellow. When we drove up closer they tossed their heads, snorted and bounded off into the tall elephant grass.

Darkness was now turning to dawn, and long ribbons of mist hung over the hills. We came upon another herd of twenty or thirty wild buffalo. It was a great stroke of luck to see so many of them up close, and Diko suggested we approach the herd on foot.

He left his rifle in the jeep. The danger was something he knew all about: a few months ago a buffalo had charged an old woman who was hoeing the garden patch behind her hut, killing her on the spot. But Diko didn't take his rifle with him. With a gun in his hand he unconsciously lost his respect for the buffalo, and dropped his guard. Of all the dangers that existed, over-confidence was the one he feared most; that was what he'd told me when I'd started up about the gorillas.

Wet grass lashed at our faces. Clouds of mosquitoes swarmed around us at every step. Acting on Diko's orders, I had put on a khaki-colored shirt with long sleeves; I was grateful to him now. He had prescribed muted colors for a very different reason, however: there was no chance of the primatologist taking us to see the great apes if we showed up wearing white or colored shirts. But although Diko had taken every conceivable precaution (I wasn't even allowed to shave, for the wild animals could smell lather and aftershave from miles away), he *still* didn't believe our expedition would come to any good.

We walked on for 100 meters. The buffalo remained standing, stock-still, heads held high in the wind. Despite all the stories about their lightning-fast charges, I had expected the buffalo of Equatorial Africa, the *Bos brachicheros*, to be something like a clumsy steer. But when we got closer I saw that they were slender, muscular and elegant after all. Like giant deer, was how one old travel report had described them.

One of the buffalo was pawing at the ground with his right front hoof, a sign that he was getting ready to attack. Diko gestured for us to retreat. I wanted to turn around and take off at a run, but Diko whispered that this would panic the buffalo. He kept his gaze levelled on the animals as he stepped back slowly, one foot behind the other. I followed his example, aware of the smell of my own fear.

It was invigorating – especially once we were safely back in the jeep. Diko drove a little way into the grass. About thirty meters from the herd he turned off the engine. A delicate pink glow appeared on the horizon.

Five or six buffalo charged the jeep. With head and horns held forward and low, they came zigzagging at us. Diko turned the key in the ignition. The engine didn't respond. I began to see how you could become addicted to the wilderness: it made you forget the headache left over from the night before, it let the air rush in and dispel your worries, it gave you eyes only for a pair of curved horns.

Just a few meters from the jeep, the buffalo suddenly swerved off.

"They're not really dangerous," said Diko. "Only when they're wounded, or when there's lightning in the air, or when they've eaten certain plants that pep them up like drugs. When they're really out to hurt you, they foam at the mouth. That charge was only a warning."

From a hillock a bit further away, the leader of the herd stood viewing the scene. A black buffalo, a cow. She snorted. The other buffalo withdrew.

"Do we still have to go to the gorillas?" Diko asked.

"Why not?"

"I don't like gorillas."

"Listen, Diko, I want to see them."

"Buffalo are dangerous sometimes. Gorillas are dangerous *all* the time. They attack you from behind and bite through your hamstrings, or your Achilles tendon."

"Like hell they do."

"That's what they say in the village. *The wild man of the jungle.* The intelligence of a human and the strength of a beast."

Reading du Chaillu, I had come across more of these superstitions. Halfway through the last century, or so the story went, gorillas had kidnapped several men from a village. A few days later the men returned, apparently safe and sound, but when they drew closer the villagers saw that the gorillas had torn the nails from their toes and fingers.

Gorillas were widely believed to steal women and girls. I asked Diko whether that story was still current among the locals. He nodded.

"They never kill women. They molest them."

"And you believe that?"

"I say they bite. But you don't believe me. You are a *moutanguani*."

Diko spoke broken French and had adopted a few typical Gabonese words. *Moutanguani* was one of them: it means 'Mr White Man', and implies klutz, nitwit, know-it-all.

Paul Belloni du Chaillu had been responsible for arousing my interest in gorillas. I read his travel accounts in the library of the Artis Zoo in Amsterdam, and halfway through the afternoon found myself hurrying off to the monkey house to be awed by the gorillas. He described them, in moving terms, as monsters. Later, two bibliophile friends presented me with a copy of the 1861 first edition of *Explorations and Adventures in Equatorial Africa*, which they'd happened across in an unlikely looking little bookshop in London. I was thrilled; with that richly illustrated book on my bedside table, the nineteenth century seemed within arm's reach.

Du Chaillu was the first white man to ever come face to face with a gorilla. He hadn't the faintest idea how the erect brute would react, but because he was just a tad more curious than he was afraid, he raised his rifle only when the gorilla had approached to within five meters, beaten its breast twice and roared loudly – 'the most awful noise heard in these African woods', a roar that 'begins with a sharp bark, like an angry dog, then glides into a deep bass roll, which literally and closely resembles the roll of distant thunder along the sky'. Descriptions don't get much more evocative than that, and the Hollywood screen-writers didn't have to change a thing when they copied his reports seventy years later: the gorillas of the Tarzan and King Kong movies are the gorillas of Paul du Chaillu.

Exploration is a thankless task; everyone has seen those films, but these days almost no one has heard of du Chaillu. But when he left the jungle, he left with the conviction that he had made history deep in the heart of Gabon. Ever since the fifth century before Christ, rumors of an ape with a strong resemblance to man, a thick pelt and a terrifying roar had been trickling into the Western world, first by way of Carthage, later from other parts of Africa as well. Du Chaillu was privileged to be able to confirm these rumors with an accurate description of the largest living primate.

Periplus, by the Carthaginian statesman Hanno, contains the first brief eyewitness account of a gorilla; according to du Chaillu, however, Hanno's animal bore all the behavioral ear-marks of a chimpanzee. Fear of the diabolical ape was further stoked by sailors' accounts. In the early eighteenth century, the Dutch sailor Willem Bosman reported being told by a West African that "These apes can speak, but refuse to do so, so as to avoid being put to work." In the course of the eighteenth century, interest shifted to the orangutan of Borneo and Sumatra, thanks to the efforts of the secretary of the scientific academy at Batavia, Baron Friedrich von Wurmb, who had the skeleton of an oran-gutan shipped to Europe. The gorilla remained the great enigma, so in 1861 Anglo-Saxon readers hastened to bookshops to get their hands on a copy of *Explorations and Adventures in Equatorial Africa* and fold out the frontispiece etching of the monster, his genitals covered with a fig leaf to keep Queen

Victoria's female subjects from swooning on the spot.

The times were in du Chaillu's favor, although he himself would have claimed exactly the opposite. His revelation came at the very moment that English clergymen and rationalists were fighting a pitched battle over Charles Darwin's theory of evolution. Du Chaillu not only received a stupendous amount of attention, but actually became party to the debate. That was more than he had bargained for. He had simply written down what he'd seen, and didn't understand why his observations were causing such a hubbub. Furthermore, he was a pious man who didn't doubt the Genesis account for a moment, and who scrupulously pointed out that he had not come across a single creature in Africa that would suggest a link between man and the gorilla. As far as he could tell, humans must belong to a different family altogether, a statement definitively refuted by Darwin when *The Descent of Man* was published in 1871.

Du Chaillu, a manly hunter, had the looks of a ladies' hairdresser. With his frail stature and neatly trimmed little mustache, he didn't appeal much to the public imagination. Perhaps that explains why he never became a hero, despite the massive interest shown by his contemporaries. The thousands of nineteenth-century men and women who saw him speak in public could hardly imagine that this drawing-room figure had covered over 12,000 kilometers on foot, shot more than two thousand birds and a thousand quadrupeds, withstood fifty attacks of fever, swallowed a total of four hundred grams of quinine and eaten out of the same bowls used by Fang cannibals to devour a member of a rival tribe. That he had stopped a gorilla in its tracks with a single shot was far too much for them to swallow. What's more, du Chaillu was modesty itself, and he combined his powers of observation with a simple, clear and lively writing style. This alone was enough to make him suspect in scientific circles. His reports smacked of the adventure novel, and although his colorfully related experiences were interspersed with masses of biological, zoological and ethnological information, many a scholarly gentleman branded him a boastful dreamer. He was too good-natured to parry these often libellous attacks. Only once, when yet another geographical society greeted him with jeers of derision, did he lose his self-control: when someone asked him a sarcastic question, he spat in their face. After this incident, du Chaillu gradually withdrew from public life to peacefully write children's books based on his travels. This was grist to the mill of his opponents; as far as they were concerned, he had been telling fairy tales all along.

But the debate was about more than just primates. In the face of prevailing opinion, du Chaillu spoke of the natives with respect; his opponents wrote this off as yet another indication of his gullible spirit. The harsher the condemnations of the civilized world, the greater became his respect for man in his natural state. In his last children's books, the natives are referred to as 'noble fellows', 'brave men' and 'faithful friends'. Their superstition and often macabre rituals elicited his pity, not his disgust. He would never have made a comment like that of the philosopher Winwood Reade, who found it a waste of time to convert the natives, 'because every Christian Negress remains a whore, and every Christian Negro a thief'. No, du Chaillu viewed the Gabonese as brothers, and hoped that one day they would be freed of their existential fears. It was the selfsame message Dr Albert Schweitzer would spread in the second decade of the next century. For the average nineteenth-century European, however, this was half-baked poppycock. It was only through the explorer Pierre de Brazza, who devoured du Chaillu's books as a young sailor and adopted his humane view of the black population, that he exerted any influence at all on the events of his century. But by then he had started on a new adventure, and was plowing through the snows of Lapland to obliterate the bitter aftertaste of his African years.

Unlike most explorers, Paul Belloni du Chaillu was neither a neurotic nor a dreamer. His interest in Africa arose naturally, not as the result of an unhappy childhood, financial cares, romantic urges or a messianic impulse. His father, a Frenchman who had lived in America for a few years, was one of the first whites to establish a trading post on the Gabonese coast. Paul was not yet seventeen when he left New Orleans to follow him. He spent four years in Gabon, helping his father trade in rubber, ivory and indigo, and learned several of the native languages through his daily contacts with the local merchants. He felt at ease among the M'Pongwe and N'Komi, and when work was finished he would remain in their company and listen to their stories of a mysterious hinterland where no white man had ever set foot. His plan to explore that unknown world germinated slowly. At the age of twenty-one he crossed the ocean, studied biology in the United States, and wangled a grant from two geographical societies to finance his expedition. To stay in the good graces of his financial backers, he became a naturalized American citizen.

Du Chaillu returned to Africa in 1855. During the next four years, with a few native guides and bearers as his only companions, he made three long journeys into the interior. Other explorers took two or three white assistants with them, and used Senegalese bearers at the very least. Du Chaillu relied on the

Gabonese, whose helpfulness, he felt, more than made up for their sometimes unpredictable behavior. The regard was mutual. His bearers called him 'Chally', and were amazed by his talent as a hunter and the ease with which he could make himself understood in various local languages.

A murderous cook once tried to poison him by putting two tablespoons of arsenic in his food, but the tribes generally welcomed him like a king, with volleys of rifle fire in the air, singing and dancing, gigantic bonfires and huge chunks of roasted meat. 'They are only cruel to each other', he wrote in his first book. He joked with an old king who had sold slaves to America, and who thought that the rivers there ran with rum; the king's brother joined in, bemoaning white men's luck at having a God friendly enough to send them rifles and gunpowder from heaven. Du Chaillu refused to sleep with the girls the village chieftains offered him out of courtesy, and deliberately chose the oldest and ugliest women as his cooks and housekeepers (a claim made so emphatically that we might do well to doubt him on this point). Deep in the jungle he sometimes went hungry for days on end, and kept his digestive juices flowing by chewing on bitter seeds. He ate honey that was crawling with worms, for when the wild animals held their cover, honey was almost the only food the jungle had to offer.

He witnessed grisly rituals. A fetish doctor singled out three women, claiming they had caused the death of a young man who in reality had died of fever. Du Chaillu was present when the women were taken to a canoe on the river and beheaded. He was there when a horde of villagers dragged an old wizard to the river and hacked him to pieces, after which his head was split open and his brains allowed to run out and float away downstream.

These ritual murders were preceded by frenzied dancing, for 'even savages cannot kill in cold blood'.

He slept in villages while the inhabitants danced around his hut all night, dancing and screaming and singing for the first white man they had ever seen. He spent a few weeks among the Fang cannibals and laid down to rest his head beneath a tableau of skulls, with the gnawed bones of human arms and legs lying next to his mat. He soon noticed that the Fang also ate fellow villagers who had been killed in hunting accidents, and people from other villages who had died of illnesses, a form of cannibalism he had never encountered elsewhere. He was told even more gruesome stories, which he refused to believe: in a village on the coast, the Fang were rumored to have dug up a recently buried body, chopped it into pieces, then roasted and eaten it. Shortly afterwards an American missionary confirmed the story, saying it was fairly common practice.

Du Chaillu found the Fang 'more cruel than brave'. Like most other tribes in Equatorial Africa, they ambushed their enemies and avoided hand-to-hand combat. Another of their tactics was to attack villages at night; the spoils included women and children, so such raids provided more meat than any war. Du Chaillu was horrified by these customs and didn't sleep a wink at night, for fear the Fang might want to find out if a white man tasted different from a black. Yet he maintained a profound interest in the rituals and customs of the people, and made detailed drawings of their musical instruments, weapons, masks and amulets.

He crossed the range of hills to the south that would later bear his name; he traversed jungles so dark he mistook a chimpanzee for a man, so dense that a machete was useless and he had to follow the paths left by elephants. Thorny branches tore his clothing to shreds, and he arrived in the next village almost as naked as the natives themselves.

He discovered sixty new varieties of birds and stuffed two hundred animals, which he took with him to Europe. He was the first Westerner to meet the Pygmies, and after weeks of searching in the highlands of Ntambounay he finally came across the gorilla, the animal which 'even the leopard of these mountains fears, and which, perhaps, has driven the lion out of this territory; for the king of beasts, so numerous elsewhere in Africa, is never met in the land of the gorilla'.

Diko drove across the high plain, straight through tall grass towards a wooded valley. The blades of grass slapped against the windshield, causing a drizzle of tiny seeds. The path he was following was nowhere to be seen; he could drive here with his eyes closed.

In the valley we crossed yet another river. A muddy path wound through heavy brush, past trees that must have been thirty meters tall. It was still quite dark in the depths of the valley. Diko sniffed. About three minutes later I smelled the strong odor of manure.

"Elephants."

Diko nodded.

Here and there large gaps had been trampled in the bushes, and young trees lay where they had fallen. Black patties more than a meter in diameter lay on the path.

"They must be close," I ventured.

"If they were, you wouldn't smell them."

They had passed this way half an hour ago, he estimated, on their way to a water hole close to the elephant graveyard.

"Graveyard?"

You had to learn to live all over again here. The words might be the same, but a different world lay behind them.

When a sickly old elephant (elephants can live to be much older than a hundred) feels its end approaching, it lets two or three other members of the herd assist it to a swamp. The elephants support the sick and shaky animal between them and, with endless patience, take it to the spot that will be its final resting place. An elephant with a high fever literally blows off steam, and the lukewarm water of the swamp alleviates its suffering. All the members of the herd remain standing around the sick animal, fanning it with their ears, waiting until it sinks from sight. Sometimes it takes days.

"That's pretty impressive."

Diko shrugged. "That's nature."

When Diko first came to Lopé, he had often gone out elephant hunting with the villagers. It was a filthy business. The hunters had barely brought down the first elephant before they cut open its stomach, yanked out the intestines and waded to their hips in the smoking entrails. Three days after the hunt was over they were still eating themselves sick on hundreds of kilos of meat. They ate, vomited and ate again. Amid the smell of vomit the little herdsman from the Sahel couldn't swallow a bite. What's more, he found the boiled meat too slushy.

Diko still went hunting these days. For panthers. He had to, to prove himself to the villagers. They only tolerated him because he killed panthers, or at least chased them away. Most

Gabonese tribes believe that panthers act on behalf of evil spirits. They're the embodiment of vengeance, never choosing their victims at random but coming back again and again to the same village or the same family. They never bother strangers.

Panthers enter villages in the dead of night and steal chickens. Whenever another coop had been plundered, Diko would be ordered to get rid of the animal. He thanked his lucky stars that the predators rarely came into the villages these days. They had a habit of pressing flat against the limb of a tree, hidden among the foliage, and you had to spend hours getting used to the dark before you could make out the glistening of their poisonous green eyes. They would fall on you, just like a python, and pythons were another animal he had no desire to run into. I had no trouble imagining that. Pythons, which can be anywhere from six to nine meters in length, can easily swallow a goat, an antelope or a human being, leaving behind only a long white turd.

"They have a head as big as a sheep's," said Diko.

I shivered. Diko checked my hut each evening for snakes and poisonous spiders: he would carefully lift the pillow from my bed, the place reptiles most like to nestle in, and before giving me the high sign he would finger the sheet at the foot of the bed and suggest that I sleep with my legs wide apart. That made it harder for a python to get you through its gullet.

We drove out of the valley. Before us lay the savanna, behind us woods from which there suddenly came a crashing sound, as though a hurricane were on its way. Diko was startled, I was startled, but most startled of all was the elephant that stepped unsuspectingly out of a dense cluster of trees twenty meters behind us. It was a cow, around three meters high at the shoulder, with a baby trotting along behind her trunk. The elephant flapped her ears, trumpeted (a blast that chilled me to the bone) and stamped her left front foot. The earth shook.

Diko didn't hesitate for a moment. He punched the gas pedal and drove out onto the flats so fast that I lost my footing and was thrown back onto the seat. When I turned around to look, the elephant was gone. The only sign of her was a black cloud of flies, now being harried by a flock of egrets.

"That was an angry elephant," remarked Diko.

He had recognized the cow by the scar down her back. The animal usually took up the chase immediately, running faster than the jeep could go in second gear.

The wildlife was getting wilder all the time.

Since the building of the Transgabonais railroad, which runs along the northern edge of the reserve, poachers had become a plague. They came from the capital and stayed at Lopé. They had heard about the area from their fathers, who were nostalgic about the interior they'd left behind. Inside every Gabonese is a hunter, a slumbering hunter who enjoys the taste of game only when he has killed it himself. In exchange for a big tip and most of the meat, the urbanites could count on the villagers' help; the poachers would make off with the ivory and the spoils of the chase. I spent five days at Lopé and heard rifle fire every night. The reserve – an area sixty kilometers long and thirty kilometers wide – is guarded by two game wardens, and when we actually ran into them one day they reminded me of nothing so much as country policemen on bicycles pedalling along in pursuit of bank robbers in sports cars. They politely touched the visors of their caps and asked whether we had come across any poachers. No, we hadn't, but then they usually work at night.

"When I first came here," Diko told me, "the elephants almost never attacked. But these days they stay in hiding, and if you happen to startle them at a water hole, they come right at you."

And when that happened, they forgot their manners.

The previous night, Diko had introduced me to a boy in Lopé who had gone elephant hunting a few months earlier with his father and two other villagers. To this day, the villagers still hunt in the traditional Pygmy fashion: they rub themselves from head to toe with elephant manure, so the animals can't smell them. The boy was told to climb a tree and warn the men when the elephants were approaching.

They were only a stone's throw from a water hole, so they waited until evening came and it was cool enough for the elephants to leave the woods. They were lucky; a herd showed up before long. The boy whistled, the villagers jumped out of the bushes, crawled under one of the elephants and drove their javelins into the animal's belly. But they didn't stab deeply enough. The elephant took three steps backwards, wrapped its trunk around the boy's father, picked him up and dashed him against a tree. He kept smashing the hunter against the tree until his head flew off, then his arms and legs. Then the elephant dropped the torso and lumbered off.

The boy hadn't gone into the bush since, he just got drunk every night in the only café in Lopé, going over the story again and again, his eyes still filled with horror. And the villagers laughed at him.

Diko was driving through the grass at a smart pace. I braced myself against the bouncing of the jeep. The elephant had truly taken him by surprise, and he saw that as a personal defeat. Nothing, and certainly no approaching danger, was supposed to escape his attention. With elephants, danger almost always comes in the form of females; the constant care for their young makes the cows aggressive. Older cows invariably headed the herd.

"Just like buffalo," he said.

"And just like gorillas?"

"You know nothing. You understand nothing."

The gorilla family is led by a male. He protects his kin, and he bites back. He bites his enemies and cripples them. That made a strong impression on Diko, who never let himself forget that he might one day have to walk back to his homeland.

It was getting light fast. The loveliest moment of the day, Diko said. He stopped at the edge of a valley and turned off the engine. As the sun came up behind the hills, the woods exploded in cacophony. It was as though thousands of birds had woken at the same moment; their whistling and chirping echoed down the valley. Enormous flocks rose from the treetops. An osprey circled above our heads, and ibises croaked 'yonga, yonga'.

A cool morning breeze ruffled the grass on the savanna. Giant butterflies in the brightest of hues drifted along on the wind. The chirping of crickets accompanied the birdsong that filled the valley, yet remained somehow distant and muted, like the windblown sound of a gramophone from a house on the opposite shore.

Diko handed me the binoculars.

The Lopé reserve consists of a few ranges of hills with broad expanses of savanna in between them. Just south of the Ogooué, the hills are as bald and blunt as giant molehills. The area is dominated by Mount Brazza, a 200-meter hill covered in short grass. Further south the hillsides steepen, the jungle rolling over them like a hairy carpet. Further still – I could see this through the binoculars – the various strips of forest merge to form jungle as dense and impenetrable as any in Gabon. That is where the gorillas live.

"Shall we get going?" I suggested.

Diko remained staring straight ahead.

"Are you afraid of the gorillas, or is it Hernandez?"

He acted as if he hadn't heard me.

"Want to bet Hernandez uses blanks?"

He swung around, like he'd been stung by a wasp.

"Real bullets are what he uses. He's crazy like a *moutanguani*, he shoots with real bullets."

"Maybe at poachers. Not at us. Anyway, he knows you, doesn't he?"

"And he told me to stay away from him. He shoots at everybody. 'That goes for you, too, Diko' – that's what he said."

"We can always try."

"Try what? Getting killed? You're as crazy as Hernandez."

"He's just trying to scare everybody away, that's all. They would have arrested him long ago if he wasn't bluffing. He's not a murderer, is he?"

"You don't believe me? Just wait and see!"

Diko started the jeep and drove off, hunched over the wheel as though trying to dodge bullets in advance. It seemed a bit overdone to me, but I had to admit that Hernandez appeared to have a certain magic power; he had succeeded single-handed in scaring almost everyone away from the area. That was more than the game wardens could say.

The woman I was looking for – Caroline, a Scottish primatologist specializing in lowland gorillas – lived more than forty kilometers from Lopé, in a house with a pointed roof, close to the primate colony. Beyond her house, civilization ended. All the paths came to a dead end, and the next 200 kilometers of forest were free of a single hut or village. There, in total isolation, she lived with Hernandez, a Frenchman of Spanish descent.

Hernandez had more respect for the dwindling gorilla population than he had for outsiders. While Caroline was out patiently studying primates, he'd go up to the top floor of his house and keep curiosity-seekers and poachers at bay with a double-barreled shotgun. And he usually skipped the formality of a warning shot.

Bizarre stories were told about Hernandez in the village. He came to Lopé no more than once a week, usually around nightfall. He never spoke a word, except to mutter the occasional threat. Diko said he had more or less forgotten how to talk; coming from Diko, that was even more surprising, for Hernandez had developed a great liking for the herdsman from Mali. When Diko drove by he would run out of the grocery store to wave to him, but nine times out of ten nothing more would come of it. Diko was every bit as afraid of the Frenchman as most of the other villagers, who regarded his determined struggle to save the gorillas from extinction as yet another white man's quirk.

Hernandez intrigued me. His life must be dominated by his obsession with poachers. Everything Diko told me about him reminded me of Dian Fossey, who had studied the last two hundred highland gorillas in Rwanda and whose loathing for poachers, as Belgian doctors in the area later reported, had driven her to inject Pygmies with gorilla feces. She completely lost touch with people, and the punishments to which she subjected the poachers were so degrading that her fight against the illegal hunters finally cost her her life. She was murdered with a machete.

According to her assistant, Kelly Stewart: 'She would torture them. She would whip their balls with stinging nettles, spit on them, kick them, put masks on them and curse them, stuff sleeping pills down their throats. She said she hated doing it, and respected the poachers for being able to live in the forest, but she got into it and liked to do it and felt guilty that she did. She hated them so much. She reduced them to quivering, quaking packages of fear, little guys in rags rolling on the ground and foaming at the mouth.'

For Dian Fossey, gorillas took the place of friends or loved ones. Whenever another gorilla lost a hand or a foot in one of the iron snares the Pygmies set for antelope, then died of gangrene a few weeks later, she took it as a personal loss. Compared to her mania, the shots Hernandez fired were harmless. Yet both reactions must have stemmed from the same kind of tunnel vision. Hernandez's sacred obsession clashed with local custom, he had forgotten how to talk, and he used his rifle to declare his intentions. I would have loved to see him in the vicinity of the gorillas with his wife, who I imagined as a charming – but equally taciturn – den mother. Could it be that they communicated more freely with primates?

"There," Diko gestured.

Sticking out above the forest was a pointed roof.

Diko brought the jeep to a halt and rested his chin on the steering wheel. As he searched the horizon, something intractable crept into his bearing. I had got to within 1000 meters of the dark valley where the gorillas hid in the undergrowth beneath the trees, and I knew I would get no closer. For Diko, this was the outer limit.

"You are my friend," he said quietly. "We are heading into deep shit. I have tried to convince you. You have not listened. You underestimate the danger. I can no longer stand by and watch. I'm sorry, very sorry, but now I must take the lead. That's not easy for me, you're older than I am and I should actually obey you. But I'm doing this for your own good. I beg your forgiveness and I will buy you the next beer."

I couldn't hold it against him. It truly was his affection for me, combined no doubt with an entirely irrational fear, that made him so cautious. He took Hernandez at his word, and he was cowed by the villagers' insistent attribution of invincible powers to the gorillas. During the ten years he had lived at Lopé, he had only once come across a gorilla, a male with a silver patch on its back. The beast immediately stood upright and pounded its chest, without averting its gaze for a moment.

Diko had taken off running.

Paul Belloni du Chaillu stood his ground, but was none the happier for his daring. Financially speaking, everything was going swimmingly. Ten thousand copies of *Explorations and Adventures in Equatorial Africa* had been sold within a two-year period, absolutely unique for the nineteenth century. He seemed to have done what he set out to do. It was not curiosity alone that had driven him into the jungle; he also enjoyed a good cigar and outside Africa chose to stay exclusively in palatial hotels. Deep in the jungle he had regarded the hardships as an investment, as the price of later reward, and that belief had helped to keep him going.

What he would soon lack was the recognition of his peers. *The Times* compared him to La Pérouse, Captain Cook and Columbus, but a host of other critics accused him of inaccuracy. The German explorer Heinrich Barth, himself the author of a yawn-inspiring book about his journey through Central Africa, claimed that the American had never been further inland than a few kilometers from the coast; a zoologist from Boston informed du Chaillu that the new variety of otter he thought he had identified, the *Potamogale velox*, clearly had the pelt of a rodent. The English philosopher William Winwood Reade, the French biologist Alfred Marche and the French geographer the Marquis de Compiègne – all three of whom attempted to retrace du Chaillu's steps – cast further doubts on the veracity of his reports. And the clergy saw du Chaillu as the popularizer of Darwin's insidious ideas, as the man behind the engravings and tall tales that the public simply could not get enough of.

The only support du Chaillu received at first was from the English Arabist, ethnologist and explorer Richard Burton – one of the most famous African explorers of his day, following his search for the sources of the Nile with John Hanning Speke. Burton was deeply impressed by the American's account, and took passage on HMS *Arrogant* in order to cross western Gabon and track down the gorillas of which du Chaillu had spoken. Although he saw only one specimen, and that from a great distance, he did not vent his disappointment on his predecessor.

Richard Burton, later Sir Richard Burton, was as different from du Chaillu as two men could be. He could talk in his sleep in seventeen languages and was fluent in twenty-nine. He had translated the *Arabian Nights* and, disguised as a Muslim, was the first Westerner to enter the forbidden cities of Mecca and

Medina. He was incredibly erudite, unfailingly pedantic, sardonically anti-Christian and unabashedly Negrophobic. The scholar nurtured an equally deep disdain for both the African native ('debauched by the slave trade and by drink, even worse than the Irish') and Victorian prudishness, and combined both hatreds by commenting on a whole slew of salient details concerning the sexual behavior of 'primitive peoples', in order to shock his English public.

His interest in the subject had been awakened by Arabic texts from the eighth century which made mention of the sexual vitality of blacks. Arab women 'of the warmest passions' surrendered themselves to the whims of African slaves, who had the reputation of being able to postpone ejaculation for an hour and repeat the feat twice a night, 'an irresistible attraction'. Burton set out to discover if there was any truth to these rumors. In Somaliland he measured the flaccid penis of a full-grown man (almost fifteen centimeters), but noted that it barely increased in size during erection. He was disappointed; so was his publisher – he only dared to publish Burton's first book on Africa after the explorer's death.

A staunch Darwinist, Burton searched for facts to confirm the naturalist's theories during his travels; he viewed the African jungle as a test laboratory for the theory of the 'survival of the fittest', and neither the gorillas nor the Fang cannibals could be cruel enough to suit him. Only twice did Africa live up to his grim expectations: the first time, when a warrior on the east coast drove a javelin through his cheek and out his jaw; the second, when a crucifixion was held in his honor, to welcome him to Benin.

Burton was a heavy drinker who often fell ill during his

journeys. In fact, he hated travelling, but as a captain in the British Army in India he'd become addicted to adventure and the sexual and alcoholic excesses that were, for him, part and parcel of it. Yet he felt a certain sympathy for the uncomplicated and somewhat bashful young du Chaillu; when the American spat in his detractor's face during that notorious geographical society meeting, Burton stood up and applauded, loudly and demonstratively. The retired captain was happiest when the well-to-do were shocked by his provocations; that was, in fact, the only reason he sided with the American hunter. He never commented on the reliability of du Chaillu's observations – a single gorilla sighting was insufficient grounds for him to rally to the American's side. Burton had hoped to bring a live gorilla back to England himself, but succeeded only in sending back the head and penis of a chimpanzee, preserved in a keg of rum.

Du Chaillu traversed a blank spot on the map. He could not immediately put a name to everything he discovered along the way. Sometimes he was just plain mistaken. But the *Potamogale velox* was in fact a true otter, and André Raponda-Walker, the leading Gabonese historian and writer of the twentieth century, would later praise the extreme accuracy of du Chaillu's observations of various tribal rituals. For the primatologists who went on to study the gorilla, du Chaillu's book remained authoritative, and they endorsed his careful conclusion that the famous chest-pounding was merely an attempt at intimidation. 'The more we use his publications, the more we are impressed by the value of his observations', was the verdict of primate specialists Robert and Ada Yerkes.

Du Chaillu was the victim of armchair explorers, and of colleagues whose reputations he overshadowed. Incensed by the criticism, he began preparing a new expedition aimed primarily at capturing a gorilla and shipping it alive to England, so the skeptical public could see the animal with their own eyes, preferably at the Crystal Palace.

He left London in July 1863, hoping to penetrate far into the jungle, perhaps even to emerge on the other side of the continent. Along with finding the sources of the Nile, this was the dream of almost every African explorer. With enough clothing in his baggage to last five years, the plan seemed feasible. During his first expedition he had run short of footwear; this time he packed seventy-two pairs of Balmoral laced boots with flexible soles and twelve pairs of linen slippers. There were twelve pairs of leggings to protect him from snakebite – Chally was phobic about snakes – and, for his further comfort, an additional twelve pairs of socks, a luxury in the jungle. Add six dozen pairs of trousers, an unspecified number of flannel shirts, around one hundred handkerchiefs to wear inside his Panama hat, a hundred pounds of hard soap and a do-it-yourself pharmacy consisting of seventy-five vials of quinine, ten gallons of castor oil, fifty pounds of Epsom salts, two quarts of the painkilling opiate tincture of laudanum (also useful as a sleeping potion) and small quantities of almost every medicine available at the time, and his personal equipment was complete. His arsenal consisted of twelve rifles, two revolvers and thirty-five thousand bullets: fifteen thousand for himself, twenty thousand for his native helpers to use in target practice before heading into the interior. Finally, he shipped eighteen crates of photographic equipment, enough chemicals to develop ten thousand plates, chronometers, thermometers, sextants, compasses and other instruments, all to knock the bottom out of the criticism that was, without a doubt, hardest for him to bear: that of Heinrich Barth, who claimed that du Chaillu was an adventurer and not a sound scientific researcher. Even in the children's book based on his second journey, *The Country of the Dwarfs*, du Chaillu reserved *three* pages for a precise inventory of the instruments he had shipped to Gabon.

But the expedition itself was a string of disasters.

The canoes bringing his baggage from the schooner to the beach capsized in the surf. All his equipment was lost, and he was forced to wait a full year for new medicines and instruments. Meanwhile, he captured a strapping, full-grown gorilla and put it on board a ship bound for England; the animal refused to eat a thing, turning up its nose even at bananas, and died four days out to sea. Once du Chaillu finally got under way, a smallpox epidemic broke out in the area he was travelling through; hundreds, thousands of natives gave up the ghost. As far as the jungle people were concerned, it could be no fluke that the stranger's arrival coincided with the outbreak of the epidemic: he must have brought evil spirits with him. He met with obstinacy, resistance, sabotage. Despite his precautions – the entire expedition was confined to a quarantine camp – the epidemic reached the guides and bearers. He had to bury many trusted friends. His expedition became associated with death and disaster, and his most faithful assistants grew increasingly demoralized.

In the Ashango region, at the village of Mouaou Kombo, one of du Chaillu's men lost control during the routine palavers concerning the payment for assistance and transport, and killed a villager with his spear. Other explorers would have shrugged off such an incident, but du Chaillu – and this is precisely what makes him so likable – struggled with it for the rest of his life. The villagers drove out the members of the expedition; during the skirmish, du Chaillu was hit by a poisoned arrow. The injury, which came on the heels of an attempted robbery, was the last straw; he, who had always made much of the comradeship shown him by the natives, had barely escaped their vengefulness. He was forced to abandon all his specimens and photographic plates and return helter-skelter to the coast.

The book du Chaillu wrote about this trip, *A Journey to Ashango-Land*, lacks the vitality of his first travel book, and his injured tone makes it as boring as a long-winded lamentation. The reviews it received came as no surprise: in the long run, even a well-meaning chap like du Chaillu couldn't stick it out among the heathens.

After this abortive journey, which lasted three and a half years, du Chaillu never returned to Africa. The five children's books he went on to write, all based on his travel experiences, echo his disappointment. In *Stories of the Gorilla Country*, he informs his young readers: 'I don't believe gorillas ever smile'.

The rest of his days were long and lazy. His interest in women seems to have been limited to animated conversation. As a frequent and welcome guest in the salons of London and New York, he enjoyed upsetting the occasional debutante with anecdotes about gorillas, but he remained single. Sometimes the urge to travel resurfaced, and he would head off to Lapland. At forty degrees below zero he hoped for a definitive recovery from Africa, and for release from the feeling of being misunderstood that he had brought back with him, like a chronic case of malaria, from his years in the tropical rain forest. In 1881 he published the account of his journeys to the north, *The Land of the Midnight*

Sun, but it was stale fare compared to Gabon. Du Chaillu reminds one of nothing so much as a poet who never lives up to his debut: his reputation was based on a single book, written in the twenty-fifth year of his life and based on travels made between the ages of twenty and twenty-four.

Life truly became a drudgery when he reached old age. He learned Russian and moved to St Petersburg. There he died in 1903, at the age of sixty-eight. By then his fame had dwindled almost completely away, and the brief obituaries recalled only the moment when, as the first white man to do so, he had stood face to face with a gorilla 'with a huge chest and great muscular arms', 'with fiercely glaring, large, deep gray eyes and a hellish expression of face', 'like some nightmare vision' that reminded him of the old artists whose depictions of the infernal regions included creatures that were 'half-man, half-beast'.

That was the kind of monster I wanted to see.

Shortly after arriving in Gabon, I rang the doorbell of the hunter who ran the camp at Lopé. He lived in an apartment in Libreville, a strange home for a hunter. He greeted me with big, frightened eyes. Two fans were rumbling in the background; the living room was as cold as ice, while outside his window the sea rippled, a coaster went sailing by and the narrow white beach across the bay lay sparkling in the sun.

The hunter drank his whisky neat, perched on the edge of the couch as though his kidneys were rejecting the alcohol. He seemed to be around sixty, and tired to the bone. He looked up with a start every time I spoke. Yet this was a hunter who had spent years in the bush, whose walls were covered with a huge array of hunting trophies.

I'd heard the story of his life. He had come to Gabon right after the war, just when they had started setting up an electricity network in the colony. For thirty years he worked with a crew of black laborers, building pylons in the jungle. A rifle was basic equipment for that kind of work; he pitched his tent in places where wild animals would come nosing around the flap each night. After work he would down a buffalo or gazelle to roast over the campfire; far from any village, sometimes with nothing but jungle around him for weeks on end, he was completely dependent on wild game for food. He became a hunter of renown, one of the most famous in all Gabon, and when the electricity network was finished there was no need for him to go back to school; he set up camp at the Lopé reserve and started organizing safaris. That was about ten years ago, when the oil boom was at its peak.

He asked me what I wanted to see. I counted off my Wildlife Top Ten.

"If you want gorillas, you have to go to that Scottish girl."

"Scottish?"

"Well, she might be English. She rolls her 'r's' whatever she is. She lives out there on the edge of the world, and studies the things. What do you call someone who does that?"

"A primatologist."

"Sounds impressive. She's the one who does gorillas."

"I'll look her up."

"She'll welcome you with open arms! Now I can guarantee you elephants and buffalo, a few lesser apes, antelope, wild boar, maybe a python – but then we turn tail and run – and a few hundred types of birds."

"I'd like to go down the Ogooué."

"Ogooué my eye! I'm not one for water. We'll see. There are bound to be a few rowers in the village. I know someone with a motorized dugout. Or are you the kind of guy who wants to hear the oarsmen sing?"

He took a quick slug of his whisky and choked.

A young woman came into the room. Her curly hair hung to her shoulders; she had dark brown eyes, a sharply chiselled face and thin lips. There wasn't an ounce of fat on her hips, and she had long, wonderfully muscular legs. These last few details were not the product of an overheated imagination; she was wearing only a thin cotton slip that reached halfway down her thighs and, when she stood in the light, made imagination irrelevant. A second Adèle. She excused herself for her casual appearance; I should have come later in the day, not at siesta time. It was almost five o'clock.

She sat down on a pouf, legs wide apart. She was a good talker, adding emphasis to her words by pitching her body forward. She accompanied the hunter on all his trips, and she showed me photos of herself, in khaki shirt and short pants, standing right next to a herd of elephants. Meanwhile, the hunter had nodded off; I was starting to warm to the adventure.

Monika – as she was called – handled the financial side of things. I had to plonk down a healthy sum of money. A ridiculously huge sum of money, in fact, enough to send a sixty-year-old man to a French health resort for a week. It was the inflation, she said, life had become shockingly expensive. She wasn't kidding. Over the next few weeks I was amazed time and again by the prices: a hotel in the interior cost almost as much as a night in downtown Paris.

We agreed to meet up in three weeks' time; she and the hunter would come down to Lopé from Libreville, giving me enough time to see the eastern and southern parts of the country. Monika promised me a couple of fantastic days, said goodbye with a firm handshake and chuckled at the burbling sounds that were now the only noises coming from the hunter.

They were fantastic days indeed, although we had to make do without the hunter. Monika was waiting for me when I climbed down from the train. With her was a slender little fellow, standing on one leg like a Sahel herdsman, left foot braced against right knee, long staff in hand. He bowed at the waist without bending his back and said: "Diko."

The hunter had fallen ill; in light of the condition I'd found him in, I was hardly surprised. But there was no need to worry; Monika knew the area as well as he did, and with Diko's help everything would turn out fine.

We settled down at one of the tables on the camp patio. The sky was turning a dark red; twenty meters below us the Ogooué clattered over rocks, the water in the rapids shining whitely. A rainbow-colored butterfly landed on my knee and far in the distance the rock badger was sounding its fearful cry. Right away I knew it was one of those unforgettable moments, and Monika beamed at me, as though finally freed of her tuckered-out partner, the hunter.

Dinner came. She couldn't eat a bite. The food was brought by an old woman so tiny she could barely see over the tabletop. Monika sniffed at her plate, then slid it over to me. Diko was repairing the jeep by the light of a petroleum lantern in the yard.

Monika sketched out the next morning's itinerary. She asked

what kind of condition I was in. She felt like taking a hike, seven kilometers or so; walking would do her good, the last few weeks had been rather tiring. She withdrew to her hut before I'd begun my banana flambé.

She sat across from me again at breakfast, with huge bags under her eyes. She'd slept badly; she kept hearing noises, so she'd woken Diko and made him promise to keep watch. But she still didn't sleep a wink. She asked whether I'd heard anything, and when I honestly admitted I hadn't, she said that was only natural; I wasn't afraid, yet. I asked what there was to be afraid of.

"Snakes," she replied quickly, "and, uh . . . those hairy ground spiders that clamp onto you."

It didn't sound very convincing. What was wrong with her?

Monika was a nervous wreck. She called off the hike after only three kilometers, ostensibly because sand fleas had got into her boots. But she'd never taken them off. Back in the jeep she jumped back and forth between the front and back seats, saw huge animals behind every blade of grass and gave Diko a ferocious scolding when he refused to follow her orders blindly. I had to exercise the patience of a therapist to calm her down.

Little by little, I found out what was bothering her.

Monika was a farmer's daughter from the Alsace. Her first husband died when she was just twenty-three. Her second marriage had hit the rocks. She'd read about Gabon in a magazine. Apparently you could earn a fortune there quite easily, and Monika had only one obsession left: money. She put her three children in a boarding school and hopped on a plane to Libreville. It was the first time she'd ever been abroad.

She found a job as an assistant nurse in a charity hospital. It was a filthy job and the pay was poor, barely enough to cover the rent and buy groceries. She took an apartment with an ocean view, and just happened to move in next door to an ageing hunter with an adventuresome life in the jungle behind him, but with too much energy left to simply sit around reminiscing.

Together they made a plan. A camp with nine huts. An airstrip. A monoplane. Two jeeps. A field radio for contact with the capital. Binoculars. It seemed like a sure bet.

Monika lobbied the top officials at the Ministry of Tourism and succeeded in getting a grant. The treasury was well padded with petrodollars at the time, and the watchword in Gabon was 'investment'. Visiting foreign businessmen were desperate to see the interior; the camp filled a gap in the market. Gabon had no intention of becoming a real tourist destination, but the bosses from Elf and Shell who visited the country had to be pampered: 'business tourism' was the official name for it.

While Monika and the hunter were busy building the huts with their own hands, the Transgabonais railroad came through. The camp was now only a seven-hour train ride from the capital, and dignitaries in a hurry could always come in by plane. The infrastructure couldn't have been better.

The money started rolling in. Monika was the perfect hostess; the hunter took care of security. The builders of offshore oil platforms came to Lopé, along with well-to-do Frenchmen from Libreville, the general managers of multinational companies and a great many of Gabon's fifty-odd cabinet ministers. Once in a while Monika was forced to box the ears of some insistent guest eager for the kind of game you didn't find on safari; otherwise, it all went like a dream.

She had grown coarse, it's true. She ate with her elbows on

the table and her legs wide apart. She smacked her lips. She helped herself to the meat first. She butted into conversations. She never laughed without howling, and when a guest proved unable to keep his hands off her tight-fitting khaki pants, she'd knee him where it hurt. Monika had sworn off sex, it was a resolution she'd made in the plane on the way to Libreville; in its place she had substituted a craving for money and the thrill of danger. She ignored the hunter's warnings and approached to within meters of the herds; when a few of the buffalo and elephants were culled each year, Monika was always there. Shouting, shooting, socking people – that had become her life.

Later she turned racist. Blacks, she said, had no feelings: her laundrywoman had lost a child, and the next day she was back at the tub, singing as she worked. It never occurred to her that Africans see death differently, and mourn differently, too. Unfair, unfeeling, unfaithful, those were the words with which she revealed her lack of understanding.

Disappointment had made a racist out of Monika. For as quickly as Gabon had become rich, so it became poor again. The country had lived beyond its means. The whites in the capital began saving their money; the blacks could no longer afford luxurious outings. The flow of clientele dried up.

The little airplane stood rusting in its hangar, its vital parts torn out. Of the cross-country vehicles, only one jeep was still running, despite a leaky radiator. Whenever Monika came down from the capital, she brought two fans with her; the rest of the equipment had been sold. Even the telephone had stopped working years ago. But what had finally beaten Monika and her business partner – for he was nothing more to her than that – was the people's hostility.

The Okanda and Adouma tribes have felt threatened for centuries. Résenzélé, a village elder from Lopé, had a convincing explanation for that fear. Gabonese slaves had originally come from the interior, almost never from the coast. Although the coastal people kept slaves themselves, they didn't sell them to the whites. The slaves for overseas trade, for Brazil and Cuba, were brought to the coast in long caravans from the heart of Gabon, with no Europeans involved. The coastal tribes, as middlemen to the slave trade, made a pretty penny on commission. They profited from the white man's arrival. As coincidence would have it – but was it really coincidence? – their mythology, which was closely allied to their religion, awarded whites a place of honor. The coastal dwellers believed that the ghosts of their dead ancestors had prompted the white man to come to Africa. The spirits had drifted across the ocean and nestled in the whites, where they patiently went to work. The white people were overpowered by an irresistible desire to explore the seas, and unconsciously set course for Africa. In this way the ancestral spirits returned to their former villages, where – in the form of white seafarers – they were welcomed like long-lost family. This belief remained intact for four centuries.

(Du Chaillu also saw a link between the friendliness of the coastal peoples and their religion. In *The Country of the Dwarfs*, he wrote that the N'Komi used the skin of a chimpanzee as a fetish. To them, the chimpanzee with its pale yellowish face was affiliated with white people, while the gorilla with its dark muzzle and black fur was associated with blacks. By revering the skin of a chimpanzee, the N'Komi hoped to lure the white sailors, with their ships full of copper bells, beads and cloth, to their villages.)

When the colonial era began, the coastal peoples were once again better off than the hunters and fishermen of the interior, who were forced to work on concessions under the rubber and lumber companies' reign of terror. Libreville became the seat of government, and although the M'Pongwe and Fang were paid very little for their services as boy, chauffeur or ticket-taker, they at least did not suffer physically from the whims of their white bosses.

"For us," Résenzélé said, "life has always been more cruel and bitter than for the people on the coast. We hoped to finally take things into our own hands after independence. But twenty years later, strangers came again."

It irritated Résenzélé to see jeeps full of city people driving through his area, to know that the World Wildlife Fund kept watch over the elephants, and that other whites were guarding the gorillas like precious gems. "Why don't they leave us alone?" he wondered. What Monika and the hunter had plucked were the bitter fruits of this feeling – that once again the jungle people were the victims of foreign intruders.

It was Diko who heard the rumor that villagers in Lopé were planning to kill the hunter. They were going to take him for a trip on the river, let the canoe capsize in the rapids and deliver a blow to the back of his head. Diko told the hunter, who only shrugged and mumbled something about 'scare tactics'. But a few days later one of the Okanda came up to him and asked: "How would you like to go canoeing on the river?" Deeply shocked, the hunter simply shook his head and said he wasn't fond of water.

Not long afterwards, Diko warned him again: the villagers were planning to poison his food. *Bilongo*; to hear the natives tell it, one out of every two Gabonese dies of it. After that, to be on the safe side, the hunter always brought his own food in from Libreville.

Three weeks before I rang his bell, he had suddenly been unable to get out of bed; his arms and legs were paralyzed. The next day he went into a coma. Monika called the doctor, who treated him for poisoning. Twenty-four hours later he regained consciousness, and after ten days the paralysis had disappeared. Monika watched over him day and night. Still in pain, pain he tried to kill with whisky, he swore never to go back to Lopé; as far as he was concerned, his years in the bush were over.

But Monika didn't give up that easily. Money was still the mainspring of her existence, so she urged him to open the door to customers. I was the first to come along, and Monika had come to Lopé simply because she couldn't refuse the money I was prepared to spend.

Every evening she heard footsteps on the path, every night she asked Diko to stand guard. When she had a plate of food in front of her, she could smell the poison; she couldn't eat at all, and grew thinner with each passing day.

She was worried about the hunter, alone back in the capital. Would he lose consciousness again, would his fever return? There are all sorts of *bilongo*, the most dangerous of which is a poison administered in minute quantities over a period of months or even years. Your body becomes addicted to it; once deprived of the poison, you slowly waste away. She wondered who was out to eliminate the hunter, and why. Had he kept a mistress on the side, then left her in the lurch without financial assistance? That was what had happened to another famous hunter in Gabon, Henri Guizard, and it had taken him six months in a Paris clinic to recover from the paralysis. Or had the hunter ticked off a village elder?

It gnawed at her, it made her furious; the future suddenly had nothing more to offer. She had promised her children a university education, a renovated farm in the French countryside for the summer holidays and a trip to Gabon every winter, to the equatorial paradise where she knew so many cabinet ministers . . .

Monika couldn't stick it out in Lopé. After two days, she went back to Libreville.

I stayed behind with Diko.

Diko remained calm and collected while all this was going on; he had been in more difficult situations back in the Sahel and during his flight south. His opinion of his bosses was something he kept to himself. I asked what he would do if the camp closed down; he shrugged and said he would worry about that when it happened. No, he preferred talking about elephants, rock badgers, civet cats and panthers, and kept silent about the new troubles looming over his life. With Monika's lamentations still ringing in my ears, I longed for quiet as well; together, we decided to make the best of things.

We got up at five every day and returned from our trips around eleven in the morning. After a siesta we would drive back into the reserve, then go into the village in the evening for a beer. Sometimes we were the center of attention; at other times the men at the bar would just stare dourly ahead. They drank a great deal, and sometimes fights broke out for no apparent reason. Except for the night I talked to Résenzélé, I always felt uneasy in the village, and I never had to twist Diko's arm to get him back to camp. I suspected that his boss-lady had made him promise to watch over me like a hawk.

But whenever we drove into the reserve I forgot the villagers, the poison, Monika's hysterical tirades and the hunter's sad fate. I floated along on a sea of light and space, inhaled the fragrance of wild celery and mused about gorillas. Despite the sense of doom hanging over the camp, those animals were on my mind all the time; I wanted to get close to the colony, somehow. Who knows, a young gorilla might lay its arm on my knee in perfect tranquillity – a scene straight out of Dian Fossey's *Gorillas in the Mist*.

Because gorillas aren't the monsters du Chaillu thought they were. It is only to frighten away unfamiliar and possibly dangerous creatures that they stand upright and produce a sound that can be heard up to five kilometers away. On the whole they are introverted, silent, morose. The chimpanzee plays the clown, the gorilla lives a life of solitude. A full-grown gorilla needs twenty to thirty kilos of food a day; a family packs away several hundred kilos of bamboo shoots, wild celery, stinging nettles, berries and nuts every twenty-four hours. The gorillas literally eat their way through the forest, at a rate of some 800 meters a day. They do little else, in other words, but chew, and primatologists are always struck by how slowly they move.

Their Herculean strength, however, is no exaggeration. In his memoirs, the hunter Henri Guizard tells of a gorilla seizing a dog that ran up to it and tearing it in half in a single movement. From Guizard, too, comes the anecdote about the gorilla who snuck up on a sleeping hunter, grabbed his rifle and broke it over its knee.

Du Chaillu once captured a gorilla that was approximately three years old (gorillas in the wild can live to be thirty-five), and it took four grown men to keep the animal under control. Two days later, the gorilla bit through the bamboo bars of its cage; eight men were needed to recapture it.

A gorilla colony consists of a number of 'families', each of which is headed by a male with a silver patch on his back. He leads the group to the best spot for finding food, and is chosen for his competence. This animal usually deals with aggressors as well; he can knock a predator or a hunter unconscious with a single blow of his paw. Yet he never lords it over members of his own family.

Gorillas spend most of their time on the ground, which is the main reason they attack. All other apes, including chimpanzees, flee from danger and make their escape through the trees; gorillas are too heavy for that. The females occasionally pluck food from tall branches and spend the night with their young in a tree, but the males can easily weigh up to two hundred kilos; they build their nest for the night amid the undergrowth.

Stories of gorillas' incredible potency and insatiable sexual appetite are pure fantasy as well. Gorillas mate once a year, and the penis of an adult male is no bigger than a thumb. The females give birth to no more than three or four young during their lives. The only truly remarkable thing about the sexual behavior of gorillas is their style of copulation: they sometimes mate facing each other, taking each other in their arms like humans.

Local lore, though, would still have them ravishing young virgins. Du Chaillu noted that the men of the jungle dried and pulverized the brains of gorillas they'd killed and used the powder in amulets; worn around the neck, the amulets improved their luck at hunting and their success with women. This native superstition would seem to be contagious: white men who have lived long in the interior apparently adopt it without question. Among older European planters, anecdotes concerning the gorilla's unhealthy interest in good-looking women are rife: when the daughter of the house takes her bath, a gorilla supposedly looks through the bathroom window at her, and one evening smashes it open with a roar; thanks to a courageous intervention, usually by the narrator himself, the young girl narrowly escapes being pawed by the ruttish beast. I have heard many such stories in Gabon, and they never fail to entertain. Tales like these somehow belong to the nineteenth century, when du Chaillu could turn a gorilla into a monster and Melville a whale into the embodiment of nature's indomitable power. Science has made life difficult for storytellers.

Most of the people who have studied primates in the wild have been women. It takes years for gorillas to accept the proximity of onlookers, and the work demands a patience that men usually lack. Jane Goodall dedicated her life to the chimpanzees of Tanzania, Biruté Galdikas studied the orangutans of Borneo and Dian Fossey, assisted by Kelly Stewart, made the mountain gorillas of Rwanda world-famous.

All primatologists live at war with poachers. In Gabon, the coastal people regard the flesh of primates as the food of slaves, and would no more think of eating it than they would the meat of snakes, crocodiles or rats; for the inhabitants of the jungle, however, there can be no finer meal. The meat of the primate is red, juicy and tender. And a live gorilla or chimpanzee still commands a great deal of money on the black market, partly because medical science continues to use primates as laboratory animals.

I asked Diko to drive me to Caroline's house once more, and promised him a reward. We left in the early hours of the morning. This time it was drizzling; by the time the jeep arrived at the house with the pointed roof two hours later, we were soaked to the skin. Diko crossed the magic 1000-meter line and saw the hand of Allah in the fact that no bullets were whistling around our ears; I maintained that poor visibility was keeping Hernandez from firing as a matter of course. Whatever the reason, we were both trembling as the jeep rolled the last few meters onto the property.

Diko honked. There was only silence in the yard.

The couple must have already gone into the dark valley, following the gorillas. I wanted to continue on foot. "Fine, go ahead, I'll wait here," Diko said. A few hundred meters along the trail, I realized I was crazy: with no experience, and with a penknife as my only weapon, I was needlessly risking my life. I turned back. At the jeep, Diko gloated that I had now found out for myself how unnerving the jungle could be once you'd disappeared into the greenery. I was shaking, but I blamed it on my wet clothing.

Back at the camp we drank three steaming cups of coffee and swallowed a few aspirins to keep the fever at bay. An hour later the sun broke through and left us reeling from the heat.

It was my last day at the reserve. I already had my train ticket, but I'd have to get up early to make it to Lambaréné in time to catch the weekly riverboat for the coast.

At the end of the day I went down to the river and sat on the little beach there. Behind me rose Mount Brazza, covered in short grass; at my feet the Ogooué clattered over worn rocks. A flock of egrets circled the little island in the middle of the rapids. But I was sick of the whole thing and nothing could cheer me up, not even the colobus monkey, with its white mustache, red eyelids and temples tufted with bright yellow fur, which dropped down from a nearby tree, looked at me, then drank from the river and waggled away calmly on all fours.

I did meet Caroline nevertheless, twenty minutes before my departure, on the platform at Lopé station.

That was all I needed to complete my disappointment.

She and Hernandez were bringing a colleague to the train, someone who had been staying with them for a few days. Caroline was about thirty-eight, with strawberry-blonde hair that fell over her shoulders. She wore wide khaki pants, a grubby T-shirt and sandals. I sized her up as a former hippie, someone who had hitchhiked to Nepal on her own in the late sixties.

Diko pointed her out to me. He walked up to the Scotswoman and said: "This *moutanguani* wants to find out everything about gorillas." I shook Caroline's hand and asked her a few questions, which she answered with a friendly smile. She was extremely sociable.

The reserve is home to eight or nine hundred lowland gorillas (*Gorilla gorilla gorilla*), about which – compared to the *Gorilla gorilla beringei* of the mountains of Rwanda – very little is known. The mountain gorillas Dian Fossey studied have gradually grown accustomed to the excessive interest shown in them by scientists and tourists, but the gorillas of Lopé's savanna will not let themselves be approached so easily. Caroline had been working on the reserve for five years. She went into the forest unarmed, without even a machete; the gorillas tolerated her presence, as long as she stayed about twelve meters away.

I tried to picture it. Five years, the length of time it took Flaubert to write *Madame Bovary*, the period in which Schubert composed half his oeuvre. Five years, almost as much time as du Chaillu ever spent in the jungle. To come within twelve meters of gorillas.

"Animals in the wild sometimes react quite fearfully," said Caroline, to the great satisfaction of Diko, who was giving me one of his 'I-told-you-so' looks. "And the gorillas here are wild in every sense of the word. You can never entirely predict what they'll do."

Of course, Caroline wasn't out to pat the gorillas on the head; she studied their relationship to the ecosystem, took samples of their excrement, studied nests and kept tabs on their eating habits. A great deal of interest was shown in her work in scientific circles, because time is of the essence if the lowland gorilla is not to go the way of the kooloo-kamba of the Gabonese coast; those animals – a cross between gorilla and chimpanzee – are already virtually extinct, without much being known about them.

While she was telling me this, Hernandez stood watching from a distance. He was a good ten years older than her, with a hawk nose and a surly expression.

"By the way," Caroline asked in her textbook French and marked British accent, "haven't I seen you before?"

I nodded.

I had been in the train with Caroline and Hernandez, less than two weeks before. They had been on their way to Libreville, to do some shopping and pick up their English colleague. They'd sat three seats down from me.

I could have spent six hours talking to the Scotswoman about gorillas. I could have carefully wangled an invitation to her house. I could have spent days close to the gorillas.

But during that trip Hernandez had looked around fiercely at me and had barked to Caroline (for no good reason that I could see): "Just you wait, we'll be getting day-trippers before you know it." He'd smoked one cigarette after the other, clenching the filter in his teeth every time he took a drag. A few hours later his rage had cooled, and he'd tossed me a cautiously inviting look. But I'd found him a strange, loudmouthed, extremely unpleasant man, and had kept my gaze fixed out of the window.

.

CHAPTER 3

The Hidden River & King Omar's Pretty Little Train

HE WAS leaning on his desk, its veneer surface so swollen with humidity that his elbows sometimes slipped away. The lapels of his jacket almost touched his shoulders, a look that had been in fashion when I was still in high school. Half a roll of adhesive tape was the only thing keeping the right earpiece of his glasses in place.

The broken window of the office had been patched with chicken wire; the map of Gabon on the wall wasn't yellowed but reddened, for the dust that blew in here was the color of cayenne pepper.

Two of the keys on his Underwood were broken. He filled in the missing letters with a pen, a detail offered only after I had bent over the machine with the interested eye of the museum-goer.

He didn't ask where I came from; he simply listened, and nodded from time to time.

Yes, that's right, the nicest story about Gabon was probably the one about the river.

"Four hundred years," he said, "four hundred years," then

raised his arms to the ceiling with its flaking paint.

But there was nothing he could do to help me.

Most of the documents in his archive were from this century, from the forties and fifties, and the struggle for independence.

"It was a period of idealism, a settling of accounts with colonialism. Of course, it's high time we settled accounts with thirty years of independence too, but these days the enemy is so much more abstract."

He smiled tiredly.

Hundreds of birds were chirping in the mango tree in the yard; the sun appeared from behind a thundercloud and, in the sudden burst of light, the room lost even the tinge of sad romanticism it had had in semidarkness.

"If you want to find out about sixteenth-century Gabon, you have to go to Lisbon. For the seventeenth century it's The Hague, for the nineteenth it's Paris."

What about here in Gabon?

"No African tribe ever used an alphabet. And there are no documents from our side that date from before this century. That makes a registrar's life a lot easier."

When I left he urged me once again to begin my search in The Hague – the archives of the Dutch East India Company, the West India Company, the libraries there.

"The Hague isn't too far from Paris, and you can get there by train."

I thanked him with a box of cigars.

"Dutch?"

"Danish."

"Hmm, the Dutch ones are supposed to be better."

Pieter van den Broecke saw the river any number of times.

He called it the Olibata, and indicated it on his map by means of a line extending back from the coast for no more than two centimeters. Taking his scale into account, that fell about eighteen centimeters short of the mark.

The van den Broecke family was originally from Antwerp. Sugar refiners, well-to-do merchants, true-blue Flemings who had headed north after the Revolt of the Netherlands.

Pieter grew up on the Warmoesstraat in Amsterdam. Stepping outside, he could smell the odor of pitch and caulking that hung over the harbor, and he had only to take a few steps to see the three-masters being unloaded upon their return from Guinea, narrow little ships with holds full of gum from Senegal, sugar from São Tomé, ivory and pepper from the Grain Coast, gold dust from the Gold Coast, skins from Cape Verde. Africa began just beyond his doorstep.

He signed on as an apprentice clerk at a merchant house which specialized in trade with Africa, and boarded a ship for Guinea at the age of twenty-one. Between 1605 and 1614 he made four long trips to Africa. He did such good business there that he was allowed to continue his career in the Orient.

Van den Broecke opened the first Dutch trading post in Arabia, and during his second journey to the Middle East set up a trading post at Mocha in present-day Yemen. His next assignment took him to Mauritius and Madagascar. On the voyage home he was shipwrecked just off the Indian port of Surat, in what is now the state of Gujarat, and with one hundred and thirty-two men and the best of his cargo he crossed the subcontinent to the east coast, in the conviction that he would meet up with a ship bound for Batavia. Despite attacks by Indians, he lost only three men during the two-month trek. His reputation was made.

The governor of the Dutch East Indies, Jan Pieterszoon Coen, appointed him commander of Fort Jacatra. The business of war called for cynicism; the good-natured van den Broecke, however, thought he could come to terms with any opponent. He set off straight away to negotiate with the ruler of Jacatra and promptly landed in prison. Once freed, he was appointed chief merchant of Surat, a position for which he was every bit as ill-suited; he hated bookkeeping with a passion.

With his glibness, his ability to make contacts and his extensive knowledge of markets and products, van den Broecke felt he was the right man to lead the trade mission to the still-uncharted kingdom of Persia. But Coen appointed someone else.

When van den Broecke returned to Amsterdam, he published a series of extracts from his West African journals to show his patrons just what an exceptional merchant they had snubbed. It was a bluff, but one that would save his career.

In 1634, less than a year after the publication of his travel book, which went through several editions and attracted attention far abroad, the Dutch East India Company once again sent him to the Indies. Six years later, during the siege of Maluku, he died of the plague.

Frans Hals painted his portrait in 1632 or 1633, a jaunty seventeenth-century man with the wind in his hair. Van den Broecke was one of those travellers who had only to stay somewhere for a day to make ten friends. He could make himself understood in French, Portuguese and English, and he could talk with his hands if necessary. He tasted every dish put before him, was as fond of palm wine as he was of rice wine, and never demurred when a Negro king offered him one of his wives. His motto was: *Every hour hath its own reward.*

On the coast of Equatorial Africa, van den Broecke had soon realized that the blacks believed their ancestors turned white after death and then 'with such shippes as we have now, returne for commerce and to seek their friends; this intent they choose not to make known, for reason of their riches'. The native mythology thus explained both who these white sailors were (the returning ancestors) and why they chose not to recognize their descendants (out of self-interest). The merchant put this knowledge to good use. A reincarnated ancestor would never do any harm to his coastal descendants, and although van den Broecke had failed to notice that the Africans regarded their ancestors as middlemen who mediated between humans and the gods, he approached the king of Loango as though he were a member of his own family, which was precisely the way to go about it.

The kingdom of Loango stretched from the Gabonese coast to the banks of the Congo and was bordered on the north by the 1200-kilometer-long Ogooué. With the arrival of the white man, the kingdom would gradually be whittled away: the slave trade poisoned relations between the tribes. But the pioneering van den Broecke traded broadcloth, yellow copper bracelets, necklaces, beads, bells and duffel for ivory and redwood – not for slaves – and he was given the opportunity to behold the king of Loango in all his glory.

The king's subjects assessed the status of a foreign guest largely on the basis of his potency. An unflagging sex drive was a sign of health and strength, essential criteria to a hunting and warring people. During the twenty-one months he spent in the kingdom of Loango, van den Broecke made it perfectly clear that he was an extremely important man; he seemed to possess almost divine capacities. The incredulous king offered him one woman after another, and he never turned down a single one. This boosted esteem for the king among his subjects, and he showered the Dutchman with gifts.

The king's sister, second in the ranks of the court, was anxious to test the visitor's prowess herself. She wasn't coy about it, but simply ordered van den Broecke to share her bed. The fact that she presented him the next day with an elephant's tusk, bananas, lemons, pineapples and other fruit suggests that the merchant lived up to her expectations; what's more, she had eighteen servants carry van den Broecke in a Portuguese hammock to her city, a half-day's journey inland. There he was expected to partake of the meat of a freshly killed elephant, which stank so badly that he 'was taken ill of it'.

But like all the other women, and like the hospitable monarch himself, the king's sister made no mention of the river; when van den Broecke returned to Cap Lopez a satisfied man, he failed to notice that, only five kilometers away from that finger of land, the second greatest river of all Equatorial Africa was flowing into the sea.

Dierick Ruiters of Middelburg thought less highly of Africans. He found them savage and uncouth, cannibals all; they were too skittish for their own good, and spent the whole day loafing about, playing games and singing incessantly. They bounded about and danced into the wee hours, then slept until a full hour or two after sunrise.

So the ship's captain from Zeeland offered his compatriots a word of advice: should they trade with the Negroes along these coasts, they must not hesitate to beat the natives on the ribs with a rope so 'that it raise welts a finger thick'. His opposition to slavery, however, was unusual for the seventeenth century.

If at all possible, Ruiters preferred to remain on board his ship a couple of kilometers off the coast; his *Toortse der Zee-vaert* ('beacon for navigators') travelogue adds little to our knowledge of the way Africans lived at the time. His enthusiasm was reserved for the sea, for the currents and the trade winds. It was precisely this obsession that led him to make an important discovery.

By simply drawing in the occasional bucket of water, Ruiters came to the conclusion that the Congo must be a vast river: the seawater nine nautical miles from its mouth was still perfectly fresh; at sixty-five kilometers, it was only partly saline.

But he didn't taste the water off the mouth of the Ogooué.

At Cap Lopez – Cap Lopo Gonçalves in full – Ruiters exchanged greetings with two other Dutch ships, then sailed back north and copied onto his map the names the Portuguese had given to two branches of the Ogooué: Rio de Nazareth and Rio de St Lucia, streamlets no more than two centimeters in length.

In 1474, Lopo Gonçalves had been the first to chart the coast of Equatorial Africa.

The Portuguese mariner gave his own name to the tongue of

land at the mouth of the Ogooué, and christened the estuary 200 kilometers to the north Gabon, because – as the story goes – he saw in it the form of a *gabâo*, or sailor's cloak.

The estuary looks nothing like a cloak. It looks more like the lower stretch of someone's digestive tract. The Portuguese origin of the name has, therefore, been the subject of a good deal of speculation. A growing number of historians believe that the key to the mystery was revealed in the *Itinerario*, published by Jan Huygen van Linschoten in 1596. He reported that the title of the supreme ruler in the estuarial region was Mani Gabam, which was later bastardized into Gabon.

Van Linschoten based his account on a book published by the Enkhuizen physician Ten Broecke, writing under the pen name Paludanus, who in turn probably received his information from Barent Erikszoon, a ship's captain from his home town.

In 1591, Erikszoon had set sail for Brazil on the *Sint Pieter*. He took the route all sea captains followed in those days: sailing along the coast of Africa to the Cape Verdes, then looping across the ocean. The journey was fraught with misfortune. First he encountered head winds, then his ship was becalmed. Below the Cape Verdes, the eastward-flowing Guinea Current dragged his ship into the Bight of Biafra; the *Sint Pieter* then drifted off the island of Principe, where the Portuguese overpowered it and took the thirty-six crew members prisoner. The men were brought to Sâo Tomé, which lived up to its reputation as the most unhealthy island off this coast: within a few months, thirty of them were dead. Only Barent Erikszoon escaped.

He brought back important news for the port of Enkhuizen. Two French fellow-prisoners had told him of a veritable gold mine located on the coast of Guinea. Forgetting his scrape with death, he asked several wealthy merchants to finance his exploration of this 'Gold Coast'. They agreed, and in 1593 Erikszoon returned to the Zuyder Zee port with holds full of pepper, ivory and gold.

By the end of that century, dozens of ships from Enkhuizen, Medemblik, Delft, Amsterdam and Middelburg had sailed to West Africa.

"They act as though they had discovered all these lands," a Portuguese merchant in Africa complained about the Dutch. The odds soon became too great for the Portuguese; unable to defend the entire coastline, they called in the help of local headhunters. A bounty was paid for every Dutchman captured or beheaded. To scare away the newcomers once and for all, they even dug up freshly interred Dutch sailors and hung them on gallows along the shore.

At the initiative of the merchant Balthasar de Moucheron of Zeeland, the Dutch shipowners put their heads together. What they needed was a safe haven for their ships in Africa. They succeeded in winning the support of the States-General. In October 1599, thirty-six warships appeared off the fort of São Tomé and put ashore a thousand soldiers and a few dozen officers. The Portuguese surrendered without a shot, but nature came to the aid of the vanquished. Dysentery and malaria did what musket and rapier had not: fourteen days after the conquest, the last Dutch bodies were tossed into a mass grave.

But de Moucheron didn't give up. He ordered that a fort be built on the island of Corisco, in the northernmost bay of present-day Gabon, and opened a trading post there. The inhabitants of the Gabonese coast didn't like what they saw; they were afraid the Dutch would lay claim to all trade in the region. In 1601, the natives attacked two ships from Delft anchored off Corisco and murdered both crews. Nearly a century later, in 1698, the Hollanders got even: they torched the huts on Mbini and Koning Eilandt (later bastardized to Coniquet) and killed the entire population, thereby wiping out the Ndiwa tribe.

The atmosphere on the coast turned grim. More than ever before, the interests of the Gabonese were served by keeping the trade artery of the Ogooué hidden from the whites. They became a bit more co-operative, however, when the Dutch offered them ten florins a slave more than the Portuguese.

In 1630, after a fierce struggle with the Portuguese, the Dutch flag was raised above Pernambuco in northern Brazil. From that moment on, the powerful African kings enjoyed golden years; the weaker tribes went to ruin. The Dutch West Indies Company, set up only nine years earlier, was suddenly desperate for cheap manpower for its sugar plantations. Mouree, Ardra, Calabar, Benin, Loanga – the Dutch trading posts, luggers and light sailing vessels were everywhere, and clerks had orders to buy not only gold and ivory, but also as many slaves as possible. Trade with Africa blossomed as never before. The merchants' only worry was the perishability of their cargo: four or five out of every ten slaves never reached the other side of the ocean, which effectively doubled their price.

By the mid-seventeenth century, the Portuguese were more or less out of the picture. The Republic of the Netherlands controlled the coast of West Africa from Mauritania to southern Angola. The last few Portuguese forts and strongholds were overrun; the Dutch only surrendered their claims to the most important of these – the castle of St George d'Elmina and the forts Axim, Dixcover and Saccondee on the Gold Coast – when they were turned over to the British in 1872.

By the time the Dutch Guinea trade reached its zenith around 1640, there were two hundred vessels from Middelburg, Amsterdam and the West Frisian ports, with a combined crew of ten thousand souls, continually plying the waters off the African coast. These ships all followed the same route: they dropped down from the island of Goeree (now Gorée) to skirt the Grain Coast (Liberia), the Ivory Coast (still the Ivory Coast), the Gold Coast (Ghana), the Slave Coast (Togo and Benin) and the Tusk and Palm Oil Coast (Nigeria and Cameroun) before arriving at Cap Lopez. For nine months of the year, the prevailing currents and trade winds prevented them from sailing any further – the three-masters that called at Angola and the mouth of the Congo usually came from the south.

The ships would turn around at Cap Lopez and sail back to the Netherlands in safe groups of three or four. That is how, for decades on end, one ship after another could anchor in that bay without a single crew member being tempted to go off looking behind the mangroves, not even to find out what the occasional loose-lipped native was talking about.

Pieter de Marees was the only one whose curiosity got the better of him.

He sailed up the Ogooué in 1602.

Could it have been something he heard while taking on fruit and fresh water?

Whatever it was, he *listened* at Cap Lopez, as attested to by the little lexicon he drew up:

siomba = buy
mondello = Dutch Nation
mokendofino = pretty woman
manimomeau = elephant tusks

And he took a great many notes concerning the people.

The men ran to thievery, the women to unchastity and whoredom. The king lay with his own daughters, while the wives of the king, 'who he hath in great number', lived in fornication with their eldest sons. The women painted their bodies red, and often highlighted one eye with white and the other with yellow or red. They wore the skins of apes, vervets and other wild animals, and bells around their necks like cows at pasture. People of both sexes usually went bareheaded, their hair shaven and plaited in wondrous patterns and occasionally woven with feathers and plumes. Both men and women had holes in the upper lip or nose in which they wore rings or pieces of ivory the size of a large coin. When the men went out hunting or to hail a stranger, the women would walk behind them, carrying the men's muskets, spears, bows and arrows. With the firearms they'd purchased from the French, the inhabitants of Cap Lopez were better armed than the Negroes of the Gold Coast. They worshiped the sun, the moon, the earth and certain trees. They slept on the ground, prompting de Marees to say they lived like animals.

Not much is known about de Marees himself. Scion of a wealthy family from the north of France or Flanders. Well educated, with an interest in Africa and Africans that went far beyond that of most of his contemporaries. It irritated him that so little was known about Guinea, 'the more that all lands and portions of the World have been described'.

De Marees had sailed to Africa on a ship belonging to a

merchant of Amsterdam. While preparing for the journey home from Cap Lopez he spied, to the south-east, 'a riuer, at half a league'. Several sloops were lowered and de Marees ordered his men to row against the current. Six kilometers in from the coast, a village loomed up; after trading for a few tusks there, they rowed back to the ship.

De Marees could barely believe his eyes. Clusters of oysters grew on branches dangling in the stream, and the river was teeming with crocodile and river horses (hippopotamuses), so that 'one thinks the Nilus haue here found its course'.

That was worth writing home about.

Like de Marees, later explorers would assume that the Ogooué was a branch of some other major river. The Congo, Brazza thought when he sailed up the Ogooué in 1875; meanwhile, thousands of kilometers to the east, Stanley searched for the sources of the Nile and stumbled upon the headwaters of the Congo.

De Marees, in other words, was two hundred and seventy years ahead of his time. Yet Olfert Dapper passed over his discovery without a word. Could de Marees's claims have been too bold?

Dapper himself never actually visited Africa. On the next-to-last day of the year 1689, he was buried in the Old North Church in Amsterdam's Jordaan neighborhood, less than eighty paces from the house on the Anjelierstraat where he was born in 1635 or 1636. He worked and spent almost his entire life in that same street, and there he wrote the most authoritative Africa reference book of his day, simply by laying side by side all the Portuguese, French, Italian and Dutch travelogues and documents he could find. He must have tallied the reports written by the man he referred to rather condescendingly as 'a certain Pieter de Marees' against those of van den Broecke and other travellers, and then concluded that the man who had described 'the Goldyn Kingdom of Guynea' was a fibber – after all, he who travels far, lies much. The Dutch, German, English and French versions of the cautious Dapper's book therefore stuck to the name by which van den Broecke and most other seamen knew the Ogooué: the Olibata, a measly little stream.

And so the people of the coast were able to keep the secret that de Marees had come close to wresting from them with his own eyes.

Thomas E. Bowdich sailed up the Gabon Estuary in 1815, in order to take on a cargo of wood.

More than a century earlier, the English and French had gained control over West Africa, with the exception of the mouth of the Congo, the coast of Angola and the Gold Coast, where the Dutch continued to do a brisk trade.

On behalf of the British government, Bowdich explored the West African coast from the Cape to Ashantee, and wrote an exhaustive report about his findings.

An English-speaking African at the mouth of the estuary told him of a people called the Paamway (Pahouin or Pangwe, another name for the Fang), who lived by 'the longest river in the world'.

The Englishman wanted to know more. Using the paths that had been cleared for slave caravans, he covered hundreds of kilometers through the interior and crossed the Ogooué on several occasions, without realizing that this was the mighty river of which he'd heard. The same fate would later befall du Chaillu, who crossed the Monts de Cristal in pursuit of the gorilla and saw the Ogooué flowing in the distance; he had come across so many rivers, however, that they all started looking the same. Imagine how his guides must have gloated! He who knew the river, knew Gabon, and beyond Gabon lay the road to Central Africa.

But the white man's maps continued to depict the area along the Equator as a blank, the domain of speculation.

A vast wasteland; that was Jules Verne's bet when he wrote *Around the World in Eighty Days*.

In 1839, the French lieutenant Edouard Bouët-Willaumez shook the hand of King Antchouwé Kowé Rapontchombo and was, to his considerable amazement, greeted in impeccable French.

Rapontchombo, son of Ongonwu Ré-Mboko, son of Résakuélé, son of Ré-Ntori, son of R'Ombonwa, ruled over three villages on the left bank of the Gabon Estuary and owned several plantations at the mouth of the Ogooué, which he seldom visited, leaving them to the attention of his wives.

Rapontchombo spoke fluent French and Spanish, and reasonable Portuguese and English. In his youth he had sailed aboard a Spanish ship; French he had learned from his brother, who had served in the French army. The two other languages were taught him by castaways to whom he had given shelter pending the arrival of a ship bound for Europe, on condition that they supplement his vocabulary with a few sentences a day.

Bouët-Willaumez was less of a polyglot. Unable to wrap his mouth around the king's name, he called him Denis. That was the name by which he would go down in history.

Denis was the first Gabonese chief to place his territory under the French flag. His age, intelligence and peace-loving nature made him a highly respected man along the coast, so other chieftains soon followed his example.

Rapontchombo, alias Denis, was probably born around 1780. "When Louis the Sixteenth was still on the throne," he told Bouët-Willaumez, "I could already wield a paddle."

This would have made him almost sixty when – after several rounds of tough negotiations – he placed his mark on the treaty with the French. But above his ash-gray beard twinkled two youthful eyes, alight with curiosity.

He collected British uniforms and ceremonial dress, and wore them on all official occasions. He also collected medals and decorations. The pride of his collection was the gold medal given to him by Queen Victoria, in thanks for securing the release of four English seamen taken captive by a tribe halfway up the Como River. *To King Denny.*

He sent the British queen a live panther in return.

The French, however, would not be outdone; they awarded him the Légion d'Honneur. But that wasn't enough for Rapontchombo. When the son of King Louis-Philippe honored Denis with a visit on his way back from retrieving the ashes of Napoleon Bonaparte at St Helena, the African chief demanded that a salute be fired every time he stepped aboard a French warship from his canoe. Furthermore, he wangled a promise from his visitor that he could sit at the right hand of the admiral during the annual banquet for French officers, in which elevated company he hoped to learn a great deal.

From Bouët-Willaumez he received the assurance that he could visit any French ship that anchored off his village. During those tours, he exhibited a great interest in the principles of canonry.

He had one final request for Bouët-Willaumez. The king had heard of a machine that produced music when you turned a crank. The barrel organ arrived on the next ship; he had it placed in front of his hut and played it himself every evening, attended by his slaves and subjects.

Rapontchombo owned four or five hundred slaves. Like his forefathers, he had earned his fortune in the slave trade. He saw nothing wrong with it. He dealt fairly with his own slaves; one of the most faithful and conscientious among them was even admitted to the circle of elders, without ever being made a freeman.

The king had forty or fifty wives, but loved only one of them with all his heart. When Agnouré-Babé died, the grieving king introduced a new ritual to the court. All visitors were to kneel before him and ask: "What is the evil God has done?" The king would answer: "Death." The visitor would then concur by replying: "Yes, death, that is the evil God has done."

Intolerable blasphemy: that was the verdict of the first French bishop of Gabon, and he talked to the king about it. Always anxious to please the French, Rapontchombo added a few new lines to the old ritual.

Visitor: "What is the evil God has done?"

King: "Death."

Visitor: "Yes, death, that is the evil God has done."

A brief pause.

Visitor: "What is the good that God has done?"

King: "Life."

Visitor: "Yes, that God may grant you life."

Antchouwé Kowé Rapontchombo died in 1876, at the age of about ninety-five. In accordance with his dying wish, he was buried near Pointe Pongara in the full dress uniform of a British general, his feet pointed towards the ocean over which his benefactors had come. It was the ultimate homage to the Europeans with whom he had got along so well, and to whom – in exchange for medals and decorations – he had told so much about the coast.

About the coast. But not about the river.

The river was finally discovered by sheer luck.

Sailing up the Rembwé in a sloop in 1862, Lieutenant Paul Serval stumbled upon the Ogooué near Lambaréné.

Two years earlier, he and Dr Griffon du Bellay had tried to navigate the estuary of the Ogooué. Their steamboat ran aground on a sandbank and sank within a few minutes. They escaped with their lives by scrambling into a canoe, with the natives' war cries echoing across the water. But this time Serval picked a tributary, and came in the back way to the lake district around Lambaréné. There he met King Rempolé, one of the interior's most affable chieftains.

For the Gabonese tribes, the die had been cast. They still pounded the tom-toms from time to time, shot the occasional poisoned arrow and kidnapped the odd traveller, but the curiosity of the Europeans had been piqued and the tide could no longer be stemmed: the exploration of the river had begun.

The English trader Bruce Walker made it as far as Lopé, having travelled partly over land.

Alfred Marche, a biologist, and the Marquis de Compiègne, a geographer, sailed another 200 kilometers upriver, to the confluence with the Ivindo.

Walker was held prisoner for months on end, while the two Frenchmen had their path blocked by the Fang, but that only made it more of a challenge for the Europeans. And, like the coastal tribes, the jungle inhabitants were now intent on figuring out a few things themselves: who, for instance, were these men with their strange pointy noses? Where did they come from, what gifts did they bear, and why-oh-why were they as white as the foam in the rapids, the clouds after a thunderstorm, the powder on a mask, why were they the color of death?

From the reports by Marche and Compiègne, Count Pierre Savorgnan de Brazza – a naturalized Frenchman of Italian birth – distilled the theory that the Ogooué was a branch of the Congo. He impressed upon his sponsors his belief that all that needed to be done to open a route for waterborne trade of a magnitude equal to the Rhine or Danube was to chart the river's course still further and win the tribes along its banks over to Western civilization with beads, cheap rum and a bit of gunpowder.

The Minister of the Navy granted him permission to organize an expedition. Brazza left in 1875 and returned to Libreville in 1878, a disappointed man. No, the Ogooué was not connected to the Congo, and the countless rapids made it an impracticable trade route. In fact, upriver from Poubara Falls – 800 kilometers from the coast – it was impassable for even the smallest dugout.

But the jungle had been laid open, and within less than a

decade the Gabonese tribes would lose their hegemony over lands which discretion and shrewdness had allowed them to keep out of reach of the civilized world for four hundred years.

Sharing in the optimism of his age, however, Brazza could never give up the idea of a trade artery from the coast of Equatorial Africa to the Congo. Trade, as he and his contemporaries believed, would automatically lead to social intercourse and commerce, the first steps towards civilization. He proposed building a railroad along the Ogooué.

After Brazza's death in 1905, the plans began to take shape.

On the eve of the First World War, the French parliament approved the construction of a railroad from Libreville to Ouesso, but saber-rattling had emptied the treasury of its last sou before the first tree could be felled.

In the 1920s, it was decided to construct a shorter, less expensive line from Brazzaville to Pointe-Noire, straight through the French Congo. The building of the railroad itself was a nightmare.

Georges Simenon visited the work in progress in the early thirties. The black contract laborers, he wrote in his report *The Hour of the Negro*, fled into the jungle en masse to escape certain death. The white engineers lay in devastatingly hot barracks, their teeth chattering with yellow fever. 'The score', he said, in a sentence that would go down in history, 'is one Negro per sleeper, one European per kilometer'.

The jungle inhabitants had discovered the meaning of civilization – fourteen thousand deaths to build a railroad.

'And no one yet knows', Simenon wrote, 'what this celebrated railroad is to carry. Cotton is on the decline, coffee is a losing proposition, no one wants rubber, the interior is no place for tourists, and the natives don't have the price of a ticket.'

Ticket or no, it rankled the Gabonese to watch the railroad being built. Although they were part of the twin colony of Congo-Gabon, they seemed about to get the short end of the stick. It was a gloomy premonition, but one which ultimately came true. By the late 1930s, all trade between the heart of Africa and the coast passed along the railroad that ran through the French Congo. Brazzaville grew to become the most important French colonial city on the Equator; Libreville remained a provincial town.

Following independence, the Gabonese inferiority complex took on a nationalistic character. Gabon could only join the ranks of nations if it had its own railroad. A railroad along the Ogooué. A railroad that would truly carve a path through the jungle. But railroads like that cost a fortune.

Jean-Michel M'Buwe told me how they built it. Jean-Michel had worked for years as a reporter for *L'Union*, the country's only daily newspaper, until he was given the boot because of the ironic tone of his articles. At the same time, a call came in from the presidential palace and the entire editorial board was fired: *L'Union* goes through an average of two editors-in-chief a year. He asked me not to disclose his identity, saying I could use the pseudonym M'Buwe, which means 'clan' in the M'Pongwe language. A year after leaving Libreville I saw Jean-Michel again, this time in a picture in the newspaper, at the head of a huge procession demonstrating for greater freedom. As an exceptionally well informed member of the anti-Bongo clan, he was considered by the regime to be one of its most dangerous opponents. Many such opponents have died under mysterious circumstances during the last twenty years: since 1967, Omar Bongo has ruled Gabon as an absolute monarch. So the afternoon Jean-Michel M'Buwe talked to me at length about the building of the Transgabonais, he was taking an enormous risk; the story itself closely traces the highways and byways of President Bongo's own political aspirations.

"I had just started working as a journalist when the plans were taken out of mothballs. That must have been in mid-1973. They expected us to extol the railroad's virtues on a daily basis; there was even a song about it that they played on the radio once an hour: *The locomotive of the Transgabonais / will ride through the jungle one of these days. Our rails, our pretty little train / will be here tomorrow, it's coming today.*

" 'Ride Along with Bongo', that was the name of the song. A rather fitting title, if you ask me. At the news desk we used to joke about the Trans*bongo*nais railroad. In the mid-70s, every African president had to have his own status symbol. For some it was a soccer stadium, for others a cathedral in their native village. But for Bongo it was a railroad. Our president had the wind at his back. What you people call the 'oil crisis' had made our economy blossom, and Gabon reacted like a shy girl who has suddenly become aware of her beauty. From one day to the next, the price of a barrel of crude quadrupled; foreign currency began pouring into the country and Gabon became the richest country in Africa, in per capita terms. Even richer than South

Africa. They nicknamed it 'Switzerland on the Equator', and Libreville actually started looking like Geneva."

At the seaside Gamba Hotel, where Jean-Michel had arranged to meet me, we were surrounded by busily conversing men in pearly white shirts, all of them with a calculator within arm's reach. Between twelve and four, when offices are closed, life in Libreville moves to the waterfront hotels. This is where civil servants and businessmen carry on their informal discussions, stuff themselves with French cuisine and wash away yesterday's hangover with bottles of rosé. The busier it was, the safer it was, as Jean-Michel well knew: the loud voices around us acted as a screen. Sitting out on the terraces of those restaurants, it's easy to forget that Libreville lies on the edge of the jungle; the city does have something of Zurich or Nice about it, even though the golden years Jean-Michel talked about have flown, and the toilets of the Gamba Hotel are overflowing.

"So President Bongo was determined to build that railroad, and the reasons he gave were economic. The first stretch would run between the coast and Booué, then tracks would be laid to the mountain of iron ore at Mékambo in the north-east. There were a hundred and fifty million tons of iron lying there, almost on the surface, and none of it had ever been extracted.

"Gabon asked the World Bank for a loan, but was turned down. Washington had grave doubts about whether access to the iron mine could ever justify building the railroad. The price of ore had been at rock bottom for years, and there was no reason to believe that would change. As usual, the pessimists were proven right: the iron mountain is still buried in the jungle. But we were good boys, so our paper railed against 'Western arrogance', 'neo-colonialism' and 'white people telling us what to do'.

"Okay, so Gabon submitted a second proposal. A shorter railroad this time, ending at Booué. And the World Bank turned it down again. Too expensive. No money in it. They said we should improve our roads instead.

"President Bongo was furious. Gabon could pay for two-thirds of the railroad itself, from its oil revenues, so he only needed to borrow a third. With or without the World Bank, the Transgabonais was going to be built. Or, as the president put it: 'If we have to sell our souls to the devil to build the railroad, then we'll sell our souls.'

"He asked South Africa for help, and got it, but it wasn't much. And what was the deal? Well, a trade embargo had been looming over the South African apartheid regime for quite some time, and Libreville could be used to get around it. France was also quick to give him a loan. President Pompidou wasn't too crazy about the idea of a railroad through the jungle, but he needed to stay on friendly terms with Gabon, which supplied ten per cent of all French oil imports. He signed a loan for a hundred and forty million francs, barely enough for ten kilometers of track. And then Bongo got converted."

Jean-Michel sipped his rosé. I'd met him twice before and knew he could go on like this for hours. He'd told me about the former first lady's toy-boys who had died mysteriously or disappeared without a trace. He had told me about the president himself, catapulted to the top when he was thirty-two. Tickled by power, the president reacted like a giggly schoolgirl; Jean-Michel had told me about Bongo's illegitimate children. Now he was going to tell me about the president's religious conversion.

"It seems Gaddafi suggested it to him. They couldn't have had much in common – the revolutionary and the reactionary, the vehement Muslim and the lukewarm Catholic – but opposites sometimes attract, and Bongo's little train had gained pitifully little support in the West. Gaddafi must have told him: listen, Bongo, change your religion, go on a pilgrimage to Mecca and you'll see, your problems will be over. Of course Bongo had been baptized in the Church, and was named after St Bernard, so he must have hesitated a little: after all, beneath his official portrait in every shop, every office and waiting room, it said 'Albert Bernard Bongo', in great big letters. But one month later, all those pictures were replaced with ones that read 'El Hadj Omar Bongo'.

"That's right, he'd flown to Mecca – a railroad *vaut bien une messe* – and dropped in on Sheikh Zayd of Abu Dhabi on the way home. The old emir lent a willing ear to the new convert. Gabon had been associated with the mission work of Dr Albert Schweitzer for decades – few African nations were considered more Christian than Gabon – and now the country was suddenly being led by a hadji who in a friendly but firm manner advised his cabinet ministers to adopt Islam. The emir ordered his finance minister to write the man a cheque, and not to worry about how many zeros came after the comma, but our friend Omar simply shook his head. Africans trust Arabs even less than they trust Europeans; he wanted cash, French francs on the nail. That evening the bank managers worked overtime; the next morning, Bongo left the emirate on the pirate coast with a whole row of bulging attaché cases.

"We couldn't write about any of this in the paper, of course. Besides, all the financial chicanery only came to light much later. The thing was, though, we had to type 'El Hadj Omar' all the time, and whenever someone got it wrong there would be these furious phone calls from the presidential palace. Otherwise there wasn't much of a fuss about the conversion. The Gabonese put up with a great deal from their presidents, and the skeptics were buried under an avalanche of propaganda. The people truly came to believe that without a railroad, Gabon would remain a backward country until the end of time.

"As soon as Bongo returned from his pilgrimage, Gabon began the huge task, for which it had neither the knowledge nor the technical wherewithal. A consortium of fifteen European firms, led by a French company, came in to do the job. The top management was white, the lower echelons consisted of Pakistanis and Africans: just like in the good old days, that was the joke at the news desk. I'll admit the consortium did everything it could to alleviate hardship. A whole town moved along through the jungle, with spick-and-span canteens, well-ventilated sleeping quarters, a movie theater, a field hospital. Doctors and nurses followed in the wake of the railroad workers – and the state-sponsored prostitutes, who they checked once a week for venereal disease.

"Machines were brought in to make the work easier. They attacked the jungle with dozens of scrapers and bulldozers, more than a hundred caterpillars and over two hundred trucks, but the jungle didn't give up that easily. Swamps appeared from under the tangled mat of branches and vines, along with strangely shaped hills that hadn't shown up on the infrared photos. Every kilometer posed new problems for the engineers, and they ran into huge delays. The cost of the project was twice what had been budgeted; it finally added up to twenty million French francs a kilometer, a grand total of something like fourteen billion francs.

"I think everyone in Gabon enjoyed the fight. The jungle still had something magic about it, something unpredictable. It was Western technology versus the primal forces. The fact that technology was going to win did nothing to detract from that; I've heard plenty of Gabonese people say that the jungle has only beaten a *temporary* retreat, that it could re-open the offensive at any moment. After all, the jungle is ruled by powerful spirits.

"By 1976, Gabon was on the verge of bankruptcy. Partly because of the railroad, but also because of the renovation of the presidential palace in Libreville. The renovation cost one and a half billion francs, the annual wage bill of the whole of Gabon. But work on the railroad continued unabated. In every speech he made, President Bongo begged his people to keep making sacrifices for the Transgabonais, which was gradually becoming a sort of sacred totem. He was obviously pursuing some mad dream – we just weren't sure exactly what. But after the first few stretches of track had been laid, Bongo let the cat out of the bag.

"He commissioned a new route. The plans for a railroad to the mountain of iron in the north-east were ditched; the Transgabonais was going to run to Franceville, in the south-east. Again, the arguments he brought to bear were economic. This time it was the manganese mine at Moanda. And the uranium mine, which was also located in the south. Not to mention lumber from the near-virgin forest between Booué and Franceville. Each argument more specious than the next.

"There was already a 120-kilometer-long cable car to transport the manganese from Moanda to the Congo-Ocean Railway. There was barely enough uranium in the south to fill more than a couple of cargo planes a year. And all the triplex mills were in Port-Gentil, our traditional transhipment port for wood, 160 kilometers south of the western terminus of the Transgabonais. There was no good reason for the new route.

"The Europeans were baffled, but the Gabonese understood all too well. A railroad to the north would only strengthen the position of the Fang, who lived there and were already Gabon's largest and traditionally most expansionist tribe. But a railroad to the south would keep the Batéké from abandoning their territory. The president himself is a Batéké.

"The railroad, a European invention, suddenly began pounding out an age-old African story. The story of a poor boy with a little Pygmy blood in his veins, who first saw the light of day in a village now known as Bongoville, in Haut-Ogooué province, just forty-five kilometers from Franceville."

Jean-Michel ordered another bottle of rosé.

"Albert Bernard Bongo never had a cradle or a nanny. He wasn't born in a hospital bed, but in the grass. His father died when other boys his age were just learning to read and write. His uncle raised him, and only allowed him to start school when he was ten. With a great deal of effort, though, he made up for lost time, and went on to Brazzaville to complete his education. He got his first job there, in the capital of the Congo, as a civil servant in the post office. There were no jobs to be found in the highlands where he came from, only dry elephant grass; like most other Batéké, Bongo became a migrant worker. He boosted his status by marrying a girl from the highest Batéké caste, and he and his new bride moved from Brazzaville to Libreville. Years later, when duty called that boy from the backwoods to assume his nation's highest office, he must have thought: 'Now I'm going to help my people. No one will stop me from making the train I've been dreaming of for so long run straight through the jungle to the place I was born, so the country of my youth will prosper and my poor fellow tribesmen will no longer have to seek a living in the Congo, or further away in Zaïre. I will preserve my homeland from abandonment, I will make my native province a part of Gabon, once and for all, and I'll head off the Fang, who occupy far too many key positions anyway, by including as many of my nephews and nieces, cousins and second cousins as possible in my administration. Thanks to the Transgabonais, my nephews, nieces and cousins will be able to travel to the capital in a single day, a trip that used to take them three or four days by car, sometimes longer during the rainy season. I will make Franceville, the city of the Batéké, a powerful city, second only to Libreville and Port-Gentil.'

"That's the way things go around here. A president who casts himself in the leading role of a sparkling fairy tale that brings his country to the verge of bankruptcy, but who never loses a minute's sleep over it; who writes an autobiographical play, *Tomorrow, a New Day*, and has it filmed right away; who publishes a comic book about his impoverished youth and his brilliant career, *Once Upon a Time, There Was . . . El Hadj Omar Bongo*, a *comic* book, mind you, so the illiterate can follow his example.

"Nothing has really changed in Gabon since the days of King Denis. President Bongo has every newly appointed cabinet minister brought to his country home in Franceville for the initiation rites that will admit him to the secret society of the *ndjobi*. Gabon has always had a lot of secret cults, and although they have lost most of their sacred character in recent years, they still serve to uphold the traditional rituals and ceremonies. The new cabinet minister has to recite a series of prayers and swear allegiance to the president. Rumor has it (the initiates have to swear a blood oath of eternal silence) that the ceremony ends with the president washing his feet in a large bowl, after which the minister drinks the water as a sign of unconditional loyalty. The ceremony is attended by the Batéké chieftains and the president's father-in-law. That last detail is a very African touch; the old man is the one who gave Bongo his power in the first place.

"That's how the new Africa blends with the old. Cabinet ministers act out the role of the Eleven Wise Men who once counseled the king; the president enjoys the status of absolute monarch. But even that's not enough for him. The Transgabonais was completed at the end of 1986. Ever since, the poor boy from the elephant grass has been nurturing a new dream: he wants to become the true king of the Batéké. The former king was deposed by the Congolese communists in the 1960s (the border between Gabon and the Congo runs straight through the tribe's territory), and the Batéké chieftains never appointed a successor. With the building of the railroad to Franceville, Omar Bongo announced his candidacy. After the humiliation the whites put him through and his pilgrimage to Mecca, he considered it his right. So the railroad was built to give the president a chance to sit someday on the lion skin, like the old Batéké kings. And even if that never actually happens, it was still the leitmotif in the construction of the Transgabonais. You have to admit that when you talk about the surreal, Africa always comes through with flying colors. This continent is like a dunghill, you see, but sometimes that's where the most beautiful flowers grow. Anyway, if you decide to take that Transgabonais, you can sing along with us: what a pretty little train!"

I took that train. Six hundred and sixty kilometers, straight through the jungle. A journey through one of the most sparsely populated areas on earth. Not a particularly long trip, no more than eleven hours. But it's the kind of travel that challenges the imagination: just think, it took Brazza three years to get from the coast to the upland plain on the other side of the country.

A taxi took me down a four-lane highway, the only decent road in Gabon, to the station at the port town of Owendo, just twenty kilometers south of Libreville. The station appealed to me right away. It was nothing compared to the ones in medium-sized cities, in fact it was nothing compared to the whistle-stops in Dutch villages; it was about the size of an electrical substation, the unmistakable first in a series of outposts along a deserted road, already part of the emptiness.

With a one-way ticket to Franceville in my pocket, I went looking for a window seat and heard the second-class passengers mumble as I walked by: "You belong in the refrigerator with the white folks." Judging from the color of my skin, they assumed I had enough money to pay for a first-class ticket; as it was, I was needlessly occupying a seat in the crowded second-class compartment, and the people around me thought that wasn't fair: I belonged in the refrigerator with the white folks. The air-conditioning in first class was truly blowing up a storm; in first class it was as cold as ice, but I was the only white person in there.

My black fellow-travellers stared rigidly ahead. Only one man spoke to me. A Senegalese.

The train pulled away from the station. Less than five minutes later we were rolling through the jungle.

Libreville has grown quickly during the last few decades, but most of that growth has taken place in a narrow strip along the coast. After a few kilometers the buildings all disappeared. Then something strange happened.

The soil turned a rusty-brown. Ferns towered over the train. Kapok trees like giant mushrooms overshadowed the undergrowth and tangled scrub. The countryside was veined with countless creeks and streams. The sky turned to lead; the air trembled.

And while the train rolled through the tropical rain forest – that brand-spanking-new train with carriages just like the ones on European intercity lines, carriages with seats standing two-by-two, comfortable, stable, air-cushioned carriages that seemed to be heading straight for some metropolis – the passengers started identifying with what was rolling by outside the window. All those men and women from the city, on their way to the villages where they were born, needed less than the time between breakfast and lunch to readopt the customs of the jungle. Standing at the bar in the club car, staring crustily at the neck of the beer bottle in front of them, the men talked about memorable hunting parties to whoever was standing next to them, the way they once had in the palaver hut. At every station they hopped out to buy game from local hunters, who carried it in on their bare shoulders. They pinched the bellies of monkey, serval and antelope, assessing the quantity of meat, negotiating a price; they shooed away their wives, looked in the animal's mouth, pushed back its lips, counted the rotten teeth, estimated its age. One monkey after another with cheery red eyebrows, yellow-tufted cheeks and shattered eyes disappeared into a burlap bag beneath the seat, classic spoils in a modern train, and I thought again of Jean-Michel M'Buwe, how he had impressed on me his countrymen's inability to choose between then and now, how he had the same problem himself and how, finding himself between a rock and a hard place, he had assumed that ironic tone.

At the top of a long incline, the train stopped. At the same moment, the music that had blasted from the loudspeakers all morning stopped too. Coincidence or no, the last vestiges of the city disappeared along with the disco drone.

The passengers moved over to the windows on the right-hand side of the compartment. The bar emptied out. Windows and doors were opened and a clammy heat rushed into the train. We were three-quarters of the way to the end of the line, not far from Ndjolé, having followed the foothills of the Monts de Cristal, the range of hills du Chaillu crossed on foot with his machete as his only prop and stay.

The train had stopped in one of the many steep culverts built to repulse the constant attacks of the rain forest. The belief of many Gabonese that technology has won only a temporary victory over nature is not as wild as it may seem. In *Journey to the End of the Night*, Céline, who spent a few seasons in southern Cameroun (where he never went outside without his revolver, and always wore mosquito netting over his face, even during the day), had a good laugh at the expense of a colonial official who lost 120 kilometers of road in a single season. Rolled macadam, swallowed up by the greenery in the time between inspections.

Above the culvert one could see only a narrow strip of foliage, lonesome treetops, high against the sky. The man next to me, a little Bantu, tilted his head to one side and cupped a hand behind his ear. He could hear something. Was it . . . running water?

113

He nodded at me. Then he smiled. He was the first Gabonese to smile at me on the train.

The light turned green. The diesel locomotives blew black smoke, and the train began crawling down the hill. The jungle turned to benign scrub, the horizon spread wide and the man next to me said: "*Voilà, m'sieur, voilà l'Ogooué.*"

As we rounded a tight curve, the river came rushing at us. A broad, brown, churning stream, pulling tree trunks and huge snarled clumps of roots along with it. When you've spent the whole morning looking at the jungle, where never a breath of wind seems to penetrate, the Ogooué means power and freedom.

The train crossed the river just past Ndjolé. The water beneath the two-kilometer-long iron trestle burst over a smooth threshold of rock; the pounding could be heard even above the roar of the locomotives. This was where the explorers had been forced to unload their rations, weapons, compasses, chronometers and sextants from the steamer and transfer them upstream and into canoes; this was where the real struggle with the elements began.

The river was to the left of the tracks now. The atmosphere of a church service still hung in the Transgabonais. Whether dressed in blue jeans or a suit, a frock or a gracefully draped *pagne*, the passengers looked at the rapids in silent awe – their respect for nature as moving as the natural surroundings themselves. Occasionally a deep sigh was heard, as though someone was wondering why he had ever turned his back on these distant shores. The Gabonese call the jungle 'the inside', the cities on the coast 'the outside'; that's why the Ogooué is often referred to as the main artery.

The train slipped into a tunnel. Back out in the open again, the light above the water seemed even clearer and keener than before.

The Transgabonais followed the river for hours. The Ogooué added a new panorama at every curve. Long verdant islands divided the stream into three or four channels, some of which came to a dead end in the jungle a few hundred meters downstream. Only an experienced oarsman could navigate a canoe through this maze. The whites had profited from such knowledge, and had kept the logbooks up to date with a compass on their knee.

While under the direct spell of the river itself, I read an excerpt from the logbook of the twenty-eight-year-old ship's surgeon and biologist Noël Ballay, one of the three Europeans who accompanied Brazza on his first expedition.

'Route, Tuesday, 3 July: 1/6 m. s.e. river N'Coni (40 meters) -1/9 m. s.-s.e. 1/3 m. e.-s.e. 1/4 s. Flat rocks in midstream, minor rapids. -1/6 m. s.-s.e. Sand bar, left bank. -1/9 s.-s.e. -1/2 m. s.-s.e. -2/3 m. s.-s.e. 1/4 s. Two small, rocky islands. -1/9 s.-s.e. -s.e.; 1/3 s.-s.e.-s.e.; -1/3 m. e.-s.e. Rock in midstream, large sand bar; right bank, fairly strong rapids, but easy to take along right bank.'

But it wasn't always that easy. The canoes often capsized in the rapids I could see flashing in the distance, and many crates of rations, clothing and footwear were lost, as well as drums containing sorely needed medicines – it never took more than a few weeks before the fever hit. Yet none of those men turned back; they washed down the bitter pill of disappointment with rum, believing it helped to kill the worst bacilli as well, then moved on, headed for the unknown. Why? Richard Burton best summed it up as he began his ascent of Mount Victoria in Cameroun: 'To be first in such matters is everything; to be second, nothing'.

The countryside grew hillier, the river wilder. It couldn't be far to the waterfalls at Booué, another of those names written in sweat and tears in the explorers' accounts.

Brazza and his Senegalese bearers gave the falls a wide berth.

'One could blaze a trail there only with the greatest difficulty. Up to our waists in water, we occasionally had to thread our way along the course of a network of creeks, the beds of which were covered in small stones. At other times we traversed swampy ground, soaked to the skin from downpours that went on all day. One of the Senegalese wounded himself on a branch, and his foot became infected; this forced us to walk more slowly. At night we huddled half-naked around a fire to dry our clothes, wiping the water off our bodies, for a constant drizzle kept up till dawn.'

Under such conditions, a breath of wind was enough to blow a man into kingdom come. The group of bearers quickly dwindled. Yet here, at the spot where the Senegalese had breathed their last, their chattering teeth seemed an improbability. The river looked so friendly.

The tracks turned south and the train started on the most spectacular leg of its journey: the 350 kilometers to Franceville.

In the sun's dying rays, the rapids turned as pink as coconut-husk embers, the sandbars a yellowish-white like ivory. Most of the passengers had left the train by now, and there was no evidence of human life along the tracks: no dugout on the water, no hut, no wisp of smoke among the stands of ebony and mahogany.

The last few thousand Pygmies lived a bit further east of here. Subsisting on hunting, they move as freely as the wild herds themselves. Their women can build a hut in two hours. They call themselves the Bongongo, the invisible ones, and their motto is: *Bongongo bwa imo-imo* – 'Beside you one moment, vanished the next'.

Even the places where the train actually stopped were as still as the grave. A few dilapidated huts leaning tiredly against each other, mangy dogs sleeping on the muddy path to the station. You could hardly call them villages: these were outposts, not much bigger than the first colonists and missionaries had left them. Back when the railroad was being built, back when the travelling circus was still on the road and a motley crew was terrorizing the bars, these places must have done a roaring trade. But that was years ago; no doubt the current inhabitants lived in the shadow of the age-old African proverb, 'A bad person is better than an empty house'. Vines wrapped themselves like countless snakes around a bridge that seemed to have fallen into disuse; almost hiding the steel trusses from sight, the greenery reached to within a few meters of the far bank. In the switchyard at Lastoursville there were flatcars piled high with okoumé, their trunks more than a meter in diameter; after that, the forest was wild and desolate.

This Africa in no way resembled the Africa I knew from earlier trips: it was not frenzied, magnanimous or exuberant, nor was it grim, hideous or defiant; it was silent, subdued, mysterious and, above all, lonely. The incessant whistle of the Transgabonais could do little to change that; nothing could breathe new life into this place, and no one seemed to want that, either. There were no children holding out their hands on the platforms, no men wheedling for a cigarette; the people of the jungle had learned to be content with little, and had learned it centuries ago.

The little Bantu sitting next to me woke from his afternoon nap and rubbed the sleep out of his eyes. I asked if he wanted to join me for a beer. He had to think about it for a minute.

We walked to the club car.

He asked whether I was a businessman, and couldn't imagine that anyone would travel for travelling's sake; you travelled to visit family or for your work, there was no sense to it otherwise. He always went first class. He had to save for months, but he had diplomas, and a man with diplomas travels first class. When I told him that I sometimes travelled second class, he asked: "Didn't you ever get your diploma?"

His gaze fell on the burlap bag at the feet of the Gabonese man standing next to us. The man had bought a serval. He showed us the animal, a beautiful wild cat with a thick, speckled tail, like a small lynx. He complained that he'd paid too much for it. Servals are protected and the railway police don't always turn a blind eye, so the deal had to be made fast, there was no time for bartering. But there was no way he would have let this catch slip through his fingers.

Then, as though he had shot the wild cat himself, he said: "The serval is a hard animal to bring down. It can disappear into the trees before you know it; just two eyes glowing in the dark, the hunter can't hesitate for a moment."

My first-class neighbor pointed to a clearing along the tracks.

"My grandfather used to take me antelope hunting. He still walked around in a loincloth. He would sneak up on the herd, stand as still as a termite mound, choose the animal he wanted, then pounce like a panther and throw his spear. He always let me finish them off. A noble animal, the gazelle, the noblest animal of the savanna, nice tasty meat. The best cut of buffalo can't hold a candle to it."

The man with the serval said he preferred elephant entrails.

"You pull them out of its stomach, right after the kill, while they're still steaming. Then grill them straight away, above the fire. A delicacy, m'sieur, a true delicacy."

The men talked about the feasts that followed the hunt, the way the hunters stuffed themselves. There was something undeniably nostalgic in their voices, but that could also have been the time of day – just before sundown, the moment for melancholy reflection.

An old Toyota was parked in front of the station at Franceville. The boy at the wheel was willing to take me to my hotel, and the little fat girl sitting next to him, his sister, named the price. After I'd agreed, she provided me with a summary of their fare criteria: 1. the distance; 2. the weather; 3. *la tête du client*. I seemed to have passed the test.

It was no more than a twenty-minute drive into town; but my hotel was on the other side of Franceville, easily another fifteen minutes. The streets were broad and illuminated by tall lampposts, but were full of potholes. The buildings were spaced far apart along the boulevard. Franceville seemed as sprawling as it was deserted.

"A city on ten hills," said the boy at the wheel.

He drove down one of the ten at full speed. When we were almost at the bottom, he suddenly slammed on the brakes as hard as he could. The tires screeched; the car skidded to a halt across the deserted stretch of road. The only thing moving was the tall grass swaying in the wind, but that didn't seem like any reason to hit the brakes.

"Something wrong?" I asked.

The boy threw the car into reverse, backed up 100 meters, slammed on the brakes again and jumped out. His sister seemed just as surprised as I was; she shook her head and wondered aloud what had gotten into him.

The boy bent over behind the car, then shouted. He shouted to his sister, and it was a cry of joy.

"*Tu vas voir et tu vas danser.*"

She jumped out.

"*Tu vas chanter et tu vas danser.*"

And dance she did. She clapped her hands and danced on the asphalt. I decided to take a look; something truly astounding must have happened.

Lying on the road was a dead animal. It was bleeding from the mouth, probably hit by a car. A rather plump animal. The boy didn't know the French name for it; he thought it was something like *hérisson*, but that means hedgehog. This thing was as big as a fox. The boy said they waddled around on the upland plain, and the farmers hated them because they ate their manioc. The meat was lovely when roasted, and you could boil it too.

He picked it up and I touched its pelt. The fur felt prickly. Wasn't this a . . .

"*Porc,*" I ventured.

The boy suddenly remembered the French word.

"That's right, it's a *porc-épi.*"

He took a banana leaf out of the trunk, wrapped it around the porcupine and carefully laid the blood-smeared trophy next to my suitcase. His sister was thrilled.

"We're going to take it to my girlfriend's and roast it, and then we're going to dance."

She must have repeated that twenty times, and every time she did she clapped her hands.

We drove on.

In front of the hotel I wished them *bon appétit* and carried my suitcase into the lobby, blood trailing behind me on the white-tiled floor.

The desk clerk looked at me wide-eyed.

"How did you get here?"

"Straight through the jungle . . . right across the country."

He wiped the blood off my suitcase with a grin, said I was the only person staying at the hotel, and asked if I was hungry.

That evening I dined on antelope, surrounded by four waiters who taught me a new French expression: *revenir bredouille*, meaning 'to come home empty-handed' from the hunt, the most shameful thing that can happen to a Gabonese.

CHAPTER 4
Men and Other Loneliness

A LAIN KAPRISKI picked me up at Moanda station. The first thing I noticed about him was the catch in his voice; the second, the way he barreled down the dark roads as though death were more welcome to him than the light of day. But I was in no position to complain: he'd saved me from a long night's wait on a deserted platform.

The station at Moanda, a mining town in southern Gabon, lies a good twelve kilometers from the nearest house. I had climbed down from the train in the middle of the evening, stepping out into the last few drops of a thundershower that had made the air heavy, but no cooler. No porter approached me, no taxi driver; there was no hut or shed to be seen, only the vague contours of giant trees. Moanda reeked of jungle, not manganese. The train disappeared, chuffing dully over the hill, and I heard a monkey scream, a cry of fear with no echo, a cry immediately smothered by the forest, and all I could do after that was get used to the silence.

It happens all the time in Gabon: you step down from a train into the void. The bare lightbulb above the station exit illuminates an empty place; the shadowy spot on the horizon is where you can rightfully assume the jungle starts, and somewhere in that jungle is the place you have to be. The problem is how to get there. During the day you simply shrug it off, but in the suffocating darkness of tropical night you suddenly understand why Brazza sometimes sat in front of his tent, sleepless, singing the Italian lullabies his mother had taught him. You start worrying that you may have to do the same, sitting there on the platform, alone in the world, leaning against your suitcase with the glimmer of the glow-worms as your only distraction.

Gabon is full of trees, and little more. From the people you have nothing to fear: the Gabonese wouldn't dream of bothering you, they're too busy averting their own misfortune with their own matchless rituals; it's the jungle you hear moving in close with a cry. The scream of a monkey, the screech of a nightbird cuts through you like a knife, and then the silence comes back hissing in your ear.

But I got lucky in Moanda. I heard an engine turn over, two beams of light swept the platform; I left my suitcase behind and took off at a run, sprinting towards the car until I heard a man shout in French: "Take it easy, dummy, I wasn't going to leave you out here."

That was Alain Kapriski. His voice had a strange, strangled quality to it. He talked a lot and coughed constantly, but it was as though a sob had got stuck in his throat. He was small and wiry, full of a restlessness that vibrated right through to the tips of his mustache. Although he was born in Poland, he had definitely learned to drive in France: he handled the car like a red-eyed commuter blasting through traffic towards the Arc de Triomphe.

Alain drummed his fingers on the wheel, nodded at the pack

of Brazzas in the glove compartment and asked me to light one for him. I passed him the burning cigarette; he took a hurried drag, coughed up phlegm, wiped his mouth on his arm and, after another smothered fit of hacking, started talking again with that sob in his voice.

Never run in this country, he said. You could pass out, just like that – it had happened to him once. The air was too heavy to breathe, especially right after a thundershower. And never leave your suitcase unattended; even if you can't see anyone, they're still there, and they can't always resist the temptation. If I thought that was meant disparagingly, I was wrong: he meant nothing bad by it – the Gabonese were all right by him.

Then, nodding at the trees flashing by, freakish bony fingers against a jet-black background, he said: "The long nights here force the people to turn inwards. They come alive at night, but we can't deal with it, we see darkness as a sort of curtain."

The sob in his voice kept him from saying more.

There was nothing Slavic about his thin features, but that didn't really mean anything; his mother was French. Perhaps that catch in his voice was the only thing his father had left him.

I braced myself for the next curve. The Peugeot 205 dribbled across the broken asphalt, and Kapriski regained control of his voice.

"These little cars have a lot of punch. I'd never drive a German car. What about you?"

"They don't rust as fast."

"They're tanks. Just like tanks. But French cars are . . . planes."

He spun the wheel, hit the gas pedal and the car swerved to the right, tires screeching.

"First I'll show you Moanda."

I snuck a look at my watch. Nine-thirty.

"Right now?"

"It doesn't matter, we work around the clock here. Let's go to the new manganese transhipment area."

We came to a large clearing in the forest. Spotlights on steel masts held the night at bay behind the trees. The manganese mine was ten kilometers away, back in the hills; the railroad couldn't get any closer, and an endless flow of orange ore was being transported by conveyor belt to the switchyard, where a huge, towering wheel scooped it into a long line of waiting cars. The machines roared, the world around us was in motion, but there wasn't a soul in sight.

Kapriski explained the fully automated process, noting dimensions, distances, tonnages. The numbers seemed to give him something to hold on to – the sob in his voice disappeared.

We drove on. Total darkness closed in around us again, until Moanda appeared in the distance. More spotlights, this time illuminating a ski-lift with ore hoppers instead of chairs. The cables ran right along the edge of town, then straight through the jungle and across the border to the Congo-Ocean railroad, forty-seven kilometers away. Once the Transgabonais came through, the cableway became obsolete. The hoppers dangled uselessly in the air.

"How do you like that?" I asked Kapriski.

He shrugged. It was their problem, not his. He didn't pay the bills.

"Let's go to the mine."

He was sounding more cheerful by the minute.

"You'll be amazed by this. It's incredible, pure science fiction."

125

A row of hills, hundreds of meters above the town. The manganese lay right on the surface, there for the scraping. Caterpillar tractors on ten-foot tires roared across the face of the mine and tossed out the contents of their buckets without ever coming to a standstill. There was something improbable about it all: such feverish activity in the tropical darkness, the clouds of orange dust, the lowing of the Cyclopean tractors against the screams of monkeys in the surrounding forest.

"This mine covers forty-five square kilometers," Kapriski said. "Along with another in the Soviet Union, it pretty much accounts for the entire world supply of manganese. At the moment, the price of ore is around forty French francs a kilo. Which isn't much. In fact, if you ask me, it's a steal."

He talked on, dropping even more facts and figures into the conversation.

"Do you work at the mine?"

He shook his head. He didn't work *at* the mine, he worked *for* the mine. The mining company, a multinational concern, handled its own transport. He worked as an instructor for the engineers who drove the manganese trains. He was a railwayman, just like his father had been on the Nord Express, and just like his two brothers and father-in-law. They were a family of railwaymen, a caste.

"All right, off to the uranium mine."

That was thirty-five kilometers down the road.

"Let's eat something first."

He thought about it for a second.

"Since you suggested it, okay. I mean, I'll pay my own way, as long as we . . ."

". . . eat together. I wouldn't have it any other way."

126

He smiled uncertainly, then tried to come up with some way to thank me.

"I need to talk," he said finally. "If I don't talk before I go to bed, I can't sleep."

We ate in the garden of the only hotel in Moanda. From the bar came the sound of slurred chatter. Between the beers we drank along with dinner, Kapriski knocked back the shots of whisky his buddies at the bar kept sending out to him. As the evening wore on, he began dumping more and more of them onto the grass.

The drinking was what bothered him most in the tropics, the drinking and the girls. He didn't want a girl. Every white man around here had a sweet young black thing on the side, but he refused to go along with it.

"You probably think that's strange."

He'd trained engineers for the French railway, too, in Paris. And he'd been an official for the local union – a reasonable union, not one of those loudmouthed organizations. The union had grown quickly. He didn't mean to blow his own horn, but he knew how to get along with railway workers: he'd worked behind the wheel of a locomotive for years, so he spoke their language, knew their problems. He was a good official and his local union had grown at the expense of the communists, even though that was the biggest union for railroad employees. Naturally, the communists were itching to get rid of him, and they finally succeeded. There were a lot of them in the railway management, in the decision-making bureaucracy, so when cuts had to be made in his department they didn't waste any time. The decision was left up to him: he could either go on half-pay, or he could go to Gabon.

All he'd known about Africa was where it was on the map. He'd never been outside Europe, not even outside of France: he knew Paris and he knew La Rochelle, his wife's home town. They always spent the summer vacation in La Rochelle, where he went fishing down at the harbor. What he knew of the rest of the world was limited to what his father had told him about Poland, and his father had always drummed it into him that life in France was the best there was. 'Living like God in France' was actually an old Polish expression meaning 'living in the lap of luxury'.

Alain had a nice house about eighty kilometers outside Paris, with a little garden. Two children, a boy and a girl. His wife was the pleasantly plump, freckle-faced daughter of a railwayman. She knew about life on the railroad. Better yet, she had a feeling for it. They both liked to play cards, and they belonged to the local bridge club. It was a nice life, none too exciting, but the children livened things up. They knew at least twenty people in the neighborhood through the card club, and they played in tournaments. Alain always came home as soon as he could after work, and in the train he would try to guess what his wife would be wearing when he got there: a tight pair of jeans, or that knitted skirt that flattered her hips.

Then he had to go to Gabon.

Fifty Europeans live in Moanda. They work in the mine all day, get drunk on whisky every night. Sometimes they leave with a black girl. Not really a whore, just a girl earning a bit on the side; an apathetic girl, one who says: wake me when it's over. Girls whose fathers send them out whoring, an age-old custom in this country; girls who just lie there staring at the ceiling with their eyes half-closed. He went with a girl like that once, but she acted so bored taking off her clothes that he just paid her and left. She cursed him to his back.

Whenever Alain had a day off he went to Booué, a town on the river about 300 kilometers north of Moanda. He would go out fishing there in a canoe with an old Gabonese fisherman. A man of the river. An Adouma.

The first month, the old fisherman never said a word; the second month, it was only "Yes" and "No"; the third month, "Yes, boss" and "No, boss." But the fourth month, he started telling stories.

Alain had picked up the language of the Adouma, word by word. He had listened. He had learned what Europeans are never taught – the meaning of patience, of tolerance. The fisherman told him: we're different, you'll never be able to completely understand me, and I'll never be able to completely understand you, but we can still fish together, you in your way, I in mine . . . as long as we catch a lot of fish together.

It gradually sank in. You started off by respecting each other, and the rest followed. He'd never stopped to think about that kind of thing before. He wasn't much of a reader; he never knew you could reflect on life and draw strength from doing so. It had helped him through some difficult times.

In fact, every day around here was difficult. The agreement was that he would stay in Gabon until his ten apprentice engineers had earned their diplomas. After a year they took the exam, and nine of his students flunked. Two whole years had gone by, and he was still stuck with eight apprentices.

They just weren't interested; they didn't listen to what he told them. They could repeat what he said and mimic everything he'd showed them during the practical lessons in the locomotive, but as soon as he turned his back they started talking about hunting. That was all they cared about, they had absolutely no feeling for trains. They couldn't tell when a diesel engine was running irregularly, they ran into parked rail cars in the switchyard – they just didn't have any feel for it. Every job that involves a sequence of steps has its own rhythm, but he couldn't teach them that; their rhythm was completely different.

He had asked the old fisherman what to do.

The fisherman said: "Let them go hunting, send them home."

"And what then?" he'd asked.

"Then there are two possibilities: either they'll come back after a while and you'll be able to teach them whatever you want; or they'll just go on hunting, in which case they're clearly happier out in the woods."

But the mining company wouldn't let him send them home.

Kapriski tossed back the contents of his glass. There were bags under his eyes. The sob in his voice returned, reminding me of how he'd sounded earlier in the evening, when he'd picked me up at the station. Had he been sitting alone in his car, crying?

He had driven a friend down to catch the train. A nice guy, a lumberjack who had spent twelve years in Gabon and had learned to view the jungle the way the Gabonese do; he knew the local names of all the plants and trees. But then, from one day to the next, the lumberjack had started acting strange. One evening after dinner, he took his rifle, went out onto the porch of his house, sat down and just started shooting. The darkness of the tropical night had become a curtain, a curtain he was trying to shoot to ribbons, and he kept firing until the sky grew light.

His friends told him to go back to France. They'd had to do a lot of talking, but they finally convinced him. Kapriski drove him to the station.

"He talked about it so clearly. He said there was something funny in the air here, something we can't handle. We may be able to stick it out for years, but one day we finally blow our tops. He said it was like an itch deep inside you, an itching in your soul."

"Do you believe that?"

"Not completely. Maybe it's just homesickness. We're all homesick for the past. My father never stopped thinking about Poland, even though he talked about France like it was heaven on earth. Way down deep, he was an outsider. We all are, only this place makes you so painfully aware of it."

The next morning Kapriski took me to the uranium mine.

Twenty-four hours later, he drove me back to the station.

As we were saying goodbye, he asked me what kind of winter we'd had in Europe.

I told him what he wanted to hear.

"Really cold."

In Lastoursville I went looking for the tomb of Lastours.

François Rigail de Lastours was born in the French town of Montauban in 1855. He came from a family of Protestant noblemen who had owned land around Rennes for ten generations and more. His early years were spent with his three sisters at the ancestral castle, and he would have remained a country gentlemen all his life if his parents hadn't died within a few months of each other. His uncle, a retired naval officer, raised the boy, broadened his horizons and taught him the meaning of wanderlust.

Lastours studied mining engineering and took part in an exploratory expedition to Mozambique. It was while living in the Portuguese colony that he developed a taste for Africa.

'The air tonight is so wonderfully mild', he wrote in his journal. 'I've never felt so strong, so happy and healthy as I do today. I see myself crossing all of Africa, from the Cape of Good Hope to Algeria.'

Those words must have flashed through his mind when the bailiff appeared at the door. Upon his return from the tropics he had regaled too many friends with his stories, and paid too dearly for the banquets at which he spun his yarns, without taking into account the waning family fortune. It had happened before he knew it, a few months at most, but that didn't interest the bailiff. He gave his creditors the slip by joining up with Brazza, who was making the final preparations for his third African expedition. Lastours said nothing, of course, about his real reasons for vanishing into the jungle in Brazza's wake. He simply signed up, sailed out of Bordeaux and away from France, leaving his sisters and uncle to pick up the tab.

Once safely in Africa, he proved a zealous explorer. He was out for glory, to negate the scandal at home. But glory didn't come easily; the only recognition Lastours received was having a settlement named after him, and he wasn't around to see that.

Acting on Brazza's orders, he navigated the Alima and explored the upper reaches of the Congo. His reports on the tribes who lived along those rivers were lively and full of observant detail.

'The Batéké are generally small, skinny to a man and extremely energetic, scrawny as bantams. They eat very little, yet occasionally knead manioc into a large ball, stuff it in their mouths, force it down with a thumb and then swallow it whole: you can see the ball sliding all the way down to their stomachs.'

He adopted the same cheerful tone when describing his journeys on the Ogooué, for he was still too young to spend much time mourning those killed along the way.

'I've run the river three times, and men have drowned during each of these convoys, six of them on the last trip alone. Yet there is no denying the thrill one feels at being swept along at full speed through rapids and cascades, at shooting through the foaming waves and whirlpools like an arrow . . . In five days of going downstream, we cover a stretch that took a whole month coming up.'

For Lastours, the real work began in 1885, when Brazza chose him to help make an old dream come true: the discovery of a route to the mysterious land of Chad. But then, of all moments, Lastours's strength deserted him. At the age of thirty, having barely set out on what was to have been the journey of a lifetime, he died of malaria in the settlement of Maadiville, later known as Lastoursville.

Before breathing his last, he whispered a few words to his subordinates. They referred to the debts he had left behind with his family: he begged his uncle and sisters for forgiveness.

As he fell back in exhaustion onto the horse blanket that had been rolled up for him as a pillow, Brazza walked into the hut.

The Italian was passing through on his way to Franceville. 'I arrived just in time', he wrote later, 'to clasp a hand no longer able to release my own, and to close eyes extinguished while gazing into mine'.

It was not until forty-six years later that *La Géographie*, the explorers' trade journal, commemorated Lastours with a lengthy article. To compensate for that long silence, the editors portrayed him as a saint. But the Adouma remember a different Lastours. Too often did his ambition get the better of the preternatural patience required in Africa. Driven by his need to discover the unknown, he had flogged reluctant porters and rowers, even seeing fit to use summary execution as a means of dealing with thievery and acts of violence.

To this day, he's still paying for that.

The neighborhood where Rigail de Lastours is buried is referred to in Adouma as Micatsha, meaning 'whiplash'.

On my way out to the Whiplash district, I was suddenly reminded of another explorer, Paul Crampel.

He left Lastoursville on 12 August 1888, headed for Cameroun with an armed escort consisting of a grand total of two sharpshooters.

The party walked into an ambush.

Both riflemen were killed, and Crampel was shot in the thigh. From then on it was a race against gangrene.

Limping and racked with fever, he completed his 300-kilometer journey to the coast carrying Niarinzhé, a Fang girl entrusted to him by a chieftain, on his back.

Crampel had a poet's love of Africa. He viewed the native dances as Dantesque tableaux, and was carried away by their hallucinatory fervor. He observed man in his natural state through the fond and idealistic eyes of a Rousseau, and excused the ease with which he went for spear and rifle as the simplicity of the unspoilt. The handmade slug that had entered his leg just below the groin apparently gave him no cause to reconsider.

Back in France he regained his strength and recuperated from his injuries. He had covered no less than 2100 kilometers on foot, through the jungle. From his sick bed he worked out the plans for his next expedition, based on one single, simple premise designed to capture the popular imagination. That, Crampel believed, was the only way to sway public opinion in one's favor. More than those who had gone before, he was aware of the power of the press; Crampel thought in headlines. From the jungle to the desert: that was a cause readers could identify with, and that was the route he planned to follow – from the heart of the Congo to the northern Sahara, then home by way of Algiers.

The reporters took to the plan immediately, but even more to the person of Crampel. After all, the man was a walking feature story. Who else would limp 300 kilometers through the jungle with a black girl on his back?

She had come with him to Paris. Wherever he went – to the opera, to the fashionable cafés and restaurants, to the Petite Vache creamery where the explorers met – the slender, boyish Niarinzhé went with him, hiding her shyness behind the poses of a nymphet. His Arabic interpreter, Ischekhad – the Tuareg who would unintentionally bring about Crampel's demise – usually accompanied him as well. His adoring wife stayed at home, however, so as not to compromise his carefully constructed image of cosmopolite and young primitive. Brazza's personal secretary, Charles de Chavannes, spoke in his memoirs of Crampel's behavior as 'quite original'; his outspoken Negrophilism branded him an outsider. Nonetheless, once back in the jungle, Crampel lost his bearings and left a trail of blood behind.

Seventeen years later, Louis-Ferdinand Céline – still plain old Dr Destouches at the time – spent time in the jungles of Cameroun. In *Journey to the End of the Night*, he wrote:

'In the European cold, under gray, puritanical northern skies, we seldom get to see our brothers' festering cruelty except in times of carnage, but when roused by the foul fevers of the tropics, their rottenness rises to the surface. That's when the frantic unbuttoning sets in, when filth triumphs and covers us entirely.'

And, he added:

'It is hard to get a faithful look at people and things in the tropics because of the colors that emanate from them. In the tropics colors and things are in a turmoil. To the eye, a small sardine tin lying in the road at noon can take on the dimensions of a catastrophe. You've got to watch out. It's not just the people who are hysterical down here, objects are the same way. Life only becomes tolerable at nightfall, but then almost immediately the darkness is taken over by swarms of mosquitoes. Not one or two or a hundred, but billions of them. Survival under those conditions is quite an achievement. A carnival by day, riddled full of holes by night, a quiet war.'

Yet this twilight war was not the only one Crampel had to fight. 'Not a day goes by', he wrote home, 'without the sound of gunfire'. He felt bad about that, yet pointed the finger at hostile chieftains, not at himself. Determined to reach his destination, every day he would order his sharpshooters to fire again.

Leaving from the Congo, he headed for Chad, then crossed the Sudan into southern Algeria. It was just the way he'd formulated it in those few simple sentences drawn up on his sick bed: were this entire area to be placed under French rule, France would possess a magnificent African empire, with Lake Chad at its heart. His prediction ultimately came true: by the late nineteenth century, the French flag flew over Central Africa and Chad, but no thanks to Crampel. His expedition was a dismal failure.

Goaded by the fear that Germans from Cameroun, Brits from the Sudan or Belgians from the Congo Free State would beat him to the punch, he left Marseilles in too great a hurry. The first thing he did when he arrived in Senegal was recruit the local station-master, Albert Nebout, and the police commissioner, Gabriel Biscarrat; Maurice Lauzière was the only member of the expedition to come with him from Paris.

At a trot whenever possible, but usually in single file, he moved through the jungle with thirty Senegalese riflemen, seventy porters, his Tuareg interpreter, Ischekhad, the Algerian guide Mohammed ben Saïd and, of course, his Niarinzhé, who he worshiped like a black goddess and who heeded him like a slave in turn. Crampel's white companions couldn't understand his devotion: Niarinzhé fraternized too much with the natives, too obviously enjoyed being back in Africa, too easily forgot the drawing-room manners she'd learned in Paris. They didn't trust the girl, but they were also afraid to call their leader to account. Morale quickly worsened. They were barely under way when Crampel had the first run-in with his porters, who were sometimes forced to march on an empty stomach for three days at a time; organizational talent was not one of his gifts.

The further north they went, the more frequent became the clashes with the natives. Ongoing tribal warfare had made the region extremely restless, but Crampel didn't waste time negotiating with local chieftains. Belgians and Germans and

Englishmen; his feverish mind was crawling with pursuers. To speed things up, he ordered punitive expeditions and put villages to the torch. Like Lastours, his fascination with Africa finally succumbed to his lust for glory; he was determined to succeed, cost what it may, and so raced on towards his demise.

The presence of an Algerian and a Tuareg caused the tribes along the border with Chad to suspect that the French had teamed up with the northern desert peoples, the cattle thieves with whom they lived in a state of permanent hostility. Crampel was given no chance to prove differently; on 9 April 1891, at the age of twenty-seven, he was murdered on the banks of the Aouk River by soldiers of the Sultan of Kouta. Forty-one days later, a similar fate overcame Biscarrat, and Lauzière died of fever. Of the white men in the expedition, only Nebout survived; Niarinzhé fled with Mohammed ben Saïd and, to save their own skins, the girl and the guide told the inhabitants of the village where they finally took refuge that they had intentionally led the white intruders into an ambush.

When news of Crampel's death reached Paris four months later, all France mourned. With his unruly beard, his cowboy hat, his short pants and his collarless shirt open flamboyantly at the neck, with the obligatory monkey on his arm and lithe Negro boy at his side in every photo – *Look, folks, here I am among the savages* – Crampel was the hero of the illustrated press. A hippie *avant la lettre*, who had studied classics at the universities of Paris, Nancy and Bordeaux, but gave it all up to test the tenor of the heroic poems against the reality of the jungle. But Crampel was too wild a romantic to be a good organizer and – despite his Negrophilism – knew too little of the tribes in the area he tried to cross, and virtually nothing of Islam. This latter shortcoming brought about his downfall once he approached the desert, and with it the most fervent Muslims. He was literally hacked to pieces.

The terrible thing was that his sponsors had seen it all coming. Crampel was barely under way when the Comité pour l'Afrique Française sent a relief expedition out after him, followed shortly afterwards by a third, announcing that he 'lacked adequate resources' and had 'insufficient knowledge of the region'. The second expedition was led by Louis Mizon, the third by Jean Dybowski, an employee of the Musée de Paris who was well acquainted with Arabic culture and the peoples of the southern Sahara. Mizon was forced to turn back, so Dybowski took the bull by the horns; when news of Crampel's murder reached him, he changed his plans and set out to avenge the death of his compatriot. Months later, when he arrived at the town where Crampel had been ambushed, Dybowski executed an innocent *marabout*, attacked a group of Muslims, killed another fifteen men and left the same day, back the way he'd come.

He too had lost his bearings, he too had suffered the itching in his soul, he too had taken to violence as the last line of defense against his fear of the unknown.

Lastours's final resting place consists of a brick tomb and a rusted iron cross, almost hidden from sight by weeds, grass and vines; the inscription is no longer legible.

I followed the slippery path back to my lodgings. The ground between the near-white trunks of fifty-meter-high kapok trees was clogged with giant ferns. Canary-yellow butterflies with black spots fluttered up from the bushes, pursued by clouds of mosquitoes.

Had I been born a century earlier, would I have done any better? Better than Lastours, better than Crampel or Dybowski? Travelling required more patience back then, and patience is something lost easily in these parts; after ten mosquito bites have been racked up in the space of five minutes, you're ready to go out of your mind. Dying for a breath of wind, you walk on, and after half a mile you ask yourself how Crampel ever kept it up for 2100 kilometers in this humid, leaden air.

'We rarely see a blue sky from late June to the end of July', wrote Albert Schweitzer in *Lambarene*. 'On the whole the sky is gray, like Europe on a dark November day. Often too dark to read or write.' And when he couldn't read, the jungle truly became depressing for Schweitzer. 'Intellectual labor is what one needs to stay on top of things in Africa. Strange as it may sound, life in the jungle is harder on the native than it is on the educated man, for the latter has means of relaxation at his disposal that the other does not . . . Woe to him who cannot find rest in this way, and so recoup his energy! For he will be destroyed by the horribly prosaic life in these parts.'

Reading was the clue, and not just the newspaper.

'Here where time stands still, such printed chit-chat made to serve the fleeting day seems just a touch ridiculous.'

To his readers, Schweitzer held up the example of the lumberjack who always took a copy of *Aurora*, by the German seventeenth-century mystic Jacob Böhme, along with him in the dugout.

'Almost all great Africa travellers carry food for thought among their supplies.'

He was probably thinking of Mary Kingsley, who read Spinoza in the jungle, or André Gide, who devoured the collected works of Racine during his eleven-month journey through the French Congo.

Beneath a barred window, I sat leafing through the Acts of the Apostles. I was staying at the mission post, the only accommodation in town. The sole hotel in Lastoursville had closed after the Transgabonais was completed. My room contained a cot, a bare table and a straight-backed wooden chair. On the chair lay what was left of a Bible. Many of the pages were missing, and I soon came to follow the example of those who had gone before me by using the Gospels for toilet paper. Little had changed since Lastours's day; at best, supplies only trickled into the interior. 'No food, no clothing, no shoes, no medicine, no quinine', Lastours had complained. But then, on the other hand, there *were* millions of tsetse flies.

Out on the porch I came across a priest with a head of kinky gray hair, dozing in a high-backed rattan chair. When I sat down next to him he awoke with a start.

"Oh, it's you. Nice to have company. Slide your chair over here; you look sad."

"What do you expect," I mumbled, "with all these wasted lives?"

He waved a hand tiredly. Talking wouldn't get us anywhere; it was enough to just sit next to each other and enjoy God's handiwork. He folded his hands, I folded mine, and we remained that way, without a word, till darkness came and the jungle awoke with the call of the rainbird, followed as if on command by the cries of a thousand others.

It must have been the crucifix above my bed that made me save my last melancholy moment of the day for the Duke of Uzès.

His mother made him go into the jungle.

The staunchly Catholic Duchess of Uzès was simply wild about Count Brazza. Bent over the newspaper in her Parisian boudoir, she followed the accounts of his civilizing expeditions as though his deeds were those of a crusading knight, and in a surge of piety decided to extricate her son from 'the wasteful life of the capital' and send him out on 'a grand mission'. With the Italian count – who was actually a great deal less papist than the duchess realized – as a lamp to guide his feet, the duke was to bring the one true faith to Africa and, on his way from Brazzaville to Abyssinia, drop in and free Khartoum from the Madhists. Wishing to leave nothing to chance, she organized the expedition herself between tea parties.

Jacques de Crussol, the Duke of Uzès, was barely an adult; he could do little but yield to the plans of his overwrought mother and – after a final blow-out with his friends – put away his patent-leather slippers and order a pair of stout boots. Meanwhile, the duchess had recruited the old Africa-hand Emile Julien, as well as a physician, an ethnologist, a quartermaster and a journalist, whose job was to engrave her son's heroic exploits in the minds of French readers for all eternity.

Thirty heavily armed Algerian sharpshooters were to ensure the safety of the members of the expedition, who wanted for nothing, save perhaps a smidgin of confidence in the success of their own enterprise. When the expedition left Marseilles in 1892, the duchess came along to the harbor to wave goodbye.

Once in the jungle, the young duke soon found himself forced to hand over command to Lieutenant Julien, for even the Algerian foot soldiers laughed in his face. When the original plan of reaching the Nile within a few months proved impossible, the expedition degenerated into a drawn-out wild-goose chase, the goal of which defied all compass technique.

Jacques de Crussol lost all control over the situation and returned to Brazzaville in February 1893, accompanied by Emile Julien. Both duke and mentor were seriously ill. Just when the young nobleman had mustered enough courage to board a ship for France and face his mother, he died of dysentery.

Less than one year later, the deeply sorrowful Duchess of Uzès published an account of the journey. *Le voyage de mon fils au Congo*.

I arrived in Ndjolé on the evening of the first of May. The driver of the beer truck was the only sober man in town. He brought me from the station to my hotel, a further twelve kilometers, in his truck laden with empty bottles.

"*La bière,*" he said. "*Ça passe ici.*"

The next morning he would drive to Libreville with the crates the local population had emptied on International Labor Day, and return the same day with fresh supplies. He drove the route three times a week, along a muddy road that was virtually impassable in the rainy season. It was a tricky business, as he chose to demonstrate: pumping the brakes, he nosed the truck downhill, thousands of empties clattering at our backs.

"Transporting beer demands concentration, m'sieur."

The locals were unfit for this kind of work. Unable to keep their hands off the cargo under the tarpaulin, they would drink themselves silly and fall asleep at the wheel. His boss only worked with foreign drivers, and his boss was Lebanese.

"The Jews of West Africa, m'sieur."

He himself came from Sâo Tomé. He knew how to work. He'd been running himself ragged in Gabon for the last twelve years. As soon as he'd put together a nice little nest egg, he was going back to Sâo Tomé. Ever since the crisis started, the Gabonese refused to give foreigners the time of day. Foreigners meaning those from Senegal, Mali, Cameroun and Sâo Tomé. Not the French.

"If you'll excuse my saying so, m'sieur, they prefer foreign masters to hard-working brothers."

Could a Gabonese have his own shop? Impossible. His whole family would start running up a tab and he'd be bankrupt before he knew it. In this part of the world, retailers were, by definition, foreigners.

"They should be grateful to us, m'sieur."

The Gabonese were lazy, suspicious and envious by nature. Alcohol, inbreeding, venereal disease and a total lack of hygiene had done the rest. I probably couldn't tell the difference, people from Sâo Tomé were just as black as the Gabonese, but to him they were worlds apart. The Gabonese showed absolutely no initiative, the Gabonese let themselves be led around by the nose, the Gabonese were far inferior to the people of Sâo Tomé; this wasn't racism, this was the gospel truth.

We pulled up at the hotel and I asked him in for a beer. He emptied his glass in less than two minutes. The Gabonese bartender was giving him dirty looks; he wasn't welcome here, he could feel it.

"Now that's what I call racism, m'sieur."

The Gabonese bartender turned out to be my waiter as well. He was courteous, but tired. Shuffling off into the kitchen, he looked like he was taking his final steps under a murderous sun, yet he came back each time and served my order attentively.

The hotel was run by two Frenchmen. The only African thing about the dining room was the mosquitoes. The walls were hung with copper pans and a clumsily painted landscape of the bay at St Tropez. The Frenchmen also ran a nightclub across the road, where the Ogooué flowed just a few meters beyond the dance floor.

Against the left wall of the restaurant was a piano, a relic from a different age and another world. I couldn't help thinking of the young, consumptive wife of the American missionary Dr Robert Hamill Nassau, who lost her startling Pre-Raphaelite beauty in less than two years in some two-bit town outside Ndjolé, confiding her melancholy to the piano with fingers that grew ever thinner; she was buried behind the new chapel during a service at which the piano sounded for the last time, for the next Mrs Nassau could read no music. Then I thought of another missionary who had played one hymn after another, encouraged by the enthusiastic singing of four Gabonese villagers, only to discover the next morning the real reason for their resounding musical support: during the performance, the four accompanists had taken turns ransacking his pantry.

I felt like playing something.

The tired old waiter said he didn't mind – I was the only customer, and he was deaf in one ear anyway. I played a Rondo by Mozart, then one of his Fantasies, and I shouldn't have done that.

Standing up from the piano, soaked in sweat, I turned around to find myself being stared at by a group of about ten men. Older white men with weathered faces, burly broad-shouldered fellows, the kind I'd come across so often, lumberjacks in filthy shirts with the sleeves rolled up and pegged corduroy trousers that had grown too short from frequent washing.

I walked up to the bar and didn't have to order a beer: the bottle was set in front of me. I didn't have to sign the meal ticket either: the bill had been paid for. While I was slowly emptying my glass, the men left the room, one by one, clearly touched. However clumsy and out of tune the music, they had heard it and come in from outside, or from the nightclub across the street, because they heard something of the past in it, something irrevocably bound up with that continent on which, for whatever reason, they had turned their backs. Mozart: that was their mother, or their cousin, or their old school teacher, and suddenly they were missing people they had almost forgotten. I had never seen so many men in one place acting so shyly, so awkwardly. They were unable to speak a word, unable to find the gesture that would allow them to strike any pose at all. One by one they slunk off, eyes averted, crumpled felt hats in hand, and I knew it: no country is more forsaken than Gabon, no country makes of loneliness a more serious ill.

That night I was awakened by shouts. I jumped out of bed and pushed open the door to the balcony. There was a fight going on in front of the nightclub. It was the same group of men. They were fighting each other. They were fighting with three, four Gabonese. Pie-eyed drunk, they staggered into the nightclub and came back out with chairs which they broke over each other's heads. They ducked, jumped up and smashed each other in the face. They cursed, swore, bled and went back into the nightclub again and again for fresh ammunition. Tables were used as shields, the legs of chairs as sabers. They roared.

I closed the shutters and the balcony door behind me and went to take a shower. That couldn't really have been going on under my window, it must have been a bad dream. By the time I had showered and was drying myself, the ruckus had stopped. I peered through the shutters. A puddle of blood was the only thing left to show there had ever been a fight. Two stray dogs were licking it dry.

CHAPTER 5

The Count and the Bastard

H<small>E HAD</small> known the Count, had seen him at work in the bush – the best place other than a man's deathbed to assess his real worth – but now he was selling pots and pans door-to-door in the suburbs of Johannesburg, with scarcely an opportunity to summon up old memories.

One day he rang the bell of the novelist Ethelreda Lewis. She wasn't really in the mood for other people's stories as she'd just written the opening line of a new chapter, but she told him he was a godsend, because she needed a new griller. While she was paying him, she heard the lilt in his voice; during the weeks to come, she would only ask him to stop talking when she needed to sharpen her pencil.

Alfred Aloysius Smith was the name. Born and raised in Lancashire. Left home at . . . well, he must have just turned eighteen, the newly employed agent for the illustrious Hatton and Cookson merchant house of Liverpool. His destination? Gabon, or, as they called it back then, the Ivory Coast, because what they were really looking for on the west coast of Africa was ivory. A remote trading post, days upriver from the coast; some-times he would go a whole rainy season without seeing another white man, and his closest neighbors were cannibals. The most upstanding race on earth, Mrs Lewis, the women chaste, the men devout.

No doubt about it, it was a hard and lonely existence. Some colleagues his age took their own lives, others took to the bottle as a substitute for human company, and most of them died of fever. But all it took to make his day was to see a gray parrot fly overhead. Nature had helped out in other ways as well: it had made him as tough as nails.

He moved to Madagascar at the end of the last century, took part in the Boer War at the beginning of this one. After all, he was an Englishman, wasn't he? Penniless and exhausted, he'd stayed behind in South Africa and, well, she knew the rest of the story by now: he'd sold pots and pans, door-to-door, until he rang her bell.

Mrs Lewis wrote it all down with a grateful smile. She sat down at her typewriter and expanded on her notes, turning them into a coherent story and giving Smith a pseudonym that seemed hacked from the right kind of tropical hardwood. Three years later, anyone who hadn't heard of Trader Horn was either illiterate or never went to the movies.

Trader Horn, subtitled *The Ivory Coast in the earlies*, was published in New York in 1928. The trader's straightforward tales about gorillas, elephants, hippos, cannibals and the kidnapped white girl Lola D. may have been rather long-winded – despite the stylistic interventions of Ethelreda Lewis – but the Hollywood screenwriters knew how to fix that. Metro-Goldwyn-Mayer bought the rights, and W. S. van Dyke's film starring Harry Carey made Trader Horn a household name. A London publisher took advantage of the public's interest by producing a cheap film tie-in edition. *Trader Horn* became one of the biggest sellers since *Uncle Tom's Cabin.*

Horn took his share of the royalties back to England, where he bought a house in the country. He was seventy-three by then, but his tongue didn't go into retirement. He could always be found down at the local pub, adding new anecdotes to his store of published memoirs, until he died of alcohol poisoning soon after.

Horn had a passionate hatred for the French, which extended to the entire Latin race. "If God ever created a worse colonial than the Frenchman, then he never told me about it," he confided to Ethelreda Lewis.

He allowed only one exception. That was Count Brazza.

The Lancashire trader had observed the Italian explorer during his final expedition.

"A gentleman through and through. Commissioned by the French, but tended to work according to his taste for adventure."

He remembered Brazza as a pensive man who never smiled, pacing back and forth on his verandah, twisting the tips of his mustache as he walked. The Africans would giggle and mimic him.

"He'd've done better at poetry," Horn ruled. "But a man, for all that. Aye, he stepped as if earth was his heritage."

'Welcome to Franceville' read the banner stretched across the asphalt road to the center of town, 'Everlasting Monument to Savorgnan de Brazza'.

That was a good sign.

At the University of Franceville I hoped to find a historian who could give me the African low-down on the explorer. The only Gabonese point of view I was familiar with was that of ethnologist Jean Emile M'Bot, who roundly referred to Brazza as a cheat – under the cloak of elevated ideals, he had turned Gabon and the Congo over to the French.

After a lot of footwork I finally met a young history teacher from a local high school. He said: "Brazza is a part of your past, not ours." When I asked whether he really had nothing good to say about the explorer, he replied: "Brazza founded Francheville, a settlement for freed slaves, but it didn't take long for them to drop the *h* entirely. The city of the free men became the city of the French, and that pretty much sums it up."

But he still took me to see the statue of Brazza, unveiled in 1980 as part of Franceville's centennial celebrations. I said I was amazed that the Gabonese had erected a statue to a swindler. He shrugged. "The government was probably fishing for a loan from the French." A little later he showed me the mosque that was being built on the same street. "We could use some help from the Arabs, too." Last of all, he took me to see the new summer residence of the Gabonese head of state. An earlier version of the building had been torn down, he said, after the president had heard rumors that its walls had been rubbed with a dangerous fetish. He'd built a whole new palace.

Three civilizations on the same street. That reminded me of an anecdote Albert Schweitzer once told about Brazza.

One day, the Italian explorer asked some natives from Haut-

Ogooué province to take the canoe down to Ndjolé to pick up some supplies. Before they left, Brazza wrote a letter to the agent at the trading post. Dear sir, please be so kind as to give these men so many muskets, so many knives, so many kegs of black powder and so many barrels of salt. "Will he really do that?" the oarsmen asked after the explorer had read his order out loud. "Most assuredly," Brazza said, "as long as you hand him this piece of paper." And it worked: the agent asked no questions, and simply gave the men the goods Brazza had asked for.

Not long after that, a village chieftain asked the mission post at Lambaréné to send a preacher to Haut-Ogooué. He and his people wished to be taught the word of God and to learn to read and write. The preacher arrived, read Bible stories to the tribespeople and taught them the alphabet and how to write letters on a slate. The villagers' religious fervor quickly cooled. "This is all wrong," they said, "you don't have to teach us how to scribble on a slate, all you have to do is show us how to write something on paper that will make the whites at the trading post in Ndjolé give us things for free."

I left Franceville riding on the bed of a pickup truck, heading west. The road snaked over the same upland plain that Brazza had walked across. The Italian liked this part of the country: the air here was drier and thinner than in the jungle, the people were friendly and helpful, and the vistas wide and uninterrupted, just like in Umbria or Tuscany.

After a little less than an hour, Mvengwé appeared on the horizon. Like almost all the villages on the plateau, it seemed deserted. The truck was headed north, and I was going south: Mvengwé marks the crossroads for the track to Poubara Falls. I hopped out at the crossing; a dog barked but kept out of sight, like its masters. I waited a few hours.

Then a dilapidated Toyota pickup pulled over. Behind the wheel was a boy of about twenty. He was willing to take me to the waterfall for twenty francs. He didn't like to ask for money, he was always ready to help a foreigner, but gas cost two-fifty a liter these days, scandalously high for a country that produced its own oil.

It had rained heavily overnight, and entire sections of the dirt road were washed out. He usually took the truck up to a hundred on this road, but now he couldn't go any faster than seventy. The shock absorbers were taking a real beating; any number of times it seemed as though we were going to flip over.

The dirt track followed a range of hills. The grass growing on either side was higher than the roof of the cab. A bird the size of a pheasant took off right in front of our bumper. It had blue feathers, a yellow breast and a fluffy brown crest – a touraco. Occasionally the grass would part and we could see for twenty kilometers in every direction: yellowish-green ridges under blue-gray clouds, without a hut, pylon or telephone wire in sight. Here, creation had stopped at Genesis 2: 'thus the heavens and the earth were finished'.

The boy asked why I wanted to go to Poubara.

"Because of Brazza."

He nodded, as though that were the only logical answer.

"Strange guy. Walked from Poubara Falls all the way to the Alima. A hundred and seventy kilometers across high-country sand. He may have been white, but he walked. In his bare feet!"

The boy grinned. His name was Mikolo, but his friends called him Charlie. He shoved a cassette into the tape deck and the sound of the blues filled the cab. It was just right for the upland plains, melancholy and slow, music that seemed to make its way up a never-ending slope. "Our music," Charlie said, and I thought about the circular course of things – by way of the slaves on the American plantations, this music had come back to Africa, electronically amplified.

Charlie was wearing a felt hat and high boots. He dealt in odds and ends, scavenged around the villages, wheeled and dealed. His old pickup was his home for days at a time, and he covered thousands of kilometers a month.

"You could call me a wanderer, just like old Brazza."

He asked me about Rome. Were the roofs there made of sheet iron? Did they drive around in big cars, like on *Dallas*? Were there mango trees? He had never been outside this part of the country, and had no desire to leave the plateau; it was way too cold on the coast, and those jokers in the capital were no better than common crooks, you could tell by the price of gas.

Even when he was still a kid he had wanted to travel through the jungle like Brazza. Life must be good on an expedition like that. No women trying to marry you all the time. A little hunting, some joking around, just a bunch of pals. His friends were always calling him a sissy. He never wanted to dance, that was too risky for him. It started off with a nice tune, but before you knew it you had a little woman at home who cursed you up and down every time you stayed away for a few days. Women? Nothing but jealousy. Like it was pounded into them while they were pounding manioc. Jealous to the bone. And where did they get you? They got you to pay off their family with meat or gas, because maybe you fooled around once. And these days gas cost two-fifty a liter!

Brazza, now he was a man's man. Okay, he was white, but what difference did that make? After all, Rambo was white, too. "You can't compare Brazza with Rambo," I said. "Brazza went out of his way to avoid a fight." But not the fight with the jungle, Charlie said, and not the fight with himself.

Charlie was a cheerful kid. He spoke French better than the local tribal language, but he still called himself a real Batéké. All the boys his age spoke French when they got together; after all, it was the official language of Gabon, or, as Charlie put it, the language of the television. 'Gabonese' didn't mean much to him; he was from 'the high country', and that didn't stop at the Congolese border.

We drove south for another twenty kilometers. At one point the road dropped sharply and Charlie said: "We're coming down off the plateau now." Suddenly the countryside changed and in an instant we were in the jungle.

The road stopped at the river, where we left the pickup and crossed a bridge of vines. Our feet kept slipping through the netting, while below us the Ogooué roiled and foamed. The bridge, the product of thousands of hours of weaving, hung between two trees. Brazza felt these vine bridges attested to 'great technical ingenuity'.

A Pygmy was waiting for us on the other side, the first Pygmy I'd ever met. He must have been about one and a half meters, short enough of course, but still taller than I had imagined Pygmies to be. He asked for money to buy alcohol. Charlie spat on the ground at his feet, which seemed to curb his expectations; he toned down his request to a couple of cigarettes. I handed him three filter cigarettes, but he handed them right back: he smoked only Brazza Bruns. When I gave him a box of matches he was just as tickled as I would have been thirty years ago with a bubblegum card.

To get to the waterfall we had to trek for a few kilometers through the jungle. Twisted branches formed a roof above the narrow, slippery path; the foliage filtered the sunlight down to dusk. The air we inhaled seemed to come straight out of a humidifier. Charlie let me take the lead, then walked so close behind me that he kept stepping on my heels. His teeth were chattering.

Ever since he'd been bitten by a snake, he believed that the forest spirits were out to get him. A fetish doctor had treated the snakebite with an extract from two different plants, and Charlie was back on his feet again an hour later, but he never got over his fear of the jungle.

"Who told you about Brazza walking barefoot?"

He said he'd heard it on the car radio.

The roar of the falls was coming closer. We climbed a hill, our feet sinking deeper into the mud with every step we took. Brambles snagged our shirts and pulled us back after a few over-hasty steps, while vines wrapped around our legs and tripped us up like children playing tricks. We had to duck under low branches, and ants and mosquitoes stung the backs of our necks. The screaming of birds echoed above the rush of the falls and our breathing came hard on the last few meters of the climb. The jungle was chilly, damp and filthy hot, and we shivered and sweated at the same time. I began to understand why Joseph Conrad equated the lust to drive deep into the heart of Africa with 'the horror'.

But just on the other side of the hill, the waterfall loomed up in a display of unbridled nature; it was the kind of dramatic landscape Brazza could become so ecstatic about, perhaps because his own nature kept him on such a tight rein. The river formed a perfect right angle, plummeting for a good twelve meters, dragging tree trunks along with it and carelessly dashing them to pieces on the rocks below. We approached the riverbank through tall grass, Charlie literally clinging to me now; he swore that the undergrowth, wet with the constant spray of the falls, was crawling with reptiles. I had no trouble believing him, in fact I spent that night dreaming of ungodly monsters, but at that moment, there beside the river, I had eyes only for the water breaking from the green wall high above us, crashing down into white foam and racing off again meters beneath our feet – a breathtakingly beautiful sight.

One hundred and eleven years ago, Brazza had stood here. Pith helmet, naval dress coat, white plus fours, boots with no soles. But he probably didn't enjoy the view much. He'd been wandering through the jungle for three years, shooting one dangerous set of rapids after another, almost breaking his neck every time his canoe capsized, avoiding the trickery of tribal chieftains with tricks of his own, suffering hunger, surviving dozens of attacks of fever – only to stand here and conclude that the Ogooué was not the trade artery he'd been dreaming of. From this point on the river was no longer navigable, not even for canoes. But he didn't despair; he walked to the Alima River in his bare feet, determined to make his way to the Congo.

That was at least one thing he had in common with the poets: his obsessions.

In secondary school Brazza had read travellers' accounts sewn into the bindings of Cornelius Nepos or Cicero. Teachers who asked him questions received a blank stare for an answer. Even before his voice started breaking, it was perfectly clear to him that his future lay at sea, his fortune beneath the flapping sails of a frigate. But Italy still had to achieve true nationhood, and its navy consisted of three officers and an old tub. So, following a chance encounter with the French admiral de Montaignac, Brazza set off to seek his fortune in France. The influential de Montaignac always remained his protector.

Pietro Paulo Francesco Camillo Savorgnano di Brazzà was born in Rome in 1852, the seventh son of Ascanio, Count of Brazzà Cergneu Savorgnano, who ultimately sired a total of twelve children. Ascanio, who hailed from Udine, was a character straight out of Stendahl's *La chartreuse de Parme*. A liberal and a nationalist, a nobleman who had moved to Rome to escape the Austrian occupation of Udine, a devoted reader of Sir Walter Scott (who he had met in England) and a fanatical traveller who brought back sketches of the statues he had seen in Greece or Egypt and copied them at home in marble. An aristocrat who believed that a sound mind was one housed in a sound body, who made his children sleep on rock-hard beds and lined them up at six-thirty each morning for an hour of mandatory gymnastics. A quarter of a century later, the explorer would thank him for that: while his companions lay prostrate with exhaustion around the campfire, he was still on his feet, as straight as a ramrod.

Brazza's youth passed without incident. He wanted for nothing. He worshiped his mother, whose big, dark eyes and intensely sweet smile he never forgot, not even in deepest Africa. She, the stately Venetian noblewoman Giacenta, was always the first person he wrote to about his successes in the wilds. And she faithfully sent him the money he always asked for. Along with his restlessness and slightly apostolic tendencies, Brazza's mother was the driving force behind his journeys of exploration. For as strict and vain as she was, she expected great things of the apple of her eye. Money was no object; after all, she was paying for her family's honor. And of all the ideals she held, family was the one she held dearest by far. It was second nature to him not to disappoint her; once, as a child, he had overcome his fear of the dark for her by spending the night in a lonely graveyard.

At the recommendation of Admiral de Montaignac, Pietro di Brazzà was admitted to the ranks of foreign cadets serving at the naval academy in Brest; he was sixteen. He had little contact with the other students. Most of them were farmers' sons from Brittany; they thought he was far too refined, far too urbane, 'too Paris' as they put it. He often defied academy discipline, just to shake things up, and he was often punished for it. He made friends with only one of the boys, the budding travel writer Pierre Loti.

In 1872 he was assigned to the *Venus* and sailed the South Atlantic. It didn't take him long to realize that, as an Italian in the French navy, he would always remain an outcast. So, having read du Chaillu, Burton and Livingstone, he decided to seek his fortune on land. He didn't even have to leave the navy to do that: all French exploration, even in the Sahara, came under the jurisdiction of the Ministry of the Navy.

At Fernan Vaz he met Marche and Compiègne, who had travelled 400 kilometers up the Ogooué. His cabin was soon full of maps and clippings from geographical magazines. He scribbled a note to de Montaignac, now Minister of the Navy, to ask for financial support for his plan to 'go looking for lakes or the river through which a great mass of water runs down below the Equator'.

With this note – the first of his kept on file – he immediately established his lack of stylistic flair. He adhered more to Italian grammar than to French, could barely spell and hobbled from one lame sentence to the next. During later expeditions he took a secretary with him to edit his letters and reports; Brazza himself never wrote a book about his travels, and his articles only began to improve after he had read Stanley's *Through the Dark Continent*. That account also made him realize that he would never be the American's journalistic equal; from that moment on, he made a virtue of his linguistic shortcomings. He veiled himself in a cloud of riddles, and the things he left unsaid served to cover his tracks for both the officials at the Ministry of the Navy and his rival Stanley.

From the very start, French officialdom did everything in its power to quash Brazza's ambitions. After all, why give money to a foreigner? But de Montaignac persisted. He promoted Brazza to lieutenant (only officers were allowed to lead an expedition) and granted him a year's advance on his pay, as well as permission to take two sailors along with him (quartermaster Victor Hamon and physician Noël Ballay), a third white assistant from the Ministry of Public Instruction (the biologist Alfred Marche) and a stipend of seventeen and a half thousand francs. Ultimately, the expedition would cost forty thousand francs; Brazza's mother made up the shortfall.

But before he could set off, Brazza had to become a naturalized French citizen. He travelled to Paris, Frenchified his name to Pierre Savorgnan de Brazza, and then was told at the Ministry of the Navy that, as a Frenchman, he was to lose the rank of officer; after all, he had gained his cadetship as a foreigner. It was an act of official chicanery, meant to torpedo his plans once and for all. After being granted French citizenship, his rank would be reduced to that of seaman first class, and he would have to take his naval exam at Brest all over again. De Montaignac once again came to his rescue, but when it became clear that he could forget about the Ogooué for the time being, Brazza fled the office to hide his tears, fell down the ministry stairs and broke his arm.

I had never thought of explorers in that way, as youngsters, giant-killers who only reached maturity in the jungle, dreamers who fell down the stairs when those in charge reacted indifferently to their idealistic plans. Only through the memoirs of their friends and companions did I come to appreciate how very little support they received. The French couldn't have cared less what Pierre Savorgnan de Brazza was looking for in Equatorial Africa. In 1875 they were thinking about giving up Gabon; their military presence along the coast was costing them a fortune without producing a sou in return. The interior might as well have been the dark side of the moon, and there were no French trading for ivory at the river's mouth: the German and English firms monopolized all dealings with the elephant hunters. France made no effort to conceal its plans to sell Gabon to the British for a bargain price, and only changed its mind under powerful protest from its clerics – the French missionaries needed protection. In fact, it wasn't until the end of the nineteenth century, when the mass production of bicycles caused the demand for rubber to rise to levels equal to that of raw materials such as coal or iron, that merchants from Le Havre and Marseilles began putting up with the hardships experienced in the forests along the Equator – and immediately made a horrible mess of things.

Brazza went to Africa in search of personal adventure, not as the pawn of an imperialist power. His family invested a total of seven hundred thousand francs in his three expeditions, millions of dollars by today's standards. For services rendered, the French government later provided him with an annual pension of six thousand francs; Brazza died in debt.

No speeches were made or salutes fired when the expedition left Bordeaux harbor on 10 August 1875. At almost the same moment, a British polar expedition was leaving Portsmouth harbor: a garrison of marines stood at attention on the quay, a hundred thousand thrill-seekers waved to the members of the expedition and a telegram from Queen Victoria was read aloud before the ships set sail. Brazza had to make do with a letter from his mother, but he didn't mind the lack of pomp and circumstance. No one had to convince him of the importance of his mission, and he had sought his support where he was sure to find it: at the Petite Vache creamery on Rue Mazarine in Paris, where explorers like Crevaux, Duveyrier, Serpa Pinto, Lamy, Burton and Cameron were among the regulars. He had spread out his map between the glasses of milk and pointed to the blank spots along the Equator; he had fired questions at the old Africa hands and taken their advice to heart. He may have set sail for the unknown with his arm in a cast, but not with his eyes closed.

The expedition left the last European settlement, Lambaréné, on 12 November. The one hundred and fifty-six crates of luggage contained beads, copper trinkets, hundreds of meters of cloth and supplies of Bengal fire – 'sparklers, Roman candles, a harmless bag of tricks'. Brazza aimed at peaceful exploration from the very start, and to save weight he had reduced his arsenal to a minimum: fourteen repeating rifles, four single-shot weapons and eight revolvers.

Acting on the advice of his comrades at the Petite Vache, he recruited Senegalese marines (*laptots*), who were accustomed to the discipline aboard French naval vessels and to staying away from home for years. The four Europeans were accompanied by twelve *laptots* to supervise and assist the local bearers, two Fang interpreters and two Gabonese guides. The military top brass had absolutely no confidence in the expedition's success: seasoned travellers like the Marquis de Compiègne, Alfred Marche and the German Dr Oskar Lenz had never been able to pass beyond the territory of the Okanda tribe, so how could a newcomer like Brazza? No officer his age had ever been sent on an official mission; he would only end up in a cannibal's pot or come racing back helter-skelter to the coast.

Brazza disappeared into the jungle in late 1875. He was unable to send Paris any sign of life for another three years. By then the officials at the Ministry of the Navy had almost forgotten about him. Only once in all that time did a civil servant scribble a note in his dossier, something to the effect of: what on earth has happened to Brazza? No one lost any sleep over his lengthy silence.

But Brazza had been in constant contact with the coast. In his summary reports and missives he complained of adversity, of conflicts with bearers who stole like magpies and kept asking for more money or goods, of tribal hostilities and the endless haggling with Negro kings who tried to squeeze him for all they could get, and of illness, illness and more illness.

Alfred Marche always travelled out ahead, with Brazza, Hamon and Ballay following his trail, but after only a few weeks Ballay, the physician, was felled by fever and had to be left behind. This posed new problems, for he could now no longer treat the bearers for the innumerable wounds to arms, feet and legs they incurred along the way.

Brazza reached Lopé and had to take to the sickbed himself. Malaria. When he finally recovered two months later, the first task which confronted him was to secure the release of Dr Oskar Lenz, who had been held captive by the Okanda for more than a year. He succeeded. Ridding himself of Lenz proved more of a challenge.

Bucked up by the arrival of other white men, the German explorer began to shadow Brazza on his scouting expeditions into the hinterland. Brazza made it clear to him that, even on journeys of discovery, the rule was every man for himself and the devil take the hindmost; Ballay, restored to health by now, hastened to warn his commander in Libreville 'that the honor of being first to accomplish the difficult journey should go to he who rightfully deserves it, and that honor belongs to Mr Brazza, and to no other'. But Lenz wasn't to be put off, he just kept trotting along behind Brazza. Only when natives shot at his canoe did Oskar Lenz return to the coast – he was to have more luck in the Sahara, where he led the first successful European expedition from Tangiers to Timbuktu.

Brazza's next headache was his own companion Marche. The biologist was eight years older than Brazza and had spent much more time in Africa. Marche was the one who had shown Brazza the ropes; along with Compiègne, he could claim the honor of being the first to explore the lower reaches of the Ogooué, and his detailed observations of plants, trees and animals and exhaustive descriptions of the native population lent the expedition a certain scientific cachet. But the twenty-three-year-old Brazza soon took the lead; it was clear to Marche that Brazza would take the glory as well. He became more frustrated with each passing kilometer. After some 'difficulties', Marche stated that he would no longer concern himself with 'anything not directly associated with biology'. Sick with fever, he was the first to arrive at Poubara Falls in 1877; sick with jealousy, he decided to return to the coast immediately. His career as an explorer ended in the Philippines.

After Marche left the party, Brazza became the trailblazer. It was he who now travelled ahead of the rest, negotiated with tribal leaders, made their mouths water with crates of pure rum or bags of beads, and promised them much more tribute if they guaranteed the expedition a safe passage. Such talks lasted at least five days, and could even run as long as four months. Brazza's expeditions more closely resembled the endless maneuvers of a professional negotiator than they did the plot of *Tin-Tin in Africa*; only when the local rulers had given their assent would Brazza give the caravan the sign to move on.

Within a few months, Brazza developed into a skilful diplomat. He loved the endless palavers. It was a game to him, a deadly earnest game of give-and-take. He never lost his patience and always remained the perfect gentleman, even after weeks of negotiation. The words of his great inspiration, David Livingstone, were firmly imprinted on his mind: 'If a man goes with a good-natured, civil tongue, he may pass through the worst

165

people in Africa unharmed'.

He made peace with the Okanda and Adouma, the much-feared oarsmen who controlled the upper reaches of the Ogooué. For though they came out to meet Brazza in full battle dress, the black kings could not withstand the temptation of a few copper bells, some brightly patterned cloth or the crack of rifles. They may have realized that this was the beginning of the end of their sovereignty, but the old rulers preferred the taste of rum to palm wine, and the strangers introduced them to a culture that glittered like real gold. They might fly into a rage when their greed remained unsated, but Brazza's boundless patience – and the fact that he was white – saved him time and again. To the jungle tribes he seemed to have fallen to earth from another planet. Or, as Stanley put it: 'Even in the midst of a battle, curiosity stronger than hate or blood-thirstiness arrested the sinewy arm which drew the bow, and delayed the flying spear . . . the savages became absorbed in contemplating a kind of being which to them must have appeared as strange as any . . . the traditions of their fathers had attempted to describe. "White men!" '

The Okanda and Adouma, the only rowers capable of safely negotiating the rapids, accompanied Brazza to Poubara. The Batéké carried his cargo across the upland plains to the Alima. Women and children also served as bearers; in those days, the only beasts of burden in Equatorial Africa were human. Horses and mules died after a single bite from a tsetse fly.

With each passing day Brazza realized more clearly that the route over the Ogooué to Stanley Pool was a lost cause. The journey from the coast took a good three months, and only a third of his equipment ever arrived at its destination; the rest was either stolen or lost in the rapids.

He finally reached the Alima, only to find that his passage was blocked by the Apfourou. Lying flat in his canoe he watched as the warriors rose up from the reeds along the riverbanks, their bodies painted white. To the rolling of tom-toms they drew back their bows, and when darkness fell their war songs rang out across the water. Brazza retreated, tried again the next day and heard the wild screams that preceded the flight of the javelins. He ordered his men to fire. At least two Apfourou were killed, and a number of Brazza's bearers were wounded. He had too few men and weapons to wage a direct battle; the expedition turned on its heels and fled.

But Brazza had no intention of having his plans foiled by such hostilities. Sending Hamon, Ballay and most of the *laptots* back to the coast, he remained behind with a few trusted servants. Hunger and thirst had drained him, his feet and legs were covered with sores – yet he continued to hope that he could change the Apfourous' minds. He began wandering aimlessly about the camp, playing the martyr with growing conviction. When his men finally shot a bird or a monkey after days of chewing on nothing but their fingernails, he would mumble something about not feeling well, withdraw to his tent and let the others divide the spoils.

In Paris, Nadar had photographed him with a staff in hand, barefooted and wearing a burlap garment that hung on his body like an old rag. The photograph makes him look like a saint grown old before his time, like a penitent monk, like the Lord Jesus himself. That was one side of his personality. Other photographs depict him as the impeccable count, a dandy who looks like he's dying for a glass of champagne.

On the whole, he was really quite down-to-earth. His men

167

were prescribed a bottle of wine at every meal and a liter of tafia a week as the best remedy against germs. But during the final phase of his first expedition, his thoughts must have been with that other great follower of rivers, David Livingstone. After two years of wandering and countless misfortunes, Livingstone had still refused to abandon his attempt to find the sources of the Nile. He had no teeth left, his skin was covered with running sores, he was starving, mere skin and bone, his bearers had all deserted him and he had lost his way – yet when Stanley finally found him, Livingstone had only one request for the American: "Let me die here in peace."

Such self-denial seems symptomatic of being an explorer, or at least of its terminal phase. Like all of the great travellers, Brazza wished to drink the African cup to its bitter dregs, and he lost the will to live. Perhaps it was because these men came face to face with death each day, and were reminded each minute of the fleeting nature of existence. The huge quantities of quinine they swallowed, doses which sometimes left them senseless in their hammocks for a full twenty-four hours, further undermined their mental resilience: they simply went a bit off their rocker.

One night Brazza heard the cry of the rainbird. He realized then that he would have to hasten his return to the coast; otherwise he would remain a prisoner of the jungle for another rainy season. Without clothing and rations, he could never survive.

I suggested to Charlie that we walk across part of the Batéké highlands. He didn't have to think too hard about it; he said, "Let's do it, just for kicks."

While picking out our route on the map, he admitted that he wasn't much of an athlete. He preferred sitting in his truck. But I was able to put his mind at ease – when I'd played soccer as a kid back in Holland, I always had to be the goalie, and I never blocked a ball. He took a good look at me and said: "Yeah, I can imagine that."

We left early in the morning, but had to slow down the pace within the first hour. It was tough going. The terrain had looked smooth enough driving by in the pickup, but there were ten-centimeter ripples hidden under the elephant grass, and the toes of our shoes bored into the sand with every step we took; it was like hiking through dunes. Charlie had warned me: "It'll give you powerful calf muscles, and after a while a pretty damn sore back, too."

My problem was my feet, which had swollen up and started stinging. "That's not so strange," Charlie said, "the sand fleas have decided to pay you a visit." But he was prepared for all eventualities. He referred to the aerosol can he had with him as 'the Johnson', after the brand of insect repellent. Every couple of kilometers I would kick off my shoes and socks and yell: "Charlie, the Johnson." While fumigating my feet, he said: "Don't forget, Brazza didn't have any Johnson." The sand fleas left Charlie's feet alone, but he attributed that to the color of his skin. "Black scares them away."

It seemed as if nothing could dampen his spirits, but once the dew had dried off the grass he started talking less; by mid-morning his gaze was fixed just as grimly as mine on the distant range of hills, which shimmered on the horizon without getting any closer.

After three hours or so, Charlie turned to me and said: "Tell me the truth now, Jan, is there really anything left for us to discover?"

"Well, not in the strict sense of the word."

"So no one would be terribly disappointed if we turned back?"

"I'm afraid not."

On the way back he warned me to keep my head covered. "You people can't take it, with those red faces of yours." But my scalp kept itching, so I had to take off my hat a few times.

We arrived back at the road where Charlie's pickup was parked. He automatically shoved a cassette into the tape deck. After a little while, the blues started sounding disturbingly faint. Back at the hotel, Charlie said he would walk me to my room. "You don't have to do that," I said, then grabbed his shoulder to keep from falling.

Lying on my bed, the last thing I felt was the ground undulating beneath my feet. I fell into a deep sleep, and when I awoke there was a wet washcloth on my forehead.

Charlie was watching a kung-fu movie on TV. He was stretched out on the couch, a can of cola in one hand and a cigarette in the other.

"Kick him up the side of the head," he mumbled.

He had turned down the sound, the images were throwing milky-white smears across the walls of the half-darkened room. Every once in a while he would get up, without taking his eyes off the screen, and freshen the washcloth on my forehead.

"Turn around, dumbo, right behind you."

I closed my eyes again and, in a flash of lucidity, told myself I should have known better. I had read the memoirs of Brazza's companions: Charles de Chavannes, for example, two volumes, six hundred pages, at least three hundred of which dealt with illnesses. Three hundred pages of bilious fever, dengue fever, swamp fever, yellow fever, blackwater fever and malaria, to say nothing of ulcers, dysentery, anemia, dizzy spells and fainting fits.

The room was much darker the next time I awoke. Charlie was still watching a kung-fu movie, the fourth or fifth that afternoon; during the day, Gabonese TV broadcasts them one after the other.

When Charlie saw me looking at him, he stood up and held his index finger before my eyes.

"You see only one of these?"

"Yes."

"Then we can go get something to drink."

The room pitched when I stood up, but righted itself after I'd held my head under the faucet. Charlie turned off the TV and mumbled: "The first one was better, this one looked like it was made in a convent."

Out on the hotel patio he ordered a roast chicken, a beer for himself and a bottle of mineral water for me. He polished off the chicken, then left. But the next morning his rust-brown pickup was waiting in front of the hotel, and he greeted me with the words: "Hey there, goalie."

After his exhausting and disappointing trip to the Alima, Brazza received a hero's welcome in Paris.

The newspapers wrote about him extensively, and in such resounding terms that the owner of the shop where he bought his clothes refused to take his check, asking only for an autograph.

171

The Ministry of the Navy may have forgotten about him completely, but when he dropped by to pay his respects and unfold his map of Equatorial Africa, a bit the worse for wear by then, he was showered with compliments. He was asked to give readings everywhere he went, and the attention he received was breathless. At the same time, however, he realized that all this interest was due only marginally to his achievements in the jungle.

The French translation of *Through the Dark Continent* had appeared shortly before his return. With his nine-hundred-and-ninety-nine-day journey from coast to coast, during which he had charted the course of the Congo, Stanley had elevated Africa to world news. All England rejoiced, while France cast about desperately for a hero of its own. The scramble for Africa had begun. Before long all the European powers would join the race, but due to domestic problems such as the war with Germany and the Paris Commune, France had gotten off to a late start, and then been humiliated by the British in Egypt to boot. Suddenly all objections to a lieutenant of Italian descent were laid aside; when Brazza arrived in Paris he was hailed as the heir to La Pérouse.

Only after he'd read Stanley did he realize that the river he had followed was a branch of the Congo. He had been only five days from the waters of that broad expanse when the Apfourou had blocked his path. He was so upset by this revelation that he briefly forgot his noblesse oblige. Insinuating that the Apfourou had taken up arms because they'd mistaken him for Stanley, he wrote to the Ministry of the Navy: 'Stanley's only legacy in the Congo has been thirty-two armed skirmishes'.

He was making it up.

He had heard nothing about Stanley while still in Africa; his accusations were based solely on the explorer's own accounts, and though Stanley *was* a bully, Apfourou country was the one place his men had held their fire.

Brazza played up the contrasts with Stanley in an extremely cunning fashion. As a representative of the old, refined Europe, he dismissed the American as a trigger-happy cowboy in the jungle, a man who looked down on the natives and understood shamefully little of what stirred their souls. He made a caricature of Stanley, who of course was perfect for the role, but he conveniently forgot the fact that initially he had used equally disparaging terms to describe the jungle inhabitants. In a letter written less than two years earlier, he had compared two Gabonese tribes to beasts of burden 'without the slightest intelligence, sense of tradition or poetry'.

Slowly but surely, however, his opposition to Stanley caused Brazza to adopt a more humane view of the black population. He was no match for Stanley as an explorer; to achieve his ends, therefore, he had to use different means. The American applied the very same rationale to defend his own methods: if he had adopted Brazza's tactics, he said, it wouldn't have taken him nine hundred and ninety-nine days to reach the Atlantic, it would have taken him until the twentieth century. (Which was another bit of hyperbole: in eastern Africa in particular, Stanley had taken advantage of thousand-year-old caravan routes – the Arabs had penetrated far into the continent as early as the eighth century.)

Humane! Brazza had been *obligated* to negotiate again and again; he had too few men and too little equipment to take on the natives. But even though he covered far fewer kilometers in the jungle and charted a much smaller area than Stanley, his was ultimately the greater achievement: he won the Africans' respect.

In the century that followed, this would earn him the reputation of *le premier tiers-mondiste*, the first development worker. No mean feat for a man who, though capable of waiting for days for a sick *laptot* to recover, also thrashed lazy bearers with a cane, caused a number of fatalities during his battles with the Apfourou, and shot and killed two men who attacked his canoe at Lopé. 'I was protecting my own skin', he wrote his mother coolly.

Brazzaville remained Brazzaville after independence, but Stanleyville became Kisangani and Stanley Pool was renamed Pool Malebo.

After a youth like something out of *David Copperfield*, Stanley became one of the most lauded men of the nineteenth century.

The German writer and philosopher Jakob Wasserman wrote:

'The world was infatuated with him: he was the hero of a generation of young men and boys. At the age of fifteen, and again at twenty, I lived through the man's triumphs; when the name "Stanley" was mentioned, it sounded like a brass band; at the time, the mere existence of such a man had something fantastic about it.'

In the twentieth century, however, Stanley fell from his pedestal with a resounding crash.

But in fact he wasn't all that well loved in the nineteenth century either. Strange rumors made the rounds; he was said to have thrown black babies into the Congo. He hadn't behaved that appallingly, but after having been married to him for quite some time, Stanley's wife was unable to resist a cautious enquiry as to the truth of those rumors. He answered her with a distraught look, realizing once again that, when it came right down to it, he remained unloved despite all the world's acclaim.

Stanley was born out of wedlock in Wales in 1841, and was named after his father, John Rowlands, a drunk. His first memories were those of St Asaph's workhouse, when he was six. 'It took me some time to learn the unimportance of tears in a workhouse', he wrote in his autobiography.

He saw his mother for the first time when he was twelve.

'Now that I was told my mother had entered the house . . . my first feeling was one of exultation that I also had a mother . . . and the next was one of curiosity to know what [she] was like . . . Francis [a teacher at the workhouse] came up to me during the dinner-hour . . . and pointing out a tall woman with an oval face, and a great coil of dark hair behind her head, asked me if I recognised her. "No, Sir," I replied. "What, do you not know your own mother?" I started, with a burning face, and directed a shy glance at her, and perceived she was regarding me with a look of cool, critical scrutiny. I had expected to feel a gush of tenderness towards her, but her expression was so chilling that the valves of my heart closed as with a snap.'

A few weeks later he ran away from the workhouse, appealed unsuccessfully to various members of his family, worked as a shepherd, a shop clerk, a butcher's assistant, then crossed the ocean to America as a cabin boy.

His life aboard the cargo ship consisted of hunger and beatings.

'I bore no grudge, and thought no evil of any person . . . and felt it an honor to be in the company of such brave men . . . but, invariably, they damned my eyes, my face, my heart, my soul, my person, my nationality . . . In the meantime, my mind was becoming as impervious to such troubles as a swan's back to a shower of rain.'

In New Orleans, a childless couple – the Stanleys – took pity on young John Rowlands. The wealthy cotton broker Henry Hope Stanley found him a job, loaned him books and taught him how to use a toothbrush.

When Stanley went to Havana on business, he left his sickly wife in the boy's care. When Mrs Stanley became deathly ill, John immediately quit his job and dedicated himself to nursing her. After she died, he was barely able to keep his head above water; Stanley returned a few months later, saw what had happened, and threw his arms around the boy. Totally unaccustomed to any sign of affection, John fell to the ground in a swoon.

At least, that's the way he told it in his autobiography. In truth, he had a falling-out with Stanley Senior less than a year after they met, and Mrs Stanley didn't die for another eighteen years.

After leaving New Orleans, he worked for a while on a plantation. In Arkansas, the Southerners left him no choice but to take part in the Civil War. He received a parcel containing a petticoat. The message wasn't lost on him: either take up arms, or put on the petticoat.

He enjoyed the Civil War even less than his later battles with the jungle.

'That which was unlawful to a civilian was lawful to the soldier; thou shalt kill, lie, steal, blaspheme, covet and hate.'

Once freed from the battlefield as a prisoner of war, he joined up with the Union Army under the name of his former Southern benefactor. He came down with dysentery, and spent weeks hovering on the verge of death before receiving a discharge.

After a long journey on foot, he finally collapsed in a field; it took the farming couple who found him two months to nurse him back to health. Deckhand on an oyster cutter, farmhand in Maryland; by the age of twenty-five Stanley had experienced more than most mercenaries do in a lifetime. Yet his sentiments had not entirely withered at the root: he went back to England for a final attempt at reconciliation with his mother. She handed him the money for a train ticket and sent him packing. His youth became such a trauma to him that later, in his private diary, he could write about it only in Swahili.

He signed on with a ship bound for Barcelona and, according to his autobiography, was shipwrecked off the coast of Spain. But this was just another of his fabrications; in actual fact, he had snuck away, jumped overboard and swum ashore.

During a trip to Turkey, he tied his American travelling companion Lewis Noe to a tree and whipped him so thoroughly that five days later the lesions still hadn't healed. He could not countenance the slightest weakness on the part of other whites in his entourage. During the Livingstone expedition, he told the deathly ill Englishman John W. Shaw: "You, sir, are simply suffering from hypochondria." Shaw limped along after the rest of the party, and died a few days later.

In late 1863, while in New York, Stanley made the following entry in his journal: 'Boarding with Judge X. Judge drunk; tried to kill his wife with hatchet; attempted three times. I held him down all night. Next morning, exhausted; lighted cigar in parlour; wife came down – insulted and raved at me for smoking in her house!'

Brazza may have been a poetic figure, but Stanley could turn a phrase. He channeled all his frustration, harshness and misanthropy into his writing. As an American Navy reporter he had covered General Terry's expedition and seen how two thousand marines scaling the walls of Fort Fishet were turned back by a harrowing artillery barrage. He was able to publish his account in a newspaper. Six months later he accompanied General Hancock's army on its mission to keep the Sioux Indians at bay while the Pacific Railroad was built across their hunting grounds. During the following year he travelled to Abyssinia with a British punitive expedition, and reported on the Cretan revolt and the Spanish Carlist uprising on his way home.

'It is only by railway celerity that I can live. Yet I feel as though the world were sliding from under my feet.'

He studied the history of every country he visited, and to compensate for his lack of formal education, read the classics with an avidity bordering on the manic. But at the same time he was a man of action, a man who gave himself no time to penetrate to the heart of the matter. He was quick, inquisitive, egocentric, hard, cold, closed; it would have been as hard for him to laugh as it was to relativize his own importance. The only joke he ever made in his life left him blushing like a schoolboy.

James Gordon Bennett, publisher of the *New York Herald*, sent him off looking for Livingstone. Nothing had been heard of the missionary for more than two years. In the suite of the Grand Hôtel in Paris, his feet on the table, cigar clenched between his teeth, Bennett told Stanley: "Find him."

Bennett was asking the impossible.

But Stanley found him. In an area the size of the combined territories of France and Spain, he found the wandering missionary who had gone off in search of the sources of the Nile. And it was then that he spoke the words for which he could have kicked himself the rest of his life: "Dr Livingstone, I presume?" He meant it neither as understatement nor as a joke. Nor was it his way of toning down the dramatic portent of the meeting; these were merely the only words the intensely shy Stanley could come up with. Every time the remark was quoted to him, he hated himself for having made it. Incredible as it may sound, the quote was the bane of Stanley's existence, and it made of him a taciturn, terrifyingly lonely and suspicious man. There is every reason to believe that Stanley returned to Africa, braved a thousand dangers and put up with dozens of attacks of fever, only to no longer have to hear the words "Mr Stanley, I presume," the standard greeting given him in London.

The suspicion he met with upon his return to England did the rest. Livingstone, who was at death's door, had chosen not to return with him, and most people refused to believe that Stanley had tracked down the missionary at all. The letters he brought back from Livingstone had to be forgeries; in Brighton, before an audience of three thousand, he was forced to defend himself like a crooked politician, and the geographers went out of their way to cast aspersions on his expedition.

After Livingstone's death eighteen months later, Stanley decided to continue in his footsteps.

'I have a spur to goad me on . . . What I have already endured in that accursed Africa amounts to nothing, in men's estimation. Here, then, is an opportunity for me to prove my veracity, and the genuineness of my narrative . . . If I can resolve any of these [problems], which such travellers as Dr Livingstone, Captains Burton, Speke and Grant . . . left unsettled, people must needs believe that I discovered Livingstone!'

He went off in search of the sources of the Nile. At a branch in a river, his guides pointed north. He decided to go south. That was how he discovered the headwaters of the Congo.

Stanley was riddled with doubts, a man who constantly had to prove himself in the face of danger. Rejected by his father, his mother, the Old World and later America as well, he felt at home only in the African wilderness. His *Through the Dark Continent* is the tersely written account of a never-ending battle. For Stanley, discovery was tantamount to possession, and he led his expeditions like a general. He destroyed more than thirty villages that lay in his path, refusing to haggle with native chieftains and simply forcing his will upon them. If he noted even the slightest hint of a threat in a chief's attitude, he viewed it as a declaration of war. Stanley regarded the 'savage' as a mixture of child and demon and, as Jakob Wasserman wrote in his biography of the explorer: 'He went to considerable lengths to conquer the white man's pride in his own breast, approached the problem from every conceivable angle, too meekly on occasion, too sharply on another, here too haughtily, there with too much amicability: everywhere he encountered unconquerable suspicion, fear, audacity and pretence'.

In every way, therefore, he was the polar opposite of the calm, patient, well-balanced Brazza, who also happened to be blessed with a healthy sense of humor. But the two men had one thing in common: they both wanted to bring civilization to Africa.

After his nine-hundred-and-ninety-nine-day journey down the Congo, Stanley returned to Africa.

'Having been the first to explore the great River, I am to be the first who shall prove its utility to the world . . . establish settlements along its banks as centers of trade and friendly intercourse, mold them into nation-states in accordance with modern opinion, and . . . destroy the slave trade at its roots.'

It was the same credo by which Brazza left for his second African expedition.

Charlie took me to the village where he was born.

The huts were no longer round, as they'd been in Brazza's day, the roofs no longer made of straw. Corrugated iron, cinder blocks and cement had transformed the village into a civilized muster of barracks.

Charlie introduced me to the village elder.

"Sheriff, Jan. Jan, this is the Sheriff."

The old man pointed to the trees in the center of the village.

In the olden days, when a son was born to a village elder, he would plant a tree in front of his hut. The Batéké believed that, safe in the shadow of that tree, the child would lead a long and healthy life. No one was allowed to tamper with its growth, for whoever hurt the tree, hurt the child.

The tree was both protector and augur. If it grew quickly, divine providence had awarded the boy a great future: he would grow to be big and strong, the father of countless generations. But if the tree was blighted, the child would meet with misfortune. If it withered or fell, the child would die within the year, and should he continue to live despite such an omen, the *n'anga*, the divine healer, would slip him a fatal poison.

"That's the way it went," the village elder said.

But didn't that seem cruel?

The word didn't mean much to him. "There was no difference between people and nature."

181

A child was like a tree, and a tree like a child, and all of life was contained within that metaphor.

Continuing the tour, he showed me a few smaller buildings at the very edge of the village. "This is where the slaves lived."

"A long time ago?"

"Not so long."

"Forty years ago? Fifty?"

"Two lifetimes, no more than that."

"Were they content to be slaves?"

"They didn't know any better."

"Do you think it was fair of people to have slaves back then?"

"It was a part of life. I can't pass judgement on it. I wasn't alive back then. You can't judge the past. What is done and gone is gone for us as well."

Slavery was a block over which the Europeans stumbled again and again.

In 1831 and 1833, the British and French signed agreements to combat the slave trade. Frigates were boarded and searched; a veritable armada was launched to inspect ships crossing the South Atlantic. All along the coast, settlements for freed slaves were established with names like Freetown or Libreville. But the local population didn't see this as a humanitarian act. In fact, the coastal tribes near Libreville refused to marry off their women to these freed slaves.

International slavery may have been curtailed, but domestic slavery was still firmly entrenched. When Paul du Chaillu went into the jungle in 1855, every one of Gabon's dominant tribes kept slaves, and it was customary to honor a chieftain by killing a few of them directly after his death. In the graveyard at Cap Lopez, du Chaillu saw a huge pile of bones, the remains of slaves who had been beheaded to accompany local rulers on their journey to the hereafter. Other tribes tied up the sacrificial slaves and smashed their testicles to a pulp with stones. As the story goes, a dying slave once screamed: "You cause me to suffer the cruelest pain in my genitals, but mark my words: you will suffer in the hereafter, just like me. You will piss fire and the disease will never leave your tribe." The story wouldn't be African if it didn't end like this: within a few months all the members of the tribe experienced a burning pain when urinating.

For Stanley and Brazza, domestic slavery was ironclad evidence of the barbarity of the tribes deep in the jungle. Both men did their best to combat slavery, feeling that abolition was the first step towards civilization. During his first expedition, Brazza bought and freed a great many slaves. During his second expedition, he proclaimed that no black man should be allowed to lose his freedom, and gave land to those he had freed. During his final expedition, he brought along a commission to help set up an administrative system that would put a definitive end to slavery. But he didn't have much luck that time, either.

When Albert Schweitzer built his hospital at Lambaréné in 1913, many Gabonese were still living in slavery. In the eyes of the law they were free, but accustomed as they were to the safety and shelter of their subordinate existence, they continued to serve their masters free of charge.

And they weren't all in such dire straits. One day a woman came into Schweitzer's clinic, accompanied by five young men. She said they were her servants, but there was no doubt about it:

these were her slaves. The next day Schweitzer saw her gathering wood near the hospital. He asked her why she had to work with so much manpower at hand, whereupon she smiled and replied: "Having slaves doesn't mean one is well served."

Officially, Brazza returned to Africa to further impede the slave trade and establish two medical stations and a scientific outpost along the Ogooué. In fact, his efforts were focused entirely on beating Stanley to the punch and planting the French flag on the banks of the Congo.

Following his nine-hundred-and-ninety-nine-day journey, Stanley made several attempts to convince merchants in London and Liverpool to set up trading posts along the Congo. He was unsuccessful. No interest was shown in British political circles either. Highly indignant, Stanley trotted off to King Leopold II of Belgium, who had just made Brazza a royal job offer. But the Italian had courteously declined; his hard-won French citizenship prevented him from entering the service of the Belgian king. So even though Leopold was more favorably disposed to Brazza – a nobleman after all, a count with refined manners who didn't sit there sweating like a peasant the way the American did – Stanley was a godsend. The king's fancy had turned to a private kingdom in Africa, stretching from the Congo to the Nile. He needed someone to procure that empire for him.

Stanley left for the Congo with half a million francs in his pocket.

A few months later, having spent the winter under his mother's wing, and having fully recovered from the liver infection and chronic bronchitis he had contracted in the jungle, Brazza took off after him.

He celebrated his twenty-eighth birthday at sea.

Two marines, a mechanical engineer and ten bearers accompanied him out of Libreville. The patience he had displayed when negotiating with local chieftains during his first expedition now bore fruit: everywhere he went, he was welcomed as an old friend. The once-so-hostile tribes now offered him all possible assistance, and he was able to cross Gabon with considerable speed. Within three months he had reached the confluence of the Ogooué and the Passa, where he established the outpost Francheville. He waited a few weeks for Mizon and Ballay to bring him fresh supplies, but they were delayed by illness and adversity. Brazza was in a hurry: Stanley had at least a four-month lead on him. Accompanied only by his Senegalese servant Malamine, he crossed the Batéké highlands on foot and, after a long and exhausting journey, found the Congo. The first thing he did on the banks of that river was drink six liters of water.

In August 1880 he began negotiations with Makoko, King of the Batéké, who ruled over the area west of the Congo. The man's official name was Eloi the First, Makoko (King) of the Batéké, but because his servants addressed him as 'Makoko', Brazza assumed that this was his first name.

The *makoko*'s subjects were so in awe of his power that they approached him only on their knees. His fetish emitted an annihilating force; according to Batéké belief, the soil became barren wherever he walked. Just as the king of the coastal nation of Dahomey was never allowed to view the sea, the *makoko* could never move at will through his kingdom. He never left the royal village, where his throne was a lion's skin. What's more, the king was forbidden to eat in public.

The *makoko* lived like a lion in a cage, with nary an opportunity for cruelty or despotism. Despite his divine power he was powerless to make any decision without the assent of the tribal elders: in their keenness for material gains, the Eleven Wise Men now felt it was time for the king to grant territorial sovereignty to 'the Great White Master'.

Besides, the reign of Eloi the First was grinding to an end. Batéké kings, elected from among the tribal elite, never ruled for longer than half a decade. Starting on coronation day, the royal cook mixed a tiny dose of poison into the *makoko*'s food, just enough to kill him in about five years' time. But Brazza knew nothing of this custom of keeping kings on death row: it wasn't until the 1960s that the last *makoko* finally revealed the secret.

Preceded by a bugler and a freed slave bearing the French flag, Brazza strode past the straw palisades that hid the clustered huts of the royal village. At the entrance to the village square, the cortege halted until the king granted permission for the strangers to approach. A bell was rung, an iron bell dating from the time when the first Portuguese missionaries had Christianized the tribes along the coast. Cordons of court attendants in old, worn-out uniforms stood at attention, spears and shields in hand.

Then the king's forty wives walked into the square. Once everyone had taken their places, the king himself appeared, a thin and stately figure moving amid a deathly silence. He wore a long robe, copper bracelets and anklets, and a woolen headdress. His face was scarred with the tribal tattoos of the Aboma and Batéké. The medicine man, carrying the royal fetish in his left hand and a beautiful medieval sword in his right, followed close behind. The king stretched out on his lion's skin, one elbow leaning on a few leather cushions and his feet resting in a copper pan: the procession of wives and children could begin. One by one, the royal family knelt down before Brazza.

The negotiations lasted twenty-five days. Makoko's wives presented the visitors with the most lavish meals. 'The king's own children would have fared no better at his hands', Brazza wrote home to Europe. On 10 September 1880 the king signed a treaty placing his territory under French protection. With this document in hand, Brazza was able to win over all the local chiefs. He had the settlement of N'Tamo built right next to Makoko's village, and a second outpost – Brazzaville – thirty kilometers to the south.

What made Makoko give in so quickly? The first bishop of Brazzaville, Monsignor Augouard, wrote him off as a fool. 'For three bales of cloth he squandered a kingdom twice the size of France.' But Makoko, who Brazza described as extremely sly, probably never realized that he was handing over his kingdom for a pittance. After all, he wasn't selling his land, he was placing it under French protection. History had taught him that tribes who traded with the whites were never worse off for doing so. Until then, the whites had remained safely on the coast, without actually taking possession of an area. Besides, the Batéké ascribed sacred powers to 'those who come from the sea', and considered it the height of incivility to refuse a request from 'one who comes from afar'.

During the final meeting with the tribal chieftains, Brazza picked up a few bullets with one hand and a bundle of cloth with the other. He told them that the whites had two hands, one for war and the other for trade, and asked the chieftains which hand they preferred. "Trade!" they shouted in unison. Brazza tossed the bullets into a hole in the ground, planted a French flag on top of them and said: "May war never come between our peoples before this tree grows bullets."

Brazza had indeed beaten Stanley to the punch. From then on, the area to the west of the Congo would belong to France. In veiled terms, he informed Paris of the expedition's success. But his letters were intercepted by agents of King Leopold, and the Belgians urged Stanley to make haste. In his diary, Stanley noted bitterly: 'Brazza. In 1874, no one had even heard of him, but in 1878 no one talks about anything else. As far as I know, all he did was accompany Messrs Compeigne [sic], March [sic] and Ballay on their trip up the Ogooué.'

On 7 November 1880 the two explorers met at Stanley's camp on the Congo. It must have been quite a comical encounter. Stanley noted in his diary: 'My French is quite miserable, and his English none too fluent'. Nonetheless, the men spent two whole days in conversation. Brazza played his cards close to his chest: he remained deferential, gave Stanley the opportunity to sing his own heroics in great detail and failed to mention his treaty with Makoko. Stanley first found out about it when he visited Batéké territory in July 1881. Only then did he realize how diplomatically Brazza had led him up the garden path.

The Belgians were furious. Their ambassador to England, Baron Solvyns, later wondered why it had not occurred to the American to 'dispose of his rival with a single bullet'. As far as Solvyns was concerned, Stanley had been as sweet and trusting as any ignorant black in the jungle. Another of King Leopold's confidants, Hoge, remarked that Stanley had put his stupidest foot forward; the first thing he should have done, of course, was to secure Stanley Pool, the most strategic spot on the Congo.

Brazza, whose pace had once been likened to that of a snail, had clearly won the race. He was now paddling up the Alima, the skirmish that had taken place during his first expedition still weighing on his mind; he had no intention of returning to France before peace was made with the Apfourou. But he was in luck: the old Apfourou king had died and been succeeded by his more amiable brother. The new king bore the scar of a bullet hole in his jaw and, as Brazza wrote, 'it seemed wiser not to ask how he had come by it'. Brazza dug deep in his pockets and – for four sabers, eighty kegs of gunpowder, five hundred yards of cloth, two hundred bells, one hundred mirrors, eight copper bowls, eight anklets and one hundred necklaces – found the Apfourou willing to bury the hatchet once and for all.

Ten years later the tribe was conquered by the Batéké; twenty years later it had disappeared from the face of the earth.

Brazza returned to Paris in a flush of self-confidence.

"I travel through the region as a friend," he told the reporters, "not as a bully. That was how I was able to make the peaceful conquests which so amazed the American explorer in the employ of the Belgian king."

When Stanley returned to Europe a few months later, he gnashed his teeth as he read how Brazza had depicted him as a brutish murderer. He decided to travel to Paris and deliver Brazza a long-overdue tongue-lashing. The speech he prepared for the 20 October 1882 gathering of the Parisian chapter of the Stanley Club was long and sarcastic. King Leopold saw trouble brewing, and did all he could to convince the American not to take up battle against the eloquent Italian count. Stanley ignored the king's warning; his reputation was at stake.

On the day of the meeting, Stanley happened to run into Brazza on the street. According to Brazza's adherents, Stanley told him: "I'm going to kill you tonight." But according to Stanley's supporters, he said: "I'm going to have the pleasure of giving you a bit of a mauling this evening." Once again, his lack of guile played right into his rival's hands. Brazza hurried back to his hotel and, drinking one cup of black coffee after another, wrote a speech in English which he spent the rest of the afternoon learning by heart.

The banquet began. Stanley, not ordinarily a drinking man, imbibed heavily and began his speech full of Dutch courage. According to his sympathizers, it was a reasonable reply to Brazza's accusations, but the assembled French press saw it as a harangue, a blustery and pompous diatribe. Stanley ended his speech by expressing his regret that he could not join the chorus proclaiming Brazza as 'the new apostle', as his competitor had introduced an 'immoral diplomacy' to a 'virgin continent'.

At that very moment, Brazza walked in.

The American cabinet member presiding over the evening asked Brazza to come and sit between him and Stanley. Brazza, who was more than two heads taller than Stanley – the American had short bow legs and a tendency to run to fat – shook his rival's hand and immediately took the floor.

He spoke of Stanley as a colleague, not an opponent. Both of them were doing their best to bring progress and civilization to Africa. In fact, everyone stood to win once France became actively involved in Africa, and a part of the continent came under French rule.

Then he raised his glass and proposed a toast. "Gentlemen, as a Frenchman and a naval officer, I would like to drink to the civilization of Africa through the concerted efforts of all nations, each under their own flag."

Paris was struck speechless. Had Anglo-Saxon hubris ever taken such a beating at the hands of Latin refinement?

Within two months the French parliament had ratified the Makoko Accord, and awarded Brazza an advance of over one million francs for his third African expedition.

Eighty-eight Europeans were to accompany Brazza on his West African Mission. Two hundred candidates responded to the advertisement in the government gazette. Among them were students, military officers, bookkeepers, policemen and *five* pharmacists.

Quartermaster Veistroffer from Compiègne, having received only a one-day leave to apply, kicked in Brazza's bedroom door – the Count was ill and not allowed any visitors. Charles de Chavannes, a Lyon lawyer who was bored by court proceedings and usually sat there reading *Le Tour du Monde*, also barged into Brazza's room. "He was bent over a topographic map," crowed Chavannes, who saw Brazza as a modern-day hero, the Columbus of the nineteenth century. The lawyer had to wait four months before hearing that he had been appointed Brazza's personal secretary. "I received a telegram ordering me to report within twenty-four hours. I didn't hesitate for a moment, I left every-thing behind."

Zeal was the order of the day, but Brazza would not let himself be bowled over. "Two or three of them may exhibit a good heart, the rest will be a source of exasperation." He was right: by the end of that year fourteen members of his expedition had been sent home for thievery, drunkenness or incompetence.

Bookkeeper Blondel had secretly requisitioned and sold al-most half the expedition's supplies.

Laporte ordered the torching of a village on the coast. Labeyrie did the same, but this time in the region of Lambaréné.

At Cap Lopez, Faucher instituted a veritable reign of terror. A bearer who had tried to steal supplies was left lying spread-eagled on the ground, manacled hand and foot, for an entire month. Every evening Faucher came by to sprinkle the man with water, so the mosquitoes wouldn't overlook him.

And everyone was puzzled by Froment. Of all Brazza's agents, he left behind the most detailed observations of native life, and was outspoken in his admiration for native society. Yet this staunch and inflexible Protestant, who performed his duties with holy zeal, also possessed a criminally vicious streak. He ordered a young Galoa girl who had committed fornication to be stripped, tied to a tree and given fifty lashes before the entire village, to purify her mind. 'He is quick in going for the whip', a colleague wrote of Froment, 'and irredeemably overbearing'.

The expedition's three hundred Senegalese bearers received sixty francs a month. At the end of the West African Mission, a few rolls of inferior cloth were 'tossed in their faces' as well. The dozens of Gabonese men taken on along the way as boy, cook, rower or guide received between fifteen and thirty francs a month. They almost all deserted before receiving a sou, and if they had to cross Fang or Okanda territory they usually didn't survive the trip home.

It was around this time that the Gabonese tribes added a new lament to their repertoire:

"Where's Lutumbi? He's off working for the whites. They offered him fifty silver coins. And we'll never see him again!"

'I have taken a woman', the biologist Attilio Pecile wrote in his diary.

Pecile was a friend of Jacques de Brazza, Pierre's younger brother. Pierre's mother had convinced him to take the two Italians along to help dispel the loneliness of the long African nights – after all, he could hardly seek the company of his subordinates. Jacques and Attilio went along to perform scientific research, but were not official members of the expeditionary staff. To keep from being accused of nepotism, Pierre did not include their findings in his reports; Pecile's highly candid journals and letters – the writings of a man travelling for his own pleasure and accountable to no one – were not published until 1940.

'I have taken a woman', he noted, 'the way the rest of them do. Her father, who brought her here, is extremely honored that I should take his daughter, who will remain with me until I leave (in a few months' time). Of course, I have to pay her a certain amount every month (twenty-five lire in goods – that's about five francs, cash). I must admit, I prefer white women. Kissing her disgusts me, I keep thinking I'm in bed with a gorilla. But they say you get used to it; we shall see . . .'

193

Brazza and Stanley married only after their exploring years were over, both of them to strict, puritanical, deeply devout women. Before turning forty, the elegant Brazza had refused all European advances; Africa, he felt, was too dangerous for the kind of spiritual woman he wished to wed, while a more worldly woman could hardly respect a man 'whose name reeked of the Congo'. But it was precisely such worldly women who kept close tabs on the explorers' achievements; during banquets in London or Paris, Brazza and Stanley could regularly be found trapped in a flush of giggling socialites. This once caused Stanley to moan that the wilderness never seemed so attractive as when one was back in civilization.

Stanley cherished a deep fondness for his Negro servant boy, Kalulu. Speculation concerning a sexual relationship between the two became persistent when Stanley took the boy with him to England and sent him to school. The slender Kalulu soon became the rage of London. The Victorian ladies couldn't keep from cuddling him; Stanley himself compared the boy to a young gazelle. Kalulu rejoined his master on the eve of his journey from the Indian Ocean to the Atlantic, but deserted halfway. Stanley regarded that act as the worst betrayal yet. A few weeks later, when the fugitive was finally apprehended, Stanley had him soundly whipped. Hundreds of kilometers further downriver, Kalulu's canoe plunged over a waterfall. Stanley's description of the accident is the only truly touching passage in his account.

'He turned around one last time, looking up at me with a smile half-impish, half-devoted.'

It remains unlikely, however, that the pathologically prudish Stanley would ever have given in to any homosexual or bisexual proclivity. In the entries in his secret diary, he continued to fantasize about a tender, charming, refined belle, a woman like his foster mother in New Orleans, a real lady.

Brazza missed his mother.

It was Pecile again who described the way they spent Christmas Eve in 1883.

'After sundown we dined royally, to say nothing of sumptuously. A bottle of Marsala that Brazza had brought along helped us through one of those African evenings when, in the company of people of whom you are fond, you speak of loved ones left behind. We rattled on till midnight, and our mothers were virtually all we talked about. At a certain point, without really realizing it, all three of us were sitting there, crying.'

But after drying his tears, Brazza still had an eye for the black girls.

Three-quarters of a century later, in the village of Ménayé near Franceville, the French ethnologist Hubert Deschamps met the octogenarian Nguimi. He remembered Brazza well: his sister Tongo had lived with the explorer for a time. Brazza had rented a hut from Tongo's father and had supplied the family with food. Because he always met his obligations on time, and because he brought peace to the region as well, the villagers gave him the nickname Moukounoungou, meaning 'tree that towers above all others'.

It was also Deschamps who traced the origin of the name of the Ogooué settlement Ndjolé. Once, when Brazza saw a girl of the Adouma tribe walk by, so the story goes, he cried out: "Oh, isn't she *jolie*, *jolie*!" And the natives cried in unison: "N'jolé! N'jolé!"

It was during his West African Mission that Brazza broke the tribes' monopoly over the Ogooué once and for all. But not without a fight. During a skirmish with Fang rowers, one of his men was killed and several others were badly wounded. Clashes in a village close to Lambaréné had left two dead and three wounded. The free trade and unrestricted access propagated by Brazza also put an end to the age-old allotment of territory, and it cost him a great deal of trouble to avert a full-scale war with the tribes. Alcohol saved the day. Although the expedition's original supplies included twelve hundred bottles of gin, in 1884 the quartermaster ordered an additional fifty thousand liters of wine from the Ministry of the Navy in Paris. 'For staff purposes', he added in his postscript.

Brazza's agents established twenty trading posts along the river, and raised the French flag at all strategic points along the western banks of the Congo and the Oubangui. The intense rivalry between the Italian and the American would ultimately result in the creation of two Congos, the Belgian Congo Free State (modern-day Zaïre) and the French Congo-Brazzaville (People's Republic of the Congo). No one was really struck by the absurdity of the situation until the next century; most of the diplomatic haggling at the Berlin conference had to do with postal rates in the new colonies.

It was at this same conference that the European powers agreed to the definitive subdivision of West and Central Africa. The Berlin Accord was signed in February 1885; the scramble for Africa was as good as over, and the explorers could feel the winds of change. Within a few years, their services would no longer be required.

Stanley plunged into what was to be his final adventure. He

set up an expedition that, like his first journey in Africa, was to be a manhunt; this time it was for the German professor Emin Pacha, who had disappeared following a clash with Madhists in Central Africa.

Brazza sent Ballay as his proxy to the Berlin conference. He himself was off at the time, exploring the Sangha and Oubangui rivers. In May he was still deep in the jungle, with no idea of the results of the deliberations in Berlin. He returned to Libreville, albeit reluctantly, only at the end of October. During the final months of his West African Mission he neglected all administrative responsibilities; he was having a hard time saying goodbye to real exploration. His agents' requests for advice and assistance became increasingly frequent; increasingly emphatic their demands that he come to their posts to solve the problems cropping up like mushrooms. But Brazza simply stepped into his canoe and had himself rowed to places unknown.

He became increasingly forgetful. His men would rather have bitten their own tongues than breathe a bad word about him; they forgave him a great deal, because 'his heart overflowed with goodness' (Charles de Chavannes), but sometimes they asked themselves what kind of lunatic was running the operation.

'Brazza is incorrigible', the agent Lastours wrote home. 'He's lost all his things. When he showed up here, he was almost naked. The worst of it is, you can be sure he'll immediately lose anything you give him.'

Brazza went into a conclave with the native chieftains, the way he had ten years earlier. The palavers gave him something to look forward to, but there was little left to negotiate now that the rulers had already granted him power over their territories. He was always in search of villages where he could be welcomed as the first white visitor, and each time the wild singing with which he was received touched him more deeply.

He was laying up stores for the nostalgia to come.

Stanley's future was every bit as bleak, and he wrote: 'Someday, along the horizon of memory will glide the figures of men squatting in torrential darkness, shivering with cold, holloweyed and emaciated with hunger, desperate in an unknown land; the groans of the dying shall resound, the rigid corpses become visible, the hopelessness of the jungle will become reality once more'.

Thirty-eight members of Brazza's West African Mission would fall prey to that same despair. But:

'Open your notebook and the white page will draw a dozen butterflies; your face harried by a horrendous gadfly, swarms of bees and wasps before your eyes, and at your feet the red and white ants; some of whom march upon you and sink their scissor-like mandibles in your neck.' (Stanley)

You don't have to be a Hieronymus Bosch to get hooked on that kind of labyrinthine wonder.

At first, Henry Morton Stanley and Pierre Savorgnan de Brazza were equally appalled by Africa. But whereas the Count overcame his horror, the Bastard continued to shiver at the 'diabolical riffraff' of the jungle. Yet in his own way, he too became enamored of the natives; his admiration was like that of a general who sings the praises of his enemy's vitality and skill. In his diaries he wrote of them with infinitely more respect than all those Britons who chattered on about Africa without the slightest clue as to what it was to live on the Equator. But when he saw them coming at him in their long canoes with eighty rowers – heads adorned with red and gray parrot feathers, tom-toms rolling, war horns bellowing, war chants lashing across the water – he automatically went for his gun. He couldn't help himself. The Count came to view Gabon and the Congo as his fealty, the natives as serfs who he hoped to lead step-by-step to freedom, with the foreseeing eye of a Tolstoy. In the world view of the Bastard, shaped as it was in the workhouse, the strong won and the disobedient were punished; that view of the world remained unshaken. No one would ever have questioned Stanley's daring and endurance; the natives called him Boula Matari, meaning 'Breaker of Rocks'. But they referred to Brazza as Rocamambo, 'the Great Commander'. It is this fact, that the nickname of 'great commander' was given to precisely the more peaceable of the two, that Brazza could regard as his greatest victory.

At the end of his West African Mission, a native chorus sang for Brazza.

SOLO:	*White men are wild;*
	Eat no locust, eat no frog.
	Ignorant of the fetish.
CHORUS:	*Poor whites! Poor whites!*
SOLO:	*Boula Matari far from us:*
	White man very mean,
	Black man want to see him go.
CHORUS:	*Mean white man! Mean white man!*
SOLO:	*Black woman like white man.*
	Some white men like black women.
	Black woman wants white child.
CHORUS:	*Nice whites! Nice whites!*

SOLO:	*Rocamambo in our midst.*
	Blacks are friends of whites.
	Whites friends of blacks.
CHORUS:	*Big white man! Big white man!*
SOLO:	*Gives good trade*
	For manioc, bananas,
	Rubber, tusks.
CHORUS:	*Big white man! Big white man!*
SOLO:	*Gives good firewater*
	To drink and play the tom-tom.
	Gives salt and tobacco.
CHORUS:	*Big white man! Big white man!*
FINAL CHORUS:	*Rocamambo in our midst.*
	Blacks are friends of whites.
	Whites friends of blacks.
	Big white man! Big white man!

For the tribes of the Congo and Gabon, evil is an external attribute. They will never say that someone is a thief, only that he has stolen.

It was Charlie who told me that. He was not at all surprised that his ancestors had been willing to forgive Brazza so much. He may have stolen their land, but he was no thief. His intentions were good, and he was a white man.

The color of the first European travellers greatly confused the jungle inhabitants. Charlie told me that the Bangala, who lived on the western banks of the Congo, conceived of God as a white creature swathed in cloth who lived in the water. When they saw their first white priest, they took him for God himself.

This amazement at the color of European skin was something

I had run across before in old travel accounts. The coastal peoples believed their ancestors had returned to their birthplace in the form of the first mariners. In 1596, Jan Huygen van Linschoten was distressed by the ease with which native chieftains offered their wives and daughters to the Dutch seamen. Three-and-a-half centuries later, the Gabonese ethnologist and historian André Raponda-Walker offered a different explanation: in order to figure out the true intentions and identity of the strangers, the kings used their wives and daughters as spies.

As a courtesy to their seafaring guests, the kings also assumed European names. They dressed in European clothing. King Kringer wore a dress coat, a white shirt with an elegant bow tie and a black stovepipe hat. The coastal people saw nothing strange in that: a king could have an *anyemba-nyemba*, a split personality. One and the same king let himself be called Denis by the French, William by the English and Antchouwé Kowé Rapontchombo by his tribespeople. This caused the Europeans to assume that the rulers immediately recognized the superiority of Western civilization. Yet though the monarchs were definitely in search of trading partners, their actions were based primarily on the same brand of curiosity that drove the explorers to distant shores. From 1760 onwards, many of the coastal kings sent a son or nephew along with the Westerners' ships, to unravel the mystery of where these white people came from. The Gabonese king Louis even demanded that his son be introduced to the king of France, and refused to sign a treaty with the French until he had received an undertaking to that effect. Those young men usually returned from Lisbon, New York or Marseilles as slave traders.

The tribes further inland were less forthcoming. Life in the jungle was a constant war. The people who lived there dropped like flies, and in their bitter struggle against underpopulation the tribes stole each other's women and slaves. Not a month went by without their warriors fending off or avenging some attack. The myriad epidemics and the chronic starvation caused many tribes to flee their territories and clash with others. Some tribes became permanent drifters. During the eighteenth century the Fang lived in the extreme north-east of Gabon; by the end of the nineteenth, they were building their villages on the coast, 600 kilometers to the west. The name Fang means 'those who move onward'.

As soon as a stranger turned up, the natives drew their bows. If a tribe hoped to survive, it had to be ready to defend itself. The color of the explorers' skin made them hesitate. For most African tribes, white symbolizes death – or rather, the transition from earthly life to the spirit realm; that is why the Fang and Pounou rubbed their masks, which represented their ancestors, with white powder. The arrival of the Europeans plunged these people straight into a crisis of faith. Their ambiguous attitude is described in the accounts of Albert Nebout: one day his group met with an extremely hostile reception from the inhabitants of a village on the river; the next day they were met by a pregnant woman who held out a calabash bowl for them to wash their hands in, and then drank the water in the hope that she would bear a white child.

When the ancestral spirits did manifest themselves, they almost always came urging reconciliation. Brazza, who became fascinated by African mythology after his initial arrogant rejection, made good use of this knowledge and always emphasized his role as the messenger of peace. Most tribes changed their tune on hearing this, and hailed him as 'the Great Commander'. They almost all had legends featuring just such a commander, a conciliator sent as an ancestral envoy.

It was not their alleged spiritual poverty, but the very scope and precision of their mythology that drove the Africans into the arms of the Europeans, who then turned around and destroyed that same system of belief.

This was too much for one French officer to bear. He warned the inhabitants of a village on the Congo: "A white man is coming. Do not trust him, for he wears no trousers but a dress, like a woman. If you receive him, he will forbid you to have more than one wife." A few weeks later, Bishop Augouard's launch came chugging upriver. The bishop called out to the natives on the shore: "I have come to bring you the truth." And the villagers shouted back: "Screw you! Keep moving! We don't need your type around here!" But in the weeks that followed, crocodiles and panthers invaded the village, and to make things even worse, an epidemic of sleeping sickness ensued. The villagers knew this could be no coincidence. They asked another French officer for advice, and he said: "You've been wrongly informed. That white man in the dress can actually help you with his prayers." So when the bishop's boat appeared on the river again a few weeks later, the villagers signalled to the cleric that he was welcome.

The first thing the priests made the natives do was burn their masks.

Because the whites weren't nice at all.

Brazza, who had meanwhile been appointed governor of the

colony, was travelling back and forth across France in search of entrepreneurs willing to invest in his twin colony, Congo-Gabon. He spoke to chambers of commerce, had dinner with shipping magnates, and was turned down everywhere he went. The merchants were waiting to see which way the wind would blow, while the politicians had fallen silent on the subject of the blessings of European civilization. The French state granted the new colony a loan of six hundred thousand francs annually, just enough to pay the salaries of the civil servants in the Congo and Gabon. The only firm willing to test the water in Brazzaville was a Dutch one: the Nieuwe Afrikaansche Handels Vennootschap built a few warehouses close to the capital.

The NAHV ran some twenty trading posts at the mouth of the Congo and plied the river with four steamers. In 1870, several years before Brazza and Stanley came on the scene, the company had considered organizing a major Dutch expedition through Equatorial Africa. The bosses in Rotterdam, however, finally decided against such a venture, firm in their conviction that Dutchmen would never be able to function in such an oppressive climate. Although it was true that the cemetery at Banana, the largest of the Dutch factories, was filled to overflowing, the real reason was that an expedition was simply too expensive.

The agent appointed by the NAHV, the red-haired Antoine Greshoff – known to his personnel as 'the boss with hair like the sun' – was for many years the only white trader in Brazzaville. That all changed in the 1890s, however, when the price of rubber tripled and an army of freebooters descended on the region.

Brazza soon found himself at loggerheads with the traders, the army, the Church (Bishop Augouard preached that blacks were lazy by nature and should be forced to work), his self-willed underlings and his profit-hungry superiors. France refused to invest a single sou in the colony, and sold rubber and lumber companies the right to exploit large concessions. Mercantile houses were granted huge monopolies, one presiding over an area in Haute-Ogooué province that was four times the size of the Netherlands. A total of forty companies took over the actual governing of the colony from the provincial administrators, established the rule of forced labor on the concessions and subjected the population to a harsh regime. Blacks who didn't tap enough rubber were beaten severely, thrown in prison or had a hand cut off; blacks who did meet their quota were lucky to earn anything at all. The laborers sent to work on the concessions were away from home for months on end. Back in the villages their wives became lax about the conjugal ethics otherwise observed so strictly in the jungle, and if they happened to become pregnant, had abortions under such primitive circumstances that they were usually unable to bear any more children. Hundreds of kilometers from home, the men contracted venereal diseases and, from the pittance they earned, were unable to afford hospital care. Entire tribes died out, others saw their numbers decimated, and the sterility to which thirty to forty percent of all Gabonese adults had fallen prey by the turn of the century is widespread even to this day.

Brazza raised his voice in protest. Having placed Gabon and the Congo under French rule, Paris was now obliged to propagate the values of a Christian nation. The reaction from Paris was one of disdain. Brazza was accused of 'Islamic politics', and the gossip columns reported that he had secretly converted to 'Mohammedanism'.

He was fired in 1898. He read about it in the government

gazette. 'Even a common servant would have received more proper notice', Charles de Chavannes wrote in his memoirs.

Embittered, and his body wasted by countless attacks of fever, Brazza retired with his young bride, Thérèse de Chambrun, to their Moorish villa in Algeria. Thérèse bore him three sons and a daughter; the oldest boy, named after Brazza's brother Jacques, died at the age of five. Brazza never recovered from the blow: his spirit was broken.

Lying on a chaise longue in his garden surrounded by pine trees and eucalyptus, he read the many articles protesting against the French concessionary politics that had already claimed thousands of victims – the British press in particular dealt with the issue at length. Whenever he closed his eyes he saw the black kings looking at him, the same kings he had convinced of the benefits of free trade. Each memory made him suffer.

In the autumn of 1904 the French government asked him to lead an investigative committee through the Congo, to determine the status of the alleged abuses. Brazza saw this as a roundabout form of rehabilitation, and although he sensed that this would be his last journey, he cast his physician's warnings to the wind and took his old explorer's outfit out of mothballs.

He left home in April 1905. He knew it would be another trying journey, but what he found in Gabon and the Congo was even worse than he had feared. Dysentery drained him of his strength. On the voyage home to France, the ship had to change course halfway to take him to a hospital in Dakar. On the afternoon of 14 September, he asked to be brought a photograph of his son Jacques. That evening he died.

The French government gave him a state funeral, but parliament never had a chance to see his report, damning as it was. It disappeared into a drawer. The country's concessionary policies came to an end only in 1925, thanks to André Gide, whose *Journey to the Congo* forced the French to see the 'horrible truth'. But by that time the jungle inhabitants' hatred of the whites had already become deeply ingrained, and the damage was irreparable.

Brazza's remains were brought to Algeria in 1908. His final wish was to be buried in African soil. It was his last chance to distinguish himself from his former rival: Stanley had been buried in 1904, in London.

Charlie knew nothing about the *makokos*.

"They used to be your people's kings."

He gave me a blank look and shoved a cassette into the tape deck. We drove on to the rhythm of the blues.

Thanks to Charlie, I'll always associate the Batéké highlands with B.B. King, along with the chagrin in his voice when he wondered aloud: "Eloi the First, why hasn't anyone ever told me about him?"

Three hours down the road we came across the first car headed in the other direction. The upland plain of the Batéké is empty, emptier than the Auvergne, emptier than the Dolomites, maybe even emptier than the Russian steppes.

"It's a prairie," Charlie said.

We stopped for a beer at a roadside bar. The heat under the sheet-iron roof weighed tons. The girl behind the bar pressed her flat nose to the back of my hand, to see how white skin smelled. "Like goat's milk," Charlie said, and she seemed to agree: "A bit sour, not really bad, but not real good either."

Past Léconi we turned off towards what the locals call the Grand Canyon, a gorge running through an escarpment of red rock along the border with the Congo. How did Brazza ever cross this country on foot? the two of us wondered aloud, and Charlie sighed: "We'll never know that either."

It began raining while we were following the narrow track back to the paved road. After the sudden shower had blown over, Charlie parked at the top of a hill and got out to sit on the hood of the pickup. I sat next to him and together we looked out at the vista of twenty or thirty hills surrounding us. "We're sitting on top of the world," said Charlie, nodding his head. This was his country, his home, and he couldn't imagine a better place on the planet. He talked about his father, who he'd barely known, then asked a bit wistfully: "Know any more stories?"

I told him about Brazza's mother.

At the same time her son passed away in Dakar, she was lying deathly ill in bed. In her feverish dreams she saw a funeral carriage rolling by. Weeks afterwards, when they were trying to break the sad tidings to her gently, she said: "I know already." A few months later she died, at the age of ninety.

Charlie thought that was a very African story.

Then I told him about the last years of Stanley's life.

The explorer retired to an estate he had bought thirty miles outside London, a place with gardens, meadows, a patch of woods and a pond fed by a little stream. He called the pond 'Stanley Pool', the woods 'the Aruwimi Jungle', the stream 'the Congo' and the meadows 'Unyamwezi' and 'Kinshasha'. Each day he would make his rounds of the property with giant, angry strides, at least when the recurrent bouts of malaria didn't confine him to the house. When that happened, the fits of shivering that preceded the fever were so violent that his bed would shake, and he would scream: "Africa is in me!"

All Charlie had to say to that was: "Weird!"

CHAPTER 6

Ibinga or the Wind

WE WERE sitting by the river one evening when Ibinga did something she would never have done the day before. She spoke without being spoken to.

Her story, like most tales of woe in Gabon, involved superstition.

Ibinga and her sister were born within minutes of each other. When her father heard that his wife had given birth to twins, he reacted as if it were a disaster: the elders said twin babies were born of two fathers. It's not a belief held by all Gabonese tribes, and Ibinga had never been able to find out whether her father, a Fang, had been prompted by suspicions of his own or by the prevailing morals of his village. But her mother decided to play it safe. She abandoned the children, fled into the jungle and never returned. One little girl died out in the bush, probably of dehydration; the other baby was taken in by an old woman who had never been able to have children herself. She took the child to her village and raised her like her own daughter.

When Ibinga was seven, her foster mother began getting stabbing pains in the chest. The old woman picked up the child and walked thirty kilometers through the jungle to the nearest mission post. "Ibinga was conceived in sin," she told the nuns, "once I'm not around, the villagers will kill her." Then she left the mission post and walked another fifty kilometers to Albert Schweitzer's hospital, where she died soon after arrival. She breathed her last breath convinced that evil had entered her house along with Ibinga, and that the spirits had now taken their revenge.

At the mission post, Ibinga was taught to read and write. She learned much more quickly than the other children, so at the age of twelve they sent her to a Catholic girls' school in Libreville. After finishing high school she studied English at the university. When she was twenty-three she got her first job as a secretary and translator. She supported herself, and turned down all proposals of marriage.

The mission paid for Ibinga's education. She believed fervently in the Lord God of the Bible, and in Jesus Christ, who died on the cross for our sins; she always said her prayers before going to bed, and on her notebooks she proudly wrote the name with which she'd been baptized: Angela. But once grown up and independent, she began studying the old beliefs and rituals of her tribe, perhaps in the hope of unraveling the mystery of why she had been disowned. She became so fascinated by her ancestral mythology that she readopted her tribal name, Ibinga, and the surname of her foster mother, N'Dong Meungane.

She told me all this much later on.

Through her work, Ibinga N'Dong Meungane regularly came into contact with white people. She dressed Western and acted Western. She had shown me around the capital with businesslike amiability, and answered my questions with businesslike courtesy. We had not met by accident; African formality rules out all such coincidence. I'd received her name and telephone number from her former employer, a French woman I'd met in Côte d'Ivoire.

Ibinga did a lot of travelling around the country. To give me an idea of the kinds of distances she covered for her work, she told me that she had to be in Lambaréné on 3 May for a meeting, and then in Port-Gentil on 8 May for another appointment. She was going to take the boat, the only way to get from Lambaréné to the coast. Acting on an impulse, I asked if I could accompany her, as I was planning to arrive in Lambaréné more or less on the same day. As always, her reaction was businesslike: she flipped open her pocket diary and suggested that we meet late in the afternoon of 5 May, in the lobby of the Ogooué Hotel in Lambaréné. I wasn't surprised that she had agreed so readily; like I said, she seemed quite Western, and even when she mentioned something in passing about relying on my *courtoisie*, it didn't sound old-fashioned or quaint to me.

But the Ibinga I met in Lambaréné was not the same self-assured woman in navy-blue skirt and pearly white blouse I'd encountered in Libreville. In the restaurant of the Ogooué Hotel, where we dined that first evening, the change was barely noticeable; she may have been wearing a brightly colored *pagne*, but the setting wasn't very different from the Western hotels in the capital. Our conversation ran smoothly, and when I complimented her on her lovely African dress, she gave a deep, throaty laugh, turned up the hem of her *pagne* and pointed to the label: 'Made in Holland after an old Javanese pattern'.

Her spontaneity vanished, however, during our first walk through Lambaréné. It seemed as if she realized only then that it was improper for a single woman like herself to be alone with a man; she should have arranged for a third party to act as chaperon. Once away from the capital's sophisticated establishments, away from her office with its portraits of Winnie Mandela and Miriam Makeba on the walls, she seemed to suddenly recall the old precepts and change from an energetic, independent woman into a shy girl. She answered all my questions, but I had to ask them before she would speak to me; worse still, she not only kept her replies brief but also limited herself to echoing my most trite observations. All my attempts to put Ibinga at ease had precisely the opposite effect. They made her giggle, which might have had its charm if she'd been sixteen rather than somewhere in her late thirties. Here in the interior, the racial and cultural differences we had side-stepped so effortlessly back in the capital stood between us like a wall. That we were of different sexes was the barbed wire completing the obstruction. During our first day together I exuded more perspiration than I had in all the weeks that had gone before, and I breathed a sigh of relief when Ibinga excused herself after dinner; she said she had a headache and wanted to go to bed early.

It wasn't until the next day and our arrival in the village on the river that her reticence disappeared. We were sitting in swaybacked rattan chairs on the narrow beach, lazily swatting at mosquitoes; the welcome we had received from the villagers had been friendly without being inquisitive, the chieftain's wife had been considerate enough to show Ibinga to a hut of her own, the dog that had growled at us was now lying asleep at our feet, the nightbird had stopped its screaming; I finally succeeded in holding my tongue, and Ibinga spoke without being spoken to.

She asked: "If I were to say:

'I sow the wind!
Yeah!
I fell the elephant!
Yeah!',
would that sound silly to you?"

I had met someone else in Lambaréné, a familiar face from my childhood. I grew up in a village where the spirit of Calvin blew through the furrows, and Lambaréné had been an intrinsic part of all that. It was the site of the leper colony of Dr Albert Schweitzer, an almost mythical figure for Protestant boys like us. Schweitzer: the doctor who continued to play Bach on his piano with organ pedals even at the edge of the primeval forest; the scholar who built his own hospital in the jungle, plank by plank; the battler against tropical illnesses who wouldn't hurt a tsetse fly; the theologian who wrote books not only about the mysticism of St Paul and the historical Jesus but also a monumental life history of Johann Sebastian Bach, a standard reference work on the art of organ-building, an essay on Goethe, a diatribe against nuclear armament, a work on the philosophy of civilization and a children's book about his pet bird, the pelican. His maxim *Respect for life* was as familiar to us as the questions and answers of the Heidelberg Catechism, and whenever I hear his name today I immediately see before me the Bible School on the Rijsdijk, the old heads on the young shoulders of the catechism students in the vestry, the polders glazed with frost, and the Irene Hall, next door to the church, where a bazaar was held every couple of years to raise money for Lambaréné. But as to where Lambaréné was? God, we had no idea. Somewhere in Africa. Somewhere in the deepest, darkest jungle. Somewhere far, far away, where poor, leprous Negroes squatted in little round huts and bumped their heads against the straw roof whenever they stood up.

I had already planned a good part of my trip to Gabon by the time I noticed Lambaréné on the map, and I had to go to Schweitzer's publications to verify that this was, indeed, the very same mythical Lambaréné of my youth. To us, Lambaréné was scarcely a real place; it stood for all of Africa, for all the burning hot countries, for poverty and horrible diseases. I can still recall my disappointment when I wasn't allowed to go along to the organ concert the great man himself was giving in the Laurens Church in Rotterdam. I was six or seven at the time, too young to sit through a whole evening of sacred music, but I remember feeling as if I was deemed too young to behold the miracle doctor in the flesh. In the week leading up to the concert, my father – who had spent a long time preaching God's word in the tropics himself – had given a lengthy sermon about Schweitzer, and on that same Sunday a blank envelope containing the unbelievable sum of one thousand guilders had fallen through the mail slot at the parsonage. The money was added to the revenue raised by the bazaar (at which I had sold two bags of marbles and a genuine Dinky car, a sacrifice I felt deeply at the time), which the whole village had attended. That evening the Dutch nurse Maria Lagendijk, Schweitzer's assistant since 1938, gave a reading right there in the Irene Hall; everyone was impressed by her, and when the collection bag was passed around, it rustled with banknotes. A delegation from our village was going to present the entire sum to the doctor after the organ concert.

My brother Michail, already in high school at the time, was allowed to go along. He hated the tropics, and with good reason. The first seven years of his life had been spent in the Dutch East Indies; the tropics reminded him of dysentery, and little else. His idea of the exotic was carrot stew and farm girls on skates, but nevertheless the dynamism of the jungle doctor affected him too. He devoured Schweitzer's books about Africa as voraciously as dime-store Westerns. From the first day of spring, when the sun was nothing but a watery spot of light in the sky, he would take off his shoes and socks and do his homework with his feet in a tub of cold water. When I asked him what he thought he was doing, he smiled condescendingly and said: "I learned this from Schweitzer – it improves your concentration." Thirty-five years later, when I announced my trip to Gabon – "You know, Lambaréné and all that" – his eyes misted over and he asked me: "Do me a favor, would you? If Schweitzer's house is still standing, see if that tub is still under his desk."

These days myths rarely last a lifetime. Little remained of the Schweitzer of my childhood; he had caught a great deal of flak during his twilight years, and after his death his memory was desecrated more often than consecrated.

The French writer Pierre Péan visited Schweitzer in 1964. He found him sitting in a corner of his study, reading his own biography. The doctor talked about Africa: he had gone there to do good, he loved the Africans "even though they remain children all their lives." During lunch, the audience of American, Swiss and Dutch nurses listened to this robust man, with his white mane combed back and his slightly overdone mustache, as if he were the Redeemer himself; four years after independence, the black personnel were still not allowed in the dining room.

The doctor cracked jokes, dropped a few pearls of wisdom and refreshed his audience's memory: yes, he was the uncle of Jean-Paul Sartre, who had just won the Nobel Prize for Literature. He himself had received the Nobel Peace Prize in 1952, but he wasn't expecting his nephew to travel to Stockholm to collect the award like he had; the rebel of the family would be sure to turn up his nose at such a bourgeois honor.

Behind the hospital, enough equipment to fill several operating theaters stood rusting away in the open air; the Africans wouldn't be able to put it to use, in Schweitzer's opinion, and he couldn't be bothered to send the equipment back to its donors. With the same sanctimonious air adopted by the Green Party a quarter of a century later when proclaiming the moral superiority of two legs over four wheels, Schweitzer rejected all forms of modern technology. He still had himself rowed to the town on the far shore of the Ogooué, and scolded his rowers for being lazy good-for-nothings. Crates full of the newest medicines arrived in Lambaréné; they never left the storeroom, Péan said, because the doctor knew absolutely nothing about the latest medical developments.

Péan depicted the doctor as a self-important prig, busy tossing his spanner in the works of progress with quixotic zeal. The fact that Schweitzer was turning ninety that year, and that the inhospitable climate had left him a total wreck, must have seemed too piddling for Péan to mention.

Schweitzer's shining example was Goethe: *in the beginning was the deed.* He wasn't overly humble, but without his tendency to overestimate himself he would never have left Europe in the first place. Walking through the center of Colmar one day, Schweitzer – a professor of theology at the University of Strasbourg and well into his thirties at the time – came face to face with the monument to Bruat, which showed a naked native crouched at the feet of the conqueror of Tahiti. "Could it be," the young academic asked himself right there on the spot, "that we are exploiting the black peoples and denying them access even to medical treatment and supplies?" He decided to study medicine and give up the security of his life in Europe in order to 'live up to the responsibility we civilized peoples have to the colored races'. At the time, it was a revolutionary act.

Schweitzer went to the African interior not as a missionary, but as a doctor. There were no medical facilities in Gabon when he arrived in 1913. He scraped together the proceeds from his organ concerts and his book about the cantor of the Thomaskirche, bought what was needed to equip two buildings and constructed his hospital on the banks of the Ogooué, assisted by local laborers 'unparalleled in their sloth'. He couldn't bear to watch the way they worked, so he 'took up the shovel' himself.

Schweitzer had taken his degree at a time when the century of the great explorers was coming to an end. He struggled against the spirit of that century, but never entirely freed himself of it; there was symbolism in the fact that he continued to play Bach in the jungle. He operated in the morning, held consultancy hours during the afternoon, and once the day's work was done, picked up his pen and worked steadily at his essays on theology and the philosophy of civilization. He also wrote beautifully about the flora and fauna of the jungle, yet paid no attention at all to indigenous culture. He was a transitional figure: he saw the black

218

man neither as a savage nor as a real person with a wealth of tradition and a culture of his own. In *At the Edge of the Primeval Forest*, he told tens of thousands of readers about the natives' illnesses, about their superstition and fear, but nothing at all about their religion or mythology. The stories that made the rounds on his very doorstep were lost on him, the rituals taking place in the jungle around the bend in the river were never incorporated into his philosophy of civilization. He studied Judaism, Christianity, Islam, Zoroastrianism, Brahmanism, Hinduism and the religions of China, but paid no attention to his patients' view of the world, because he found it only pitiable.

'The European cannot understand how grim the lives of these poor people are, filled as they are with the fear of such fetishes as can be used against them. Only he who has seen this misery at close range can realize that it is our human duty to bring these primitive peoples a new way of looking at the world, to liberate them from their agonizing delusions. In this regard, even the greatest skeptics, if they could but witness these things on the spot, would become the warmest advocates of mission work.'

Like many missionaries from around the turn of the century, Schweitzer seemed almost to derive pleasure from detailing the grisly acts committed by jungle peoples in their primitive appeasement of evil spirits, and shook his head in amazement at their childish superstition. The smaller fetishes, he wrote, consisted of 'red feathers, packets of red earth, leopard's claws and leopard's fangs and . . . bells from Europe of an ancient model, left over from eighteenth-century bartering'. The larger fetishes 'regularly include a fragment of human skull. Such fetishes must, however, be taken from persons wilfully murdered. Last summer, two hours downstream from our post, an old man was

When Schweitzer tapped and palpitated his patients, he heard only the sounds coming from inside. After he had made his last rounds through the hospital buildings, the African's older brother would literally close all doors behind him.

'My table is next to the screen door leading onto the verandah, so I can breathe as much of the gentle evening breeze as possible. The palm trees rustle softly through the loud music of the crickets and toads, while the jungle emits its gruesome, terrifying screams. Caramba, my faithful dog, growls softly from his place on the porch to indicate his watchfulness, and under the table a pygmy antelope rests at my feet. In this solitude I attempt to express those thoughts which have occupied me since 1900, and to help reconstruct civilization. Oh, jungle loneliness, how can I ever thank you for what you have bestowed on me!'

The only thing he notes about the blacks is that they are deeper than we are, 'because they read no newspapers'.

During the ride in the bush taxi from Ndjolé to Lambaréné, however, I forgave the jungle doctor a great deal.

The taxi-bus left from the marketplace. 'Safe as an ambulance' was the phrase the driver used to extol the virtues of his battered vehicle. He ordered an old man to surrender the comfortable seat he was occupying next to him in the cab, so that I could sit there. Outside the capital, whites are still regarded as all-powerful yet delicate creatures, with buttocks too pampered to withstand the hard benches in the open backs of pickups; they automatically receive the soft, springy seat next to the driver. The only time I heard anyone comment on this, a young boy in the bush taxi taking me from Lastoursville to Booué, his father boxed his ears. *Il faut être poli.*

Before setting off, the driver had to show his papers to a policeman. He'd forgotten them. No problem, he lived only fifteen kilometers from Ndjolé, we could go and pick them up. Back in town again, he took on two stranded passengers, a mother with her sick child. I gave my seat to mother and daughter, climbed into the back of the pickup and met with cold stares. I had violated convention.

A few hours later it began to rain. Like all the other passengers, I sat there shivering. In a cautious attempt at rapprochement, an old woman offered me a banana. To keep me warm, she said. The other passengers mumbled in agreement: "Eat, eat, not to get sick." The driver stopped to stretch a tarpaulin over our heads, and from that moment on I had more bananas than hands to eat them with. The other passengers automatically assumed that it was my presence that was keeping them dry: the driver wished to do the foreigner a service. *Il est poli.*

Never have I heard the word *poli* used as frequently as it is in the jungle. The villagers remind each other in great detail of the dictates of courtesy, an assiduousness all the more striking in view of the fact that their broken French makes them rather coarse of speech. New passengers climbed aboard at every cluster of huts, and once they'd found a place for their chickens, dried fish and bulging crates of baggage, they would shout to the driver: *"Tu peux démerder!"* – Move this fucking thing!

The old woman sitting next to me was shivering with fever; I could feel her body heat radiating through the leg of my trousers. The woman directly across from her was obviously on her way to Schweitzer Hospital too: the toddler on her knee leaned against her weakly and didn't suck when she put her nipple in his mouth. The man with the paralyzed leg spoke proudly of his injury, informing us he had been "Bitten by an adder, yesterday, during the hunt."

The two men with saws and planes were going to help build an infirmary at Lambaréné. They told me why. Gabon's state hospitals demanded a down payment before admitting a patient; Schweitzer Hospital presented the bill after treatment. If a patient couldn't pay, the medical director asked that two or three family members come and perform a few chores. Carpentry, for instance. Or like that young woman over there with her buckets and scrubbing brushes, who would clean one of the wards for a week.

My fellow passengers had nothing good to say about the Gabonese state hospitals. Filthy. Screamingly expensive. Unreliable. The nursing staff cut corners wherever possible. The only place to get adequate assistance was in a private clinic, or at Schweitzer Hospital. Not only the poor from the immediate surroundings went to Lambaréné these days; people from the capital would even walk the 250 kilometers to save the twenty-dollar bush-taxi fare.

Who among them gave a second thought to Schweitzer's paternalism? No one. Many a jungle inhabitant would have died prematurely without his hospital, for modern-day Gabon still had no alternative to offer. "And it's nicer there than at other hospitals," one old man confided. "It's like a village, the family cooks for the patient, the huts are built around a square; it's just like being at home in the forest."

I walked past the former leper colony and onto the hospital grounds. After a few steps I was already panting like an old man. The first thing that strikes you in Lambaréné is the humidity. Climate is a difficult thing to describe, one kind of heat being different from another, but this was like having a noose around your neck. Fortunately, however, distraction came soon enough; before I knew it I was back in the Irene Hall.

A little black woman, one of the many mental patients housed by the hospital, came up to me and took my hand. She asked where I was from, then led me straight to Sister Lagendijk. The eighty-two-year-old nurse embraced me as though I were the prodigal son.

"You must work for Shell."

It took me a moment to get over my amazement, but with the same ease with which she had once spoken to our congregation, the old lady started to tell her story.

She grew up in Rotterdam, where her father was an engineer at the shipyards. In the mid-thirties she'd read *At the Edge of the Primeval Forest* and knew right away that her destination was Lambaréné.

She attended nursing school in Holland, trained as a midwife at the British Hospital in London (which offered an internationally recognized diploma) and then as a theater assistant at a hospital in Brussels – "That was good for my French." She boarded a ship for Gabon in 1938.

Dr Schweitzer himself helped her out of the canoe. He didn't ask about her papers: there were only three things he wanted to know before taking her on. "One. Do you sleep well? Two. How's your sense of humor? Three. Do you have a hobby?" Crossword puzzles, she'd said. He told her she could start right away; doing puzzles would keep her mind limber.

The war kept her from returning on leave to the Netherlands. In 1945 she flew to Europe in a Lockheed, along with the doctor and his wife. She was taken into custody when they landed in Paris. Anyone could claim that they helped poor Negroes in Africa, but post-liberation France was crawling with spies. She spent six weeks in a castle, a sort of internment camp, before they finally put her on the repatriation train for Holland. She held readings there and collected clothing and second-hand bicycles; in mid-1946 she resumed her duties in Lambaréné.

She still lived in the hospital grounds, in the oldest wing, built by Schweitzer himself, in a room big enough for only one person. She had to slide the stool under her desk before I could sit down in the armchair. Once I was seated, a text by St Francis of Assisi hanging above her bed caught my eye. Hadn't she been brought up in the Dutch Reformed Church? "I turn to St Francis for strength." And the saint was the very model of renunciation. The Polish nurse who popped in for a moment spoke of Sister Lagendijk as "the living memory of Lambaréné"; she was the only one left on the nursing staff to have worked with Schweitzer himself.

She had spoken German with the doctor. It was the language he spoke best, although he had written his work on Bach in French. He translated it into German himself, and it became a completely different book. "You know what, Maria, if you translate it literally it becomes a mishmash." She imitated his voice, and for a moment it was like hearing the man speak.

"We got along so well." Before she left for Africa she'd gone to Alsace. She knew the Alsatian mentality, and Schweitzer was an Alsatian through and through. "He came from a family of preachers and teachers; that determined his whole attitude towards life."

Was he authoritarian? "Not at all!" He was a man of many talents, and exceptionally intelligent. At the end of his life, with a clear and realistic eye, he had predicted the problems to come. And he'd been right. The nurses he had trained went into retirement, and their successors soon chose to work for the state hospitals, where they earned more and didn't have to work as hard. Not a single Gabonese doctor worked at Lambaréné. "They're all in the capital." Lambaréné lost its luster after Schweitzer died, and the flow of money from Europe and America petered out. His daughter Rhena ran the hospital for a few years, but, as Sister Lagendijk so nicely put it, "It's hard being the child of a celebrity." The hospital received only two replies when it advertised for a new director.

What was the biggest change she'd seen? There was no need for her to think for a second. "When Gabon finally became free in 1960." But how did the Gabonese themselves react? The French governor's ban on alcohol consumption was finally lifted! Intoxicating freedom. She had expected something other than drinking, drinking and more drinking. When the price of oil began rising in the late sixties, "Gabon finally got rolling." They began importing labor. The Gabonese themselves contributed little to the country's development; they sat back and watched it happen. "Dr Schweitzer said it was the climate. In the rain forests along the Equator, people are doomed to idleness."

She was panting a bit. The climate had exhausted her too. She had to go back to the Netherlands every two years, because malaria pills no longer helped prevent the fever. In Amsterdam she stayed with Franciscan nuns. "These days there's almost nowhere for mission people to go."

She belonged to another era, to the mission, the vocation and a life of service. Half a century earlier, Schweitzer had "brought about a change in me by pointing out the responsibility we all bear." These days, sitting in front of the TV at night, she caught snatches of the president's speeches in which he fulminated against the laxity of his fellow countrymen. Gabon was so rich, but the money flowed out of the country like water through the rapids. Once again, the needy were coming all the way from Libreville because, just like in the 1930s, there was no one to help them in the capital; events had come full circle, the disease called lethargy was spreading like wildfire, and that made her sad.

Just before he died, Dr Schweitzer had asked her to set up a geriatrics ward. She remained faithful to her master's principles. A clinic in the form of an African village, the huts aligned east-west so the sun could never shine in directly, double roofing for insulation and screened windows for natural ventilation. The Gabonese wanted to put in fans, but she'd stopped that ("those contraptions are always breaking down"), and she didn't get much help from the Swiss hospital management either. "The Swiss always know best."

Once the clinic was off to a good start, she'd been able to take things a bit easier. Her day began at six with letter writing, when her thoughts would wander to Amsterdam, the most beautiful city in the world. She recalled how she'd cried as a girl when her father turned down an offer to work for an Amsterdam shipyard. "I still dream about the canals, at least once a week, every week."

In the 1950s she had gone to the Netherlands with one suitcase, and come back with a dozen crates full of clothing and other supplies. When I told her about the Irene Hall, she nodded absently and sighed: "That's right, Lambaréné had a name in Holland." In 1967, she was given a royal decoration. She'd had to pick it up herself at the consul's office in Port-Gentil.

She still attended the occasional operation. Yesterday she'd gone to look at a man who'd been bitten by a snake. "Of course he waited two days instead of coming in immediately." But she left the nursing to the young people. There were eight white doctors working at the hospital, but white people usually didn't last much longer than two years in Lambaréné – a flash in the pan compared with the fifty-two years Dr Schweitzer worked here, give or take the odd break.

He had known he was going to die at the age of ninety. He'd said: "Then it will be my time to go." He was struck down by a brain tumor. It took two weeks for him to die. He was unable to speak, but he remained conscious and he could still hear. The assistants who were most faithful to him placed a gramophone next to his bed and played records. He died to the strains of Bach.

Maria Lagendijk was put in charge of the historical department, the museum. The old operating room, the pharmacy, Dr Schweitzer's study, his bedroom, everything was preserved just as it had been back then. His reading glasses lay on the desk, as though the doctor could come in any moment and pick them up, and the piano with organ pedals still stood, half-rotted away, in the shadowy parlor.

She led me around the rooms. My enthusiasm seemed to do her good, but she was rather puzzled by my inordinate interest in an enameled basin in one corner of the study.

"It's just a tub," she said.

And that's what it was: just a tub.

A motorized pirogue took me to the town across the river.

Ibinga was waiting for me in the lobby of the Hotel Ogooué. She sang out a greeting and clapped her hands. Had I encountered difficulties along the way? Had the people been polite? Wasn't I suffering from the heat? Wasn't I dying of thirst? Wouldn't I like to lie down for an hour? Wouldn't it be better for me to take a shower and put on some clean clothes? I could have kissed her, but refrained – with her white lace gloves, there was something touchingly demure about her.

At dinner I told her about the Lambaréné of my childhood. Ibinga refused to put up with even the slightest levity when it came to *le grand docteur*, she wanted to hear only good things about him. Every now and then she would shake her head. Why mock the elderly? In passing, she mentioned another self-sacrificing old man, this time "one of us." He may not have achieved the white doctor's fame, and he had never been nominated for a Nobel Prize, "but we honor him." She was talking about André Raponda-Walker.

"Bruce Walker's son."

In the accounts of nineteenth-century explorers, that name has the same self-explanatory ring as a brand of whisky. Robert Bruce Napoleon Walker set up the first trading posts in Gabon for the firm of Hatton and Cookson, and reached Lopé – still a major slave market at the time – by travelling partly overland. He did it all on his own, relying on his abilities as a fast talker, but his smooth talk didn't prevent the Enenga from holding him hostage for six months. In keeping with white custom, he had a black mistress. But he distinguished himself from other traders by marrying her when she became pregnant. André was born in 1871.

The Raponda family belonged to the highest caste of the M'Pongwe. André's mother was cousin to a ruler whom the British – for the sake of convenience – referred to as King George. She was also related to a king with whom the French had signed a treaty in 1843, and who considered it a great honor to bear the name of the French ruler of the day, Louis-Philippe. André was born just outside Libreville, in the village of that same King Louis.

The child spent his pre-school years afloat. Bruce had discovered an effective way to prevent theft: he ran his office aboard a little steamboat. The *Princess Royal* was anchored off the island of Elobey, near the coast of Spanish Guinea. The black employees worked in the storerooms beneath the bridge, and had to empty their pockets whenever they went ashore. Bruce had built comfortable quarters on the afterdeck, including an extensive library consisting largely of books about Africa. He liked to say that he was married not only to a black woman but to the entire dark continent.

That didn't keep him from sending André to Europe at the age of four. His son may have had skin as brown as chocolate, but nothing would keep him from having an English public school education. The fact that the boy had been baptized a Catholic at his mother's request didn't matter to Bruce; a British education was a Protestant education, and André was plucked away from under the palm trees and sent to one of the strictest boarding schools in Southampton. Of all the family members he missed while he was there, he missed his mother the most. She was the one who clapped her hands when she spoke, and sang when she had something important to say. Bruce began feeling sorry for the lad, and brought him back to Gabon less than two years later.

But he didn't really fit in there anymore, either. English had become his first language, he spoke it more readily than his maternal M'Pongwe, and he would spend the rest of his days trying to blot out that disgrace.

For a white man, Bruce Walker stuck it out for a long time in Equatorial Africa, but he didn't spend his whole life there. As the French grip on the colony became increasingly firm, the numerous excise taxes chipped away at the British traders' margins until there was barely any profit left. Walker went back to England for good, leaving his wife and child behind. Soon after, Mrs Walker sent her son to the Sainte Marie mission school; he was a boisterous child, far too disobedient for a little black boy. At the mission school André learned a third language, French, the language in which he would later write his opus.

He grew up in the shadow of the episcopal residence with its wooden verandah, the planks for which had been sawed from the wreck of a frigate that had run aground just off the coast. The Libreville of his youth was little different from when it had been established as a settlement for freed slaves a few decades earlier. The floors of the houses, which were built on wooden pilings, still reeked of tar, the peppery smell of indigo mingled with the sweet odor of palm oil on the quayside, and the stench of rubber had not yet wafted in. Raponda-Walker later became a bishop, a living monument in the front row when the French flag was lowered for the very last time; yet he also belonged unequivocally to the pioneering era, and to the Gabonese he would always remain the son of the freebooter Bruce Napoleon Walker.

André attended the preparatory and senior seminaries, and in 1899 was the first Gabonese to be ordained to the priesthood. His superiors sent him to set up a mission post at Sindara, on the

231

Ngounié River. There, just fifty kilometers south of Lambaréné, lived six different tribes about whom nothing was known in the capital. With a few choirboys as bearers and a collapsible altar in his baggage, he penetrated the territory, waded through the swamps, hacked his way through the jungle like Brazza and du Chaillu before him, climbed mountains and came across miserable villages deep in the bush, where he preached the gospel to little effect. He seemed to be the wrong man for the job, small, squat and bashful as he was, and he lacked the one thing that turned other missionaries into an attraction: white skin. So he kept his Bible closed for the time being and tried instead to win the natives' confidence by studying their customs and habits and learning their language. He realized that he was the first – but also one of the last – to come into contact with the autonomous civilizations of the Eshira, Ivili and Tshogo, and he took up his pen in an effort to preserve at least some of their culture.

Back in Libreville, where he had been appointed to a teaching position at the preparatory seminary, Raponda-Walker began working from his notes. His typewriter rattled on into the wee hours, and he catalogued his material with the zeal of a medieval monk. Six years later, when the work was finished, the French bishop decided to send him back into the bush to continue his linguistic and ethnographic quest.

He spent four years in Rio Muni, five years in Donguila, four years in Lambaréné and another five in Sindara; he lived among the Apindji people for seven years, and spent eight years at Fernan Vaz. His first articles began appearing in obscure missionary journals in the 1930s. It took him until the 1960s to complete his two standard works, by which time he was so old that he had to call in the help of the ethno-botanist Roger Sillans to complete his task. When it was finished he was able to die in peace, which he did, at the age of ninety-seven.

He compiled four dictionaries, wrote a brief history of Gabon and a six-hundred-page botanical guide, an essay on secret rituals, three anthologies of fables, sayings, proverbs, riddles, mottos, solemn oaths and war cries, and two treatises, one dealing with native astronomy, the other with tattooing and funeral rites. He went through a typewriter a year.

Perhaps Raponda-Walker would have achieved greater fame if he had gone in for polemics. In thousands of pages he painstakingly documented what Schweitzer had dismissed as woefully primitive in less than half a volume, and his utterly serious approach to native cultures cut the ground from under the doctor's findings. He made an in-depth study of the esoteric values of the native religions, and placed superstition in the context of the tropical rain forest, where everything – from the shadowy light beneath the foliage and the unreal silence in the daytime to the ominously black nights and macabre screams of apes and birds in the darkness – contributed to the ancestral belief in spirits, and the uncertainty regarding their places of residence. In order to maintain their footing in these terrifying surroundings, the natives had designed a system of self-defence with the aid of talismans, witchcraft, taboos and rituals. Striving for unity, they formed secret societies and devised initiation rites which tested the newcomer's moral, physical and intellectual mettle. They searched for relations between the things they saw, imposed order on their conclusions, and expressed their convictions in the form of ceremonies and dances, 'because primitive man is, above all, an artist'. All natural phenomena were subjected to interpretation: a dead muskrat in the middle of the path, a yellow snake crossing the trail or a chameleon burrowing its way through the sand were evil omens; the nocturnal screech of an owl or the shriek of a blue touraco sounded notes of warning; smelling the noxious odor of the *invimbizi* ant while out in the bush could have disastrous consequences; stubbing your left foot against a tree root or stone bode ill, while doing the same with your right foot meant the future had only good things in store.

Ibinga thought I should read as much of Raponda-Walker's work as possible; it would bring about a profound change in my view of primitive peoples. I would come to see, for example, that the jungle inhabitants were great experts in the medicinal properties of plants, that their knowledge covered both botanical and mineralogical aspects, and that Raponda-Walker had met a *n'anga*, a divine healer, a man familiar with the names and powers of every medicinal plant. "That healer was a walking encyclopedia."

She spoke of Raponda-Walker in the same tone of voice the elderly Sister Lagendijk had used when speaking of Albert Schweitzer. Ibinga had visited the bishop once, when she was still a girl. He was living in a little room behind the Church of St Pierre in Libreville. The doors and windows were always open, anyone could just walk in. Between the piles of books, magazines and pages of typed manuscript were two chairs, and a little altar at which he was allowed to perform mass by papal dispensation – he'd had a bad fall once, and had been lame in one leg ever since. He helped schoolchildren and seminarians with their homework, provided inspiration to disillusioned clergymen, handed out advice to young foreign researchers. But despite his many visitors he always seemed rather lonely, his face always had something melancholy about it. A face that was darker than his soutane, but lighter than that of the average Gabonese; he belonged to both Europe *and* Africa, the Catholic Church *and* indigenous belief, the pioneers *and* the Negro kings. "Maybe he felt like he didn't belong anywhere," Ibinga said, "maybe he needed all those thousands of pages to find that out."

The boat from Port-Gentil was running late. It wouldn't be heading back to the coast before Friday, twenty-four hours later than scheduled. We had to spend another whole day in Lambaréné, so we went wandering through town to pass the time. Long lines of schoolchildren in neat navy-blue or canary-yellow uniforms ran past us; the girls in particular turned to stare, and Ibinga widened the distance between us. At one point she was almost walking behind me. The paths were slippery; halfway up a hill I turned to give Ibinga a hand, to keep her from losing her footing. She reacted as though her honor were being threatened.

We continued uphill, walking in the shadows of decaying colonial houses. Ibinga was silent. The concrete bridge across the Ogooué was barely visible in the distance. After dark, no Gabonese would dare use that bridge, crossing water at night was asking for trouble – but it wasn't Ibinga who told me that, nor was she the one who offered an explanation for the name Lambaréné. The explanation I heard was this: the Galoa were on their way north in search of a place to settle when suddenly the tip of a peninsula came into view, and one of them shouted,

235

"*Lembaréni!*", 'let's try over there'.

Later that afternoon I tried again. A boat trip on the lakes might mollify Ibinga. She agreed to the plan, but in the pirogue she took a seat behind me, where I couldn't see her. The wind caressed my face, and after the very first bend in the river the world was only water and sky and the motionless greenery along the banks. These days the well-to-do Gabonese regards Lambaréné as the ideal vacation spot; the Ogooué and Ngounié converge just beyond the peninsula, and a few kilometers south of town the river branches into dozens of lakes, ponds, streams and creeks; he can fish there, or watch birds in the hope that a white pelican will fly over, or a pippio, 'the most beautiful bird in the world . . . a mass of green and gold' (Trader Horn). After the trip in the motorized pirogue, he disembarks at the defiantly luxurious four-star hotel built directly opposite the Schweitzer Hospital; in the lobby an ice-cold wind strikes him full in the face, and he quickly orders a brandy to nip the flu in the bud. Thanks to air conditioning, the belly-warmer is now in demand along the Equator as well.

Back in Lambaréné a woman in the market had scolded me sharply: I'd had the nerve to bargain with her, when I was obviously wealthy enough to keep a black woman on the side. Ibinga had lowered her eyes, and I'd realized my mistake. I shouldn't have been with her. In Gabon, women belong with women and men with men, it's a barrier that can't be broken. What is a woman to the Fang? 'A dry ear of corn. He who has teeth takes a bite.' And the women confirm that belief in one of their dancing songs, when they submissively sing: "I'm nothing compared to a man, I'm nothing but a dumb cluck."

Ibinga made a scene at dinner. We ordered avocados, but

itself, swung down from the bow and the melee began. A woman fainted and had to be carried off; a man vomited. The passengers had spent a day and a night at the quay, waiting for the delayed departure, and most of them had long abandoned all semblance of sobriety. A half-naked boy with a bottle of beer in his hand was trying to drive a herd of goats onto the boat. The animals attempted to run, children were knocked down in the panic, mothers became enraged. Burly men toted air-conditioners and refrigerators on board; boxes of provisions burst open, their contents scattering along the quay; an old woman squatted down and moaned. From the bridge, the captain shouted to a soldier to come to our assistance, but his uniform didn't make much of an impression; he only made it halfway through the crowd. To reach the steps that led to the top deck we had to pass through the entire second-class section, which took us a good fifteen minutes of exertion. Ibinga likened her countrymen to a herd of buffalo: nice to look at from a distance, but a bit too rambunctious up close.

The captain welcomed us aboard with a tap to his visor. "Don't mind the others, I personally guarantee your safety. Tonight you can sleep in one of the two cabins." He was talking to me, not to Ibinga. I was the only white person on board. The boat trip usually took twenty-five hours, the captain explained, but we would arrive at the bay of Cap Lopez just as the tide was going out; that meant we would have to wait at the mouth of the river for a few hours before crossing to Port-Gentil. "So the whole trip will probably take about thirty hours." At least there was no danger of running aground on a sandbank, like in the dry season. "When that happens, it sometimes takes a day or two before we're afloat again." He wiped a drop of sweat from his deep-black forehead and looked up at the sky. A thunderstorm was on its way, you could tell from the way the clouds flocked together: the heavens were one big palaver.

The boat strained away from the shore, the stamping of the engines shaking the whole vessel, until it reached midstream and was lifted by the current. The little brick church quickly receded behind the foliage, a final glimpse of Dutch Reformed Holland in the tropics. The afternoon before we left I had walked among the crooked gravestones, counting the missionaries who had died before the age of forty. I got up to seven. Poor fellows. First they had struggled against the Protestants – whose church was just one kilometer away upriver – then against the fever. Meanwhile their parishioners simply couldn't understand why they weren't allowed to keep a whole flock of wives; after all, it was there in black and white in the priests' big book: the patriarch Abraham himself had more than one.

Things had quietened down on the lower deck. Most of the passengers had settled in and regrouped in families lying around their baggage. We had found a spot in the shade of the pilothouse, where we hoped to catch some wind. The passengers around us were mostly old men and women. They sat gnawing toothlessly on drumsticks and passing us bread and fruit. An old woman poured milk from a thermos flask; it was really for her grandchild, but she wanted me to taste some. A Gabonese never eats alone; Sister Lagendijk had told me that, adding: "Even if he's dying of starvation." A wondrous people, crude and mild-mannered, social and secretive. Just like the elements that surround them – the sky was overcast, shut tight as a drum.

The river was narrow at first. Hanging out over the water, the trees along the banks fought for every inch of space, their branches groaning under a cargo of vines. The boat headed due south, only turning to the west a good four hours later. I told Ibinga, whose eyes were half-closed as she watched the waves roll away towards the curtain of foliage that lined the shore, that I had felt sorry when leaving Franceville, Lastoursville and Lopé, and that Lambaréné was now making me feel the same way. Without really knowing why, I would have liked to have spent months in all those places. Was there something about remote places that made me feel at home? Or was loneliness like beer: you take a sip, then you feel like taking another, until after a while you're drunk? Ibinga shook her head groggily; she found it a bit too early in the day for reflection.

As though to soften the blow of departure, another spire suddenly loomed up among the treetops. This had to be the church at Ngomo, once the site of an important factory. There was little left of the trading post these days; the warehouse roofs had collapsed under the weight of the greenery and, against the background of tall white trunks, the church steeple seemed about ready to bow out as well. The boat slid out of the main channel and came to an abrupt halt. Motorized canoes skimmed towards us from all sides, bearing new passengers, fruit and fish. The ferry-boat passengers hung over the railings to do their shopping. One man wanted to look in a fish's mouth before he bought it, but the eighty-centimeter-long beast was still alive and snapped its sawtoothed jaws. A scream, a bleeding thumb, and the boat-men in the pirogues laughed. You had to be a city boy to let yourself be bitten by a fish on dry land; their delight knew no bounds, and the roars of laughter were still echoing across the water when they headed for shore. The man had his hand bandaged by an old woman, "A sorceress," the people around us whispered. A little later she came to the rescue again, to calm a girl who was writhing spastically across the deck.

The ferry passed a log drive – hundreds of tree trunks floating behind a tug that barely needed to use its engines as it was heading downstream. The captain called out orders to the helmsman; it wasn't easy to pass a float of trunks a meter-and-a-half in diameter and at least twenty-five meters long. The current in this stretch of river pulled and eddied: one clumsy maneuvre and an okoumé would drill itself through the hull. Entire villages once moved along the river this way; the natives would build huts on the logs and be floated down to the coast with their wives and children in six weeks. Workers were always losing their footing on the slippery trunks, and if they happened to fall between the drifting logs they didn't live to talk about it. The crocodiles on the sandbars waited patiently for their meal. Another danger was malaria mosquitoes, for whom the floating villages were a paradise. Most victims, however, were claimed by the last leg across open sea; during the crossing to Port-Gentil, the swell knocked one villager after another into the water. By journey's end, the population of the log raft had been halved.

With the current as its faithless ally, the boat swung back and forth across the river. We sat on the steel deck and the diesel engines rattled us to the bone. Wooden benches must once have stood along the railings and lounge chairs on the middle deck, but now the boat had been stripped of everything useful, except for the bridge and engine room. When the river split into three, the boat took the middle branch; the view became monotonous, forest and more forest under an occasionally rumbling gray sky. Ibinga was suffering from the heat as well; she leaned listlessly against the wall of the pilothouse, dropped off to sleep and awoke with a start when her head touched my shoulder.

Around noon the passengers began building little fires on the lower deck to roast chicken and fish. The smoke made it seem as though the ship were on fire. The spicy smell of food wafted up from below, and crates of beer were brought up from the hold and passed through the crowd; this was making me thirsty, so one of the boys raced off to bring me a bottle of Régab. A papyrus-covered island and a bowl-shaped lake had receded far beyond the horizon by the time he returned; he'd met a nice girl at the bar, and besides, there was a fight happening on the rear deck. Really? "Sure, but they'll be laughing again before you know it, and tonight we'll see them dancing together. Want to bet?"

Ibinga took a cautious sip and wrinkled her face in disgust. She never drank alcohol, *une question de principe*. In Lambaréné we had spoken English together, but in order to avoid anything that would draw attention to us while on board, she spoke French with me, and Fang or M'Pongwe with the other passengers. That gave me the chance to learn a greeting in Fang: *kor-kor*, 'may your days be long'.

She had to raise her voice to make herself heard. The quiet on board hadn't lasted long; music was now blaring out of oversized transistor radios, six or seven of them doing their best to drown out each other. Most of the old people had been forced to leave the upper deck; they hadn't paid for a first-class passage and the captain didn't want to hear about their rheumatism, frauds belonged in the hold. A group of seven travellers from Ngomo came and sat next to us, young men who seized on my presence as an opportunity to submit the injured hamstrings of soccer player Ruud Gullit to further diagnosis. I had to draw a little map to show them where Holland actually was, but they knew everything there was to know about the Dutch soccer star.

As the afternoon wore on they became increasingly boisterous. They homed in on Ibinga in their local dialect, and her reactions indicated that their speech was none too refined; she stuttered with indignation and called the boys "drunken idiots," which wasn't really the best way to quiet them down. We moved to the port side of the pilothouse, but even there the boys didn't leave her alone. Ibinga had become their prime remedy for boredom, and she seemed to be the only one not to realize it. She responded to every joke and comment, threatened to complain to the captain and told them that their infantile behavior was bound to give me a very low opinion of the Gabonese. I couldn't keep a straight face the whole time either, and that enraged Ibinga even more; she thought everyone was poking fun at her and, being already rather unsure of herself, she felt humiliated.

She wanted to go ashore. This "trash" was irritating her no end, and nothing was going to change her mind. A village loomed up, the boat slowed down, canoes shot alongside and Ibinga leapt to her feet, grabbed her things and made her way down the steps. The boys seemed just as shocked as I was and called out that they would leave her alone, but Ibinga's mind was made up. The captain came over to me and asked what was going on; I told him that my friend wasn't feeling well . . . not to worry, he said, they had aspirin on board and she could rest in one of the cabins, there was a cot in there and no one would bother her. Besides, it was almost evening and the worst of the heat would soon be over . . . on the lower deck I saw Ibinga climb over the railing and step into a canoe. "Please, stay on board yourself in any case," the captain said, but I couldn't leave Ibinga behind in some

243

cluster of huts by the river.

By the time we climbed out of the canoe the look in her eyes had mellowed. She must have acted on the spur of the moment, but her mind was still made up. In the distance, the captain stood gesturing to us from the boat, but Ibinga turned her back on him and began negotiating with the village chief about the price of lodgings. I was given the guest hut, while she received the former women's lodge at the very edge of the village; in the olden days, women had to remain in a separate hut while menstruating. The boat soon disappeared from view but half an hour later I could still hear its whistle.

We ate in silence. After dinner one of the chief's sons dragged two chairs down to the beach, the only place where we could catch a waft of the lukewarm evening breeze. I finished my pack of cigarettes, smoking to keep the mosquitoes away, and as if she sensed my uneasiness, Ibinga began speaking of her own accord. She sowed the wind, she felled an elephant, she asked whether it might sound silly to me, then she quoted a few more lines:

> *The mouth cannot say everything!*
> *The mouth only speaks with words!*
> *The heart alone can speak.*
> *The heart alone can say everything.*
> *Oh . . . if only the heart was a mouth,*
> *Then people would understand the* mvett!

The *mvett*, that's what it was all about. She promised to tell me more about it. That sounded hopeful.

There was an old-fashioned bedstead in my hut. (At the end of the last century, Mary Kingsley had come across Windsor chairs in some huts, causing her to conclude that the Gabonese were ripe for English civilization.) I slept miserably. Rats chased each other across the sheet-iron roof all night. Despite the mosquito netting, I feared the giant spider that eats mice and little birds, and the ground spider that clamps its mandibles in your groin and leaves you with testicles the size of papayas. After being bitten by one of them, you die in hellish pain within a few hours. And I jumped when a rock badger screamed, even though I'd heard them so often at Lopé. That little animal, no bigger than a guinea pig, has a triangle of tough, scaly skin on its back that resonates when it screams. It's a sound that conjures up images of a dungeon where someone is being skinned alive.

The men had all gone fishing by the time I woke up. The women gave me some manioc and a dried fish they called 'stink fish' – with good reason, as it turned out. One of the women produced a jar of Nescafé, another went to her hut and brought back some sugar. All the scanty village supplies were shared with me, and what struck me most was the completely natural way it was done.

There was a touch of blue to the sky this morning; the afternoon promised to be less overcast than the day before. The women boiled water on the smoldering fire, talking busily as they worked, and I was once again reminded of Mary Kingsley. 'The African has no writing, so he talks it out.' When Ibinga showed up half an hour later, she took a sip of my coffee and stuffed some manioc in her mouth. She too had slept badly; the rats had actually come into her hut, and that had summoned up many of her earliest memories. "Everything was bad then, really bad." A few minutes later she ran down to the river, where she'd heard the whine of an outboard motor.

Massandé wore blue overalls with ELF GABON printed in big letters on the back; his father worked for the oil company in Port-Gentil. As he was pulling the dugout up onto the bank I saw that he was lame in one leg, although he tried to hide it as best he could. Massandé must have been about twenty, much younger than Ibinga, but from the moment their eyes met he blushed like a schoolboy in love. He called her 'my little one' and 'my sister', shooed a fly away from her curly reddish-brown hair and sprang to her assistance every time she tried to pick something up. Ibinga was more pleased by his attentions than I had expected; even though we were about to leave, she went back to the hut to put on a clean *pagne*. While she was walking away, bent slightly at the knee as usual, as if she might start dancing at any moment, Massandé followed her wistfully with his eyes and breathed a sigh that came straight from the heart: "What a pretty girl." He enquired cautiously into our relationship, and I was able to put his mind at ease. He was less pleased to hear that Ibinga lived in the capital; he had never been to Libreville in his life. When she returned wearing her most colorful *pagne*, with a rolled-up bandanna tied around her frizzy hair, she gave Massandé a broad smile and I felt something stab me, right under the ribs.

Massandé claimed to be the best boatman in the delta. We were in luck, he knew every current and creek in the labyrinth. He had just picked up some supplies at Ngomo and was on his way back to his village, about forty kilometers downstream. If we went with him we could eat the most wonderful spareribs that evening, and he nodded at Ibinga: "Just for you, sister, just for you." There were two children's chairs in the pirogue; Ibinga sat in the middle, I sat in the bow. When we set off, the women and children waving from the riverbank, the wind immediately made life a great deal more bearable.

Massandé kept his speed down in order not to strain the outboard. He soon left the main channel and began following the smaller streams flowing parallel to it. One island was covered in swaying papyrus; on the next, dozens of tall, bare trunks pointed at the sky like the fingers of an open hand. Only bushes could grow on the swampier shores, but directly behind them the grim green battlements rose straight up on both sides of the river. Some of the islands were partially submerged, making the trees and bushes on them appear to float; vines hung sluggishly from the branches. The river split off endlessly, forming channels that converged again kilometers downstream, where they emptied into lakes. Searching for the fastest way out, the brown channel narrowed and widened again in the constantly shifting light. In narrow passages it could be as dusky as the last minutes before sundown, while above the lakes piles of trade cumuli spoke of the sky's truly immeasurable reach. In such surroundings I sometimes caught myself calculating distances and proportions for no apparent reason, except perhaps as a way to pin down the boundless spaces. Everything here seemed without limit: the sky, the greenery, the water. Despite the vastness of our surroundings, I wasn't scared. I couldn't have cared less whether we would ever find our way out of this maze of channels and streams, or where we would end up if the outboard should give up the ghost. All I felt was the desire to see more, and the growing ecstasy that such utter desolation brought.

Imagine clearing a little plot of ground here along the shoreline, I mused, and building yourself a house on stilts; what would life be like then? Miserable; at least that's what Mary Kingsley said. She described the fate of the young agent at Osoamokita. A plucky fellow in his early twenties, but not really cut out for such a lonely existence. He came down with swamp fever. The trading house sent him a doctor, who insisted that he go back to Europe to recover. But the young man had no one at home to take care of him. The doctor left, and three days later the agent committed suicide. 'No one knows, who has not been to visit Africa, how terrible is the life of a white man in one of these out-of-the-way factories, with no white society, and with nothing to look at, day out and day in, but that one set of objects: the forest, the river, and the beach.'

But when taken in doses of a day or a week, loneliness has a certain cathartic effect; with every kilometer you travel, you feel yourself becoming less and less significant. What do you know of the currents, the dangers? Nothing. The boatman's knowledge and experience are all you can rely on.

Hours went by before we passed another boat, and the morning was half over by the time we met three pirogues rowing upstream. Creeping along in the shadow of the overhanging branches close to shore, where the current is less powerful, the oarsmen were peering up into the branches to make sure no snakes would come slithering down into their canoe. They had to watch out for hippopotamuses too. Hippos will surface when they feel a dugout gliding through the water above them and, if enraged, can easily smash a boat to pieces. Motorized canoes, which usually stick to the middle of the river, have nothing to fear; hippos get out of the way as quickly as possible when they hear a motor in the distance. There aren't many of the old river horses left in the estuary these days, their flesh was too tender, their teeth too much in demand. The same fate has overcome the crocodiles and caimans, whose expensive skins drove them to extinction in large parts of the delta. But we still caught a whiff of one: a heavy, musky odor wafted across the river, and Massandé pointed to a tree trunk that seemed to be floating away from us. A little later we saw another crocodile, a dead one this time. The stench was unbearable.

We went ashore at Ngoumbi. The motor needed time to cool off, and Massandé figured we were ready to stretch our legs. The only bad thing about dugouts is that you can't budge once you're in them; the slightest movement rocks the hollow log almost to the point of capsizing. Ngoumbi was as shabby as the smattering of other villages we'd passed in the delta, which is emptier now than when Mary Kingsley was here. All attempts by modern-day travellers to follow her route straight through the Ogooué delta to the Rembwé have failed. The villages she visited have long since disappeared, and in a number of places the little rivers she took have been smothered by the advancing jungle.

We sat down for a drink. When a fly landed on Massandé's shoulder, Ibinga killed it with a single swat. "A tsetse," she shouted triumphantly. Our boatman's adoring glances had livened her up greatly. I bent to examine the dreaded carrier of sleeping sickness. Not much bigger than a common housefly: to the naked eye, the tsetse is barely distinguishable from other flies. "They don't zoom," Ibinga said, "and their wings open and close like a pair of scissors." But the tsetse is a secret racist: it seldom lands on a light-colored surface, and avoids white shirts and skin.

Massandé's village was another three hours downriver. While we were navigating one of the broader channels, a tangle of roots became snarled in the propeller. Massandé cut the engine and the current carried the boat to the downstream side of an island. He paddled the last few meters to shore. Once we had pulled the dugout onto the bank, Massandé crawled under the boat and began hacking with his machete at the tough roots. Despite his bad leg, he was fast and agile. The chore completed, he put his white cap back on again, carefully this time, as though looking at himself in a mirror.

We sat down in the shade of a tree and had a bite to eat. Massandé said that being on the river always reminded him of the story of Muvungu.

Muvungu was an ugly boy, so ugly that his mother sometimes refused to feed him for days on end. One day he'd had enough; he decided to take his canoe upriver and never return. After paddling for hours, his dugout bumped into a branch of a *fuba* tree. Muvungu grabbed hold of the branch and pulled it roughly. At that very moment he heard a little voice: "Stop, please, you're hurting me, you're breaking my arms and legs." Amazed, Muvungu picked a leaf from the tree, and the leaf turned into a beautiful young maiden. She asked Muvungu to marry her, and promised him that, if he kept their secret, he would be the happiest and richest man in the world. She used her fetish to turn him into a strikingly handsome fellow, dressed in the most beautiful clothes. She built a hut for their wedding night and another hut for their servants – she built a whole town for him. Muvungu was beside himself with joy. He decided to return to his old village, to show off his good fortune to his relatives. He had been in the village for hours before his mother recognized his voice. She tried every trick in the book to find out what had brought about his metamorphosis. She cooked him the most delicious dishes. Then the little voice of Muvungu's tree-woman warned him: "Don't eat anything your mother has made for you, she has put a poison in the food that will make you betray our secret." But Muvungu became ravenous when he smelled the dishes set before him; he gave in, and ate. With every bite he revealed more of the secret; his cap flew away, then his jacket and his trousers. Naked at last he ran back to his town and found that the huts had vanished, along with his wife and servants. He was just as lonely, poor and ugly as ever.

Ibinga looked at me. "Do you understand the story?" she asked. I tried to come up with an interpretation . . . the power of love can transform even the ugliest of creatures, on condition that that love never fade . . . but I was wrong. "Almost all our legends are about the respect we have for our ancestors." The journey across water symbolized the road to death, the *fuba* tree was the place where the initiation rites were held, the talking leaves were the voices of the ancestors, the ban on sharing the secret was the initiate's oath of silence. Then Massandé chimed in: "If you listen to the voices of your ancestors you will be beautiful and rich, but if you violate the trust they have placed in you, you will be unhappy." That's why he was often reminded of Muvungu when he was out on the river. Both his grandfather and great-grandfather had been oarsmen. Out here he felt their presence more strongly than anywhere else; he heard their voices, so he was never afraid on the water.

We continued downstream.

As we navigated another bend in the river, a gray parrot with a fiery red tail came and flew along beside us, circling above the boat. Massandé slowed down and imitated the cry of the bird, which gave a long cackle before landing on a little island covered in hippo grass.

'Along these banks', Mary Kingsley wrote, 'one forgets every sense of human individualism, all recollections of human life, with its sorrows, and its worries, and its doubts'.

Other travellers saw the jungle as something sinister, but this was where Kingsley found peace. Her heart pounded no faster when she landed at a village where everything pointed to cannibalistic practices. In one of the huts she found a human hand, three big toes, four eyeballs, two ears and other assorted body parts. 'The hand was fresh, the others so-so, and shrivelled.' It didn't faze her in the least. Whatever happened in Africa was better than what happened at home, because at home – being rural England – nothing had happened at all. Looked at in retrospect, the life she'd led until then had been an empty one.

As a child her life had stopped at the garden gate. Her father, George Kingsley, travelled through Asia and America as private physician to well-to-do globetrotters, and was sometimes away from home for years at a time. Her mother suffered from depression and seldom got out of bed. Mary cared for her, did the housekeeping and experienced her only moments of pleasure when reading her father's letters. She never went to school, and the little home-tutoring she enjoyed came when she sat at the table where her older brother was learning to read and write. Everything else she learned from her father's library. Mary almost never left the house. Social events, birthday parties, boyfriends – none of that for her. Her own life only started at the age of thirty, when her father and mother died within a few weeks of each other and her only brother took off as fast as he could to India. She boarded a ship for West Africa, 'to die there', as she wrote to an acquaintance. Eight years later, she did indeed die in Africa; but it was in South Africa, where she had gone to nurse wounded British soldiers during the Boer War.

"Deep inside I am truly a very melancholy person," she once confessed. "But I rarely allow that side of myself to be seen. I feel that I have no right to the sympathy of another."

This modesty, bordering almost on self-contempt, made her much-loved during her two trips through West Africa. Beneath her long black skirts and petticoat – she dressed just as respectably in the jungle as she did in East Anglia, to demonstrate to the natives the exemplary English way of life – she packed a loaded pistol, but never had to use it. The crocodiles and hippopotamuses were her dear friends, Fang cannibals her most faithful guides. Back in England she characterized herself as a 'staunch African'; she found that Africans looked at life in a much more spiritual way than 'materialistic' Europeans, and in their contemplative character she recognized something of herself.

Her account of her journeys, *Travels in West Africa*, was published in 1897. Three years later she contracted typhoid near the front lines. She asked to be buried at sea, sent the doctors away and died alone.

This countryside was a reminder of that life.

We were sitting around the fire. Behind us the fishing nets were hanging out to dry, and the ramshackle huts leaned against each other for support. It looked as if one good gust of wind could blow the whole village to smithereens. When we arrived that afternoon, the villagers subjected me to a barrage of about thirty questions, my replies to all of which resulted in uncontrollable laughter. After this cheerful intermezzo – during which I was the center of attention, like some travelling clown – the women hurried off to prepare the meal, or, as Massandé put it, "The high point of the welcome." The men returned just before nightfall, lugging a huge catch after their long day out on the river. These fishermen were worn and tattered, half-naked and filthy, their arms and legs covered with scars, the brown stumps in their mouths all that remained of their teeth. Some of them were covered with sores, the open phase of what I feared was syphilis. They hung up their hammocks, started drinking beer and, at Massandé's request, left us alone. For reasons I would later discover, Massandé had little in common with these villagers. Besides being a good boatman, he also turned out to be a good host: he tasted the spicy spareribs himself before telling the women to set them before us, he took account of the fact that I might not want to eat with my fingers and dug up a fork from somewhere, and he kept Ibinga – who he pampered like a young bride – richly supplied with cola. We ate three roasted fish apiece, and if Massandé had had his way we would have eaten ten. We could no longer smell the fishy stench hanging over the village and, with the smoldering fire as our only source of light, we soon forgot our impoverished surroundings. There are two Africas: one in the daytime, the other at night. When the moon comes out, the people huddle closer together and talk, to forget the ominous rustling of the leaves; that nocturnal Africa is ruled by the shiver of fear, and that is precisely what makes for a deep sense of intimacy.

On his father's side, Massandé told us, he was an Urundu, the tribe that lives at the mouth of the Ogooué. On his mother's side he was a Fang.

"So you're half cannibal," I said. He laughed, but a few minutes later asked in great earnest just how much I knew about cannibalism.

"Too much to be afraid of it," I said, "and too little to go upriver without a boatman."

He told me not to worry, I could go upriver on my own. Headhunting was a thing of the past, and even then it had been the exception rather than the rule.

To his ancestors a skull was a powerful thing, Massandé explained without taking his eyes off Ibinga, who had crossed her legs and was nodding to him encouragingly. A Fang honored the skulls of his relatives, his loved ones, his servants and the enemies he had killed in battle. Before going on a hunt, he would offer sacrifices to the skulls of panthers and gorillas. Strangers catching a glimpse of this confused the cult of skulls with cannibalism. The Fang didn't bother to correct them on this point, for their terrifying reputation offered them a certain degree of protection. They inspired fear, and most tribes ran for cover when the Fang appeared. When rowing on the river, they did not sing the way the M'Pongwe, Galoa or Urungu did; they didn't mix with other tribes, and their villages were built inside a circular palisade of poisoned spikes. For centuries they had sold the tusks they'd gathered on their exhausting journeys through the jungle to the river people, who then brought the ivory to the coast. But there came a point when the Fang had had enough of the middlemen's fickle demands and decided to head for the coast themselves, in order to make contact with the white men they called their 'big brothers'.

Big brothers? That sounded like something Schweitzer would have said.

"It was part of their religion. In one of the Fang legends, God speaks to his beloved black people just before he dies: 'When I'm no longer around to take care of you, you must go to the south-east. There you will find people as white as ocean foam, as white as ghosts. They are extremely rich, and they are your big brothers.' The Fang did just that. During their migration they destroyed everything in their path, villages, cultures, sometimes entire tribes. They ate their vanquished enemies to take on their power and courage, but the women and children were not allowed to watch, just as they were not allowed to eat from plates that had held human flesh. It was a ritual for grown men, for warriors, with no outsiders allowed."

Indeed, no traveller has ever seen a Fang eat human flesh. The stories Europeans told about them were based on a combination of rumors that made the rounds and the gnawed bones they occasionally came across in a hut. Ibinga thought many of the tall tales sprang from purely semantic differences. When a Fang warrior had killed an enemy, he would say that he had 'eaten his soul', or simply that he had 'eaten him'. The metaphorical twist was lost on most Europeans.

More confusion arose when the Europeans failed to see the difference between cannibalism and another phenomenon: the Fang dissected family members who had died of witchcraft or other sorcery; in other words, people who had been poisoned. They performed autopsies to determine the cause of death.

"Death by natural causes was very rare in the jungle," said Massandé. "Every accident, every illness and every fatality was blamed on poison or angry spirits. To find out whether traces of poison were left in the stomach or intestines, a priest would cut open the body of a victim. These were secret rituals, but the Europeans must have picked up on some of it without knowing exactly what was going on."

In other words, it was all a big misunderstanding.

Massandé smiled. "When the Fang finally reached the coast and saw their first white men, they thought the Europeans were wearing clothes to hide their physical shortcomings. The Europeans, on the other hand, concluded that these jungle people must be at least a little ashamed of their nakedness, because some of the women wore bunches of straw in front of their genitals. But those bunches of straw were only there to indicate that they lived with a man, and that they had borne children."

It had been an educational evening. But a few things were still unclear to me. The Fang's cannibalism may have been greatly exaggerated, for example, but it was nevertheless a fact. And the Fang showed no mercy, either to their enemies or to their own tribesmen. Was Massandé proud of his ancestors?

"Listen, and try to understand what I'm saying. The old people fought their way through the jungle. Their lives consisted of fear, and they were always on the lookout for ways to keep that fear within bounds. They did that in thousands of different ways. It's not fair to take one of those traditions and place it out of context. When you look at it as a whole, my ancestors deserve respect. They survived under hostile conditions. Along with famines, influenza and smallpox epidemics sometimes wiped out a third of the tribe. Sure, they occasionally turned a blind eye [the Fang expression for committing incest, as Ibinga explained later] to keep the tribe going, and they stole women from other tribes too. You can condemn that, but you would have to ignore just how terrible life in the jungle really was. To me, the important thing is that once their migration was over, the old people swore off the *evus*, the magic power that prompted them to commit acts of cannibalism. There was no longer any reason for that kind of brutality. The Fang adopted the Christian faith, buried their masks or let them be devoured by the white ants."

You should hear the whole *mvett*, Ibinga said. Because in the *mvett* it says:

> *We see everything on man's earth!*
> *We see the light!*
> *We see the darkness!*
> *And the* mvett *was the light in that darkness.*

According to oral tradition, the Fang once lived on the banks of the Nile, but were driven from their home by the Mvélé. During their flight, the warrior and musician Oyono Ada Ngono fell unconscious. They laid him on a stretcher and hurried on across the savanna. A week later, Oyono awoke. During his coma, he told his tribesmen, he had found a way to keep up his courage. He took a length of bamboo, stripped off four long fibers and strung them across a calabash. He played on the instrument, and he sang:

> *I sow the wind!*
> *Yeah!*
> *I fell the elephant!*

Yeah!
That the ears may hear!
That they may listen to the mvett!

And while he strummed, Oyono Ada Ngono sang the story of a warrior people he called 'the People of Iron', who had fought their way across the territories of the southern tribes. They followed the Ouellé River and the Oubangui, then turned off to the west to where a gigantic tree, the *kam-elone* (which is where the name 'Cameroun' originally comes from), blocked their path. To get around the obstacle, the Fang split into groups and followed the trails to the north-east, south and west.

"The *mvett*," Ibinga said, "is our *Odyssey*."

There are dozens of versions of the heroic epic, the length of which ranges in relation to the bard's stamina. Experienced *mvett* singers once recited for forty-eight hours at a stretch; these days the version heard at Fang tribal meetings is usually much shorter.

"For decades we neglected the *mvett*," Ibinga said. "Until we realized that our white brothers could give us everything, except a history of our own."

That was what had made her start talking about the *mvett* the night before. She had felt out of place, she hadn't known how to act, she had felt inferior, and she had remembered the *mvett*, the source of power and self-confidence.

I didn't come anywhere near understanding everything Massandé and Ibinga were telling me. Europeans aren't that much more materialistic than Africans – everyone's materialistic

– but we are much more literal-minded, and what Massandé said about the *evus*, for example, the magic power of the Fang, was far beyond my grasp. But that night I felt close to Africa. I heard the poetry of the continent, which I had only *seen* before in the anthropological museums of Paris and Berlin: in their masks, statues, jewelry and weapons, these savage Fang had achieved a purity of form unequalled by any other West African tribe.

Massandé lived and worked in Port-Gentil. In the late 1970s he had left for the city with his parents, brothers and sisters and his grandmother. They rarely saw each other in town, but on the first day of the long school vacation they all returned to their native village, and the family ties were restored. The men fished in the river as they always had, the women worked in the vegetable gardens with their sisters who had remained behind. They never worked harder than they did during those four weeks off, and in the evening they would gather around the fire and tell each other stories; there was no radio or TV, none of that constant stream of news that silences modern man or makes of him a brusque commentator on events that hardly concern him. Their stories were about people they knew or had known, about events still fresh in their memories, about their river and their village. So Massandé lived in two worlds, which he referred to as 'the inside' and 'the outside'. The outside was the big city, long trousers, white shirts, the office, the Christian faith, in-dividualism; the inside was tradition, life on the river, rubbing elbows with his ancestors, the group, amulets and talismans, the *bwiti*. The Gabonese will show the outside to anyone; the inside is only for those dear to them. Massandé must have given a great deal of thought to that dichotomy; what he was saying sounded very plausible to me. But when I asked him to tell me about the *bwiti*, he made a gesture of refusal.

"The *bwiti* is our secret. Because that's what the inside is all about, it's the part that truly belongs to us, the part we've never lost, despite all the Western influences. A Gabonese isn't even allowed to pronounce the name *bwiti*, so . . ."

He stood up, told one of his sisters to wash the dishes, and wished me a good night; he couldn't have come up with a better illustration of his theory if he'd tried. Ibinga followed his example; it had been a long and tiring day, and we would need our rest for tomorrow. It sounded as though she were apologizing for Massandé.

I went to my hut. My bed was a mat on the ground. The moon was shining through a hole in the roof, and in the walls I discovered even bigger holes through which rodents and other unwanted visitors could come and go at will. Forewarned by the example of Charles de Chavannes, who had once spent an hour hunting down and wringing the neck of the rat that had gnawed its way through his mosquito netting and bitten him on the calf, I decided to stay awake. An hour went by, and thanks to the faint rustling in the background it was the longest hour I believe I ever spent. When I heard the scratching sound at the door, I shot upright.

It was a relief to hear Ibinga's voice. She came in and sat on the mat with her legs crossed; in the light of the kerosene lantern all I could see clearly were her wakeful eyes darting to and fro. She was too nervous to fall asleep either, and she knew only one way to get through the night: talking. Before long we had touched on the *bwiti*.

She had mixed feelings about the secret society. It had originally been something sacred, connected with the cult of fire practiced by many primitive peoples, and with the bringing together of the living and the dead, which was the essence of almost every African religion. The *bwiti* belonged to the inside, as Massandé would say, but what bothered Ibinga was that the society had begun to tamper with the outside as well. Since independence, members of the *bwiti* had begun playing a formative role in the nation's politics, and the society had become a breeding ground for power, rather like Freemasonry in Europe in the eighteenth and nineteenth centuries. The *bwiti* had become a secular society, even though it maintained the old religious rituals.

Boys between the ages of ten and twelve were admitted to the *bwiti* after enduring initiation rites held in remote parts of the forest, which lasted for four or five days. The initiates were not allowed to eat, and had to chew a plant, the *iboga*, which caused them to quickly lose consciousness and see visions of a whole procession of spirits. *Iboga* produces extremely violent nightmares, and the boys would scream in terror. When they awoke, the interrogation began. Had they seen the *bwiti*? Was it a little human creature that danced and made faces, and was it the color of fire? When the novice gave a satisfactory answer, the elders would call out: "*Ai! Ai! Ai!* He has seen the *bwiti*, the great *bwiti*, the all-powerful *bwiti*!" Then the boys had to stare straight into the sun, to discover the secrets of the other world which remains hidden to the uninitiated and which is where the spirits of the forefathers live. The ceremony would end with dancing, and with a song about a dead man, meaning the ignorant, the uninitiated. 'It is the dead man we are going to bury. We think he walks too slowly; we want him to pick up his pace, for the sun is sinking and it won't be long before it disappears behind the horizon.'

The *bwiti* was laden with symbolism; it contained all the elements of the jungle people's former religion. But unfortunately, these days the secret society was more interested in power than in the knowledge of spirit and matter; its meetings were devoted almost entirely to discussions of who would get which job, and nepotism, vested interests and financial transactions overshadowed the cult of the ancestors.

"The *ndjèmbè* has remained much purer."

And Ibinga, suddenly glowing with self-confidence, told me about the *ndjèmbè*.

In that female counterpart to the *bwiti*, not power but love in all its manifestations is the central issue. During the *ndjèmbè* ceremonies, a circle of naked women perform a lascivious dance around a fish, an electric catfish, which symbolizes the foetus. In rousing chorus they sing of the genitals of both men and women, to familiarize the almost fully grown maidens with those parts of the human anatomy. During the initiation rites associated with the *ndjèmbè*, the older women spread their buttocks and roll on the ground, to give the girls a good view of both anus and vagina. At the ceremonial climax the girls must kneel down before the 'mothers', place their heads between the women's thighs and lick, while the mothers call out: "Eat the poison! Eat the poison!" That's how it used to go in the jungle, and that's the way it still goes today; the *ndjèmbè* is much more popular than the *bwiti* and, just like centuries ago, the man who catches even a glimpse of the forest ceremonies will be poisoned, by his own wife if need be. Outboard motors, airplanes, oil refineries, apartment buildings – none of these things have been able to snuff out the jungle cults, which Ibinga said "are much more in evidence today than they were ten or twenty years ago."

That night was the first time she brought up her own private history. With no visible sign of emotion, she set about analyzing why she had been disowned: her father's outrage, her mother's panic, the abandoning of the twins and her foster mother's fear.

"For the Fang, twins are a sign of iniquity. It's even a part of our creation myth. In the beginning was the omnipotent creator, Mebere, who gave life to Nzame, who in turn lost his power by committing incest with his sister Oyémé-Nam. The twins born of this illicit union were the ancestors of the various tribes, black and white . . ."

She hadn't been able to find out much more, other than that the northern tribes always kill twins, and often the mother as well.

Wasn't this a painful thing for her to think about?

"My ancestors were tough, maybe that's the main thing they passed on to me."

She got up to go, but before leaving she asked me to do her a favor.

"Don't tell Massandé that I talked to you about the *bwiti*. It would hurt his pride, he'd be upset."

I promised, then asked one last question of my own.

"Do you belong to a *ndjèmbè*?"

"No," she laughed. "That's why I know nothing about love."

The Fang used to make a mask called the *ngontang*. A mask with four faces, each with a different shape and expression but also closely related: a father and mother, a son and daughter, or the symbols for life and suffering, birth and death. The mask was rotated during the dance, and the faces would flash by.

Ibinga was like a *ngontang*. She had been afraid to look me straight in the eye for days, then without inhibition had provided me with the prurient details of rousing sexual rites; she had not spoken without being spoken to, then she had spontaneously told me all about her childhood. She had been shy, angry, compliant, and as if that weren't confusing enough already, the next morning she added a fourth face to the series.

I had dozed off briefly just before sunrise, and was wakened by voices. I jumped up from my mat, squashed a cockroach with my foot, went outside and found Massandé and Ibinga down by the river, holding hands. Ibinga smiled, a bit anxiously it seemed to me, and I smiled back. At that very moment I heard the call of the rainbird – a mournful cry.

Two young boys took me out in their dugout. Paddling with slow and even strokes along the steaming banks, they hummed a tune that was as monotonous as the lowering gray sky, as melancholy as the litany with which the rainbird announced the approaching downpour. There was a rumbling in the distance, the wind picked up and the boys decided to return to the village. As we were pulling the canoe up onto the shore, the rain came clattering down.

Massandé and Ibinga had disappeared. Soaked to the skin, I walked past the huts. Nowhere did I hear their cries of love.

The women in the biggest hut were pounding manioc roots.

"How's it going, brother?"

"Come in and eat something, brother, you look hungry."

They gave me a mango and went on pounding. There's rhythm in everything along the Ogooué, the pounding of manioc, the steady strokes of the paddles, the songs sung at weddings or funerals, all of life, gray and lonely as it is.

Around midday, Ibinga came walking across the circular field that surrounded the tallest and oldest tree in the village, her shoulders hunched. She went into her hut and emerged with her baggage. Lugging her plastic suitcase, which gleamed the way cars or apartment buildings gleam, she came over to me. She said a motor launch would be coming any minute, and that it would be a good idea for me to get my things together if we didn't want to miss the boat.

"And what about Massandé?"

"I have an appointment in Port-Gentil, remember?"

The launch arrived moments later.

Could I really leave without saying goodbye to Massandé? He had not only been friendly and helpful, but also as honest as the day was long; he'd handed me back half of the two hundred francs I'd given him for the trip in the dugout, the gas, the food, the lodgings. I at least owed him a handshake.

The boatman signalled that he was ready to go.

"Time's up," Ibinga said.

"He'll wait if I promise him a tip."

She tossed me a withering glance and said: "Oh, men."

We climbed aboard. Before we had even found a seat, the village had disappeared behind a bend in the river.

"We're in luck," Ibinga said. "It could have taken days for a boat to come along. This launch only runs twice a week."

The sound of children crying could be heard coming from the forecastle. The covered section amidships provided shelter for a cluster of about twenty passengers; we were sitting on the rear deck between barrels of gasoline, and the rain was beating down.

Ibinga unrolled her bandanna and held it over our heads like a canopy. She was leaning against me, so I asked her quietly: "You're not mad at him, are you?"

"That's not the kind of question you ask, brother, that's nobody's business."

"But you did think he was nice."

"That's not for you to say, those kinds of things are better left unsaid."

"My lips are sealed."

"Your lips are sealed, and you're not going to mention his name again."

"Poor kid."

"And you don't call him a poor kid, either. All you say is 'Poor, poor Ibinga,' otherwise you keep your mouth shut."

The four outboards roared.

The only beacons the helmsman had were islands shining dimly through the veil of rain. He was seated high above the passengers on a swivel chair that seemed to serve no function; he never turned around, not even when signalling to the bosun. After every new stretch of water he had to choose once again from the river's myriad branches, which were barely visible to anyone else. He kept an eye on the long ripples that indicated current: where there is current, there is depth. The boat zigzagged across the water, dodging invisible sandbanks, sometimes crossing at right angles to the stream.

It took hours before the launch moored at the next village. Ten huts. The fishermen there lived as they had a hundred years ago, in dirt and scarcity. The young women had all been sent away; only the grandmothers – toothless old women, bent, skinny to the point of emaciation – were allowed to remain. The village chief, who still walked around in a loincloth, began scolding the helmsman: "You almost never stop here, how are we supposed to earn a living?"

Civilization had brought this place beer and paper money, and nothing else. The river? Eternal darkness. Even during the hottest hours of the day, the sun seems to have just set. Occasionally a bolt of lightning flashes across a mop-gray sky that never clears, not even after a thunderstorm. The gods cannot be well disposed under skies like these, simply because nature itself forgoes all friendliness. It was here, or ten kilometers downstream, or twenty kilometers upstream, that du Chaillu had to stand and watch as three women were beheaded. The way he wrote about it was heartrending.

As this stubborn stream reaches its end, all thoughts turn to doom. Nothing glistens, nothing shines; the heat presses down and you become heavy in spirit, heavy-headed, heavy in body and soul.

The launch passed tall, bare, white trunks.

"Mangrove skeletons," Ibinga said.

The river stank.

'Unvarying in color, unvarying in form, unvarying in height', Mary Kingsley wrote of the mangroves.

And her views on man?

'A potential fossil.'

A ghostly silence hangs in the mangrove swamp during the dry season; during the rainy season, the catfish shoot out of the water, thunder crackles, the trees creak, thousands of crabs scratch their carapaces against the trunks and crocodiles sigh, making a sound like a never-ending '*boo*'. No one lives here, there is no unhealthier place on earth.

White poles and brown water, murky as coffee grounds, 'tea-colored' the British called it. A mass grave under water. Birds go out of their way to fly around these swamps; only the gray parrot screeches on unperturbed.

Sludge dripped from the wicker-like bushes as we drew near the coast. The channels narrowed into rivulets. The launch headed north, then veered back south shortly afterwards, twisting like a snake through the last few kilometers of delta where land was now no longer land, water no longer water.

We could feel the sea before we saw it. The slight rocking woke Ibinga from her afternoon nap. She sniffed the air and said: "We've left the forest." The fetid smell of decomposition mingled with the salty breeze. Through a narrow opening in a long stretch of peninsula, the boat moved out onto the Bay of Cap Lopez. The water glistened like silver in the last rays of the sun. I couldn't see a thing without squinting, and only then did I fully realize just how dark the jungle had been.

The lumberjacks called Port-Gentil 'Le Petit St Tropez'. Three months in the port city and they would blow the one million francs it had taken them three years to earn in the jungle. Some of them became millionaires eight times over, and died in the poorhouse. The rarefied air of Port-Gentil made them frisky; the proprietress of Le Wharf used to serve a hundred bottles of champagne in a single evening.

'A hick town', according to Georges Simenon, but then he was from Paris. For those who came there straight from the backwoods, Port-Gentil was St Tropez.

The town still has a bit of that feel to it.

Flashy blondes sip lazily at long drinks on the swimming-pool patios while black nannies watch over their children, and in Le Wharf it seems as if the locals will at any moment raise their voices in a chorus of '*Non, je ne regrette rien*'. The chalets along the seaside boulevard are hidden behind spicebushes and showy pilocarpus. The church is called the Cathedral of St Louis, and eight dragons gape from its spire. Despite the oil platforms off the coast, the refinery at the northernmost tip of the narrow spit of land, the hospital that looks like a grain silo and the bunker-like presidential palace, history simply refuses to start a new chapter around here, and the wind sometimes even catches its pages and blows them back a decade or two. Port-Gentil is like its own red-and-white striped lighthouse: largely obscured behind giant palm trees but there all the same, revealed only when the wind picks up and parts the crowns of the coconut palms.

We checked into Le Méridien, directly across from the timber docks.

Ibinga went to her room to change, and when she came back down to the lounge in a white dress, I felt a twinge of regret; her *pagne* had made her look more girlish. She was bent on eating in an Asian restaurant; except for the staff, she was the only non-white in there. The Dutch sitting at the table behind me talked about aphrodisiac plants and about their employer, Royal Dutch Shell. I was almost home, but though I'd longed for this moment last night in my hut, now I constantly kept reminding Ibinga of the river.

As we walked back along the seaside boulevard to our hotel, she slipped her arm through mine. She liked walking down the street on someone's arm, it was a sign of being close, but I shouldn't read any more into it than that. Was I mistaken, or did I detect a touch of regret in her voice? Most of our journey was behind us now, and maybe that's what she meant later when she said: "There's still so much left to tell."

"Such as?"

"Such as how the Fang told each other for centuries that reaching the sea would only make them unhappy."

"And did their prediction come true?"

"Unfortunately, yes. Once the Fang settled down on the coast they became as sterile as most of the other tribes. When they reached the sea, their numbers dwindled."

The next morning, with a newspaper clipping in my pocket, I went off looking for a French priest.

In 1986, the journalist Patrick Sery had investigated a series of morbid rumors making the rounds in the cities on the Gabonese coast. Necrophagy. Cannibalism. Poisonings. Ritual murders. He quoted a magistrate who told him that during a routine traffic inspection, the body of a ten-year-old boy had been found in the trunk of a cabinet minister's Mercedes. The boy had been ritually beheaded. The investigation was finally abandoned, following orders from on high.

A priest, who wished to remain nameless, had told Sery: "I've seen mutilated corpses in Port-Gentil. Mostly women, adolescent girls, children, babies. Liver, heart, clitoris, brains cut out.

271

They're all organs people use as talismans against the evil eye. Dried or salted, they're made into potions that give people strength and power, that make sterile women fertile . . ."

I spoke to a clergyman at the Cathedral of St Louis.

He said: "It would be better for you not to poke your nose into these things. The journalist you're talking about was deported after a few days."

Ibinga didn't seem at all surprised when I told her about it that evening. "These days the city is more occult than the jungle," she said with uncharacteristic firmness. "We met a boy on the river, as you may recall. Do you remember him saying something about the inside and the outside? Well, that equilibrium doesn't exist anymore. Gabon has turned itself inside-out."

It all started about ten years ago with the woman in the black Mercedes. She would be waiting at the curb when school let out at the end of the day. Children vanished. The country's only daily newspaper reported on it extensively for a few weeks, which made the abrupt silence that followed even more suspect. Soon after, the grapevine began carrying news of another woman. Was she black or white? The eyewitnesses could never agree on it. She limited her hunting to the poor neighborhoods of the capital. Whenever she knocked on the door of a hut and asked for a sip of water or some salt, the youngest child in the family would die a few hours later. The daily *L'Union* ran spasmodic reports on the case as well. Concerned parents organized a night watch and sent their children to school with palm fronds tied to their wrists, the tried-and-true remedy against the evil eye.

The Gabonese constitution forbids sorcery. The national anthem contains a stanza condemning superstition. On the outside, post-independence Gabon strives for a rational society, but the authorities have never been able to clear themselves of all suspicion of sinister practices. Who rides in black Mercedes? Cabinet ministers, or their wives.

The country's first president faced particularly serious charges. As a young civil servant in 1933, Léon M'Ba became involved in a scandal. A lively trade in human flesh was uncovered in Libreville and the colonial magistrates ruled that M'Ba was an accessory after the fact. He was banished to the Oubangui-Chari region, and allowed to return to Gabon only in 1946. His official biography claims that he was charged with tax evasion before the war.

M'Ba was a regular participant in *bwiti* ceremonies. His successor demands that his newly appointed ministers join a secret Batéké society. No one knows exactly what transpires within the society, or what rituals the officials must undergo. To avoid all semblance of complicity, and to quash the persistent rumors about black Mercedes, the government opposes occult practices. A Gabonese man was recently found guilty of six ritual murders; his trial received a great deal of attention on radio and TV. Meanwhile, the black market continues to trade in talismans made from human organs.

"It's because of sterility," Ibinga said. "Four out of every ten Gabonese couples remain childless. We have the whites to thank for that; their ideal of free trade disrupted the balance between the tribes. Tribal boundaries collapsed, and morals along with them. People who live in isolation for centuries are as fragile as butterflies. Alcohol undermined their immune systems, so venereal disease – another present from the whites – could take on epidemic proportions. Now we're stuck with the consequences. Sterility is endemic to parts of Central Africa, but nowhere

273

is it as common as in Gabon. Medical science is powerless to help, so people revert to old methods. That's the tangible reason, anyway. But in a more general sense, what's behind it is an identity crisis. Who are we? Africans or black Frenchmen? Our world view has been mutilated. By the colonials, by the priests, and, last of all, by ourselves."

It was in the 1940s that the Mademoiselle sect arose and began spreading its destruction. Its thousands of members believed that they could only combat the white man effectively by adopting certain elements of Western culture. They opposed sorcery, forbade participation in the *bwiti* and burned those masks and statues not yet destroyed on the orders of priests and missionaries. To underscore the depravity of the old rituals, the Mademoiselle camouflaged some of its terrorist acts as attacks by the once notorious 'leopard people', drugged slaves who used iron hooks or the claws of animals to kill their masters' rivals by inflicting mortal wounds to the neck. Characterised by self-hatred, religious extremism and nationalism, the crusade of the Mademoiselle put a definitive end to the jungle religions. The movement fell apart after independence and Gabon became as Christian as a Baptist conference ground. At least, on the outside.

'They remayne a veritable Race of Canibals', Dierick Ruiters complained in *Toortse der Zee-vaert*.

Having reached a cruising speed of seventy kilometers an hour, we made the crossing to Libreville. The hovercraft bumped and rattled like a train. From Port-Gentil, Libreville can only be reached by travelling by air or across water; there are no roads between the two cities. The old ferry boats have been replaced by hovercraft furnished like jumbo jets; black girls punch your ticket, the rest of the crew is Swedish.

Drilling platforms shot by. The ash-gray vapors above the coastline made it look as if the mangroves on the horizon were on fire.

In the early seventeenth century, Dierick Ruiters of Zeeland sailed into the Gulf of Guinea.

'These peoples', he wrote when he was back home, 'in making offers to the Devil and adoring the newe Moone, make such an unsavory rowe when inclyned to sacrifice, as would make a Christian's haires stand aright from the haueling of their dogs, as I hearde when we layd off their Shoares'.

Ibinga was watching *Jaws IV*. She had gone to sit with the other women in the front row. They screamed, grabbed each other's arms, fell off their chairs and covered their eyes. It was the right film to watch at sea, and whenever the monster appeared, the women would go into a trance.

The boat rounded Pointe Pongara (popularly known as Pointe Denis) and turned into the Gabon Estuary, tearing past the deserted beaches. The lighthouse and the short, deep green grass that surrounded it reminded me of Ireland. The apartment buildings of Libreville were coming up fast.

As we were going ashore, Ibinga said: "And that crippled boy wanted me to stay in his village!"

I found the city more impressive than when I'd left. Ibinga said that was because I had learned to see things like a Gabonese, from a bush perspective. When you arrive in Libreville fresh from the interior, it looks like a metropolis.

I saw Ibinga four or five times after that. We would go out for dinner with her friends at inexpensive little restaurants in working-class neighborhoods. She always introduced me as *mon frère blanc*, and the evening I told her the date of my departure she laughed and said: "So before long I'll be without a family again."

Ibinga's friends wore shirts with gold cufflinks, but as soon as they'd had a few beers they rolled up their sleeves; they all knew each other from university. Later in the evening we would usually go to a disco, because music and talking went together. Their analyses of the economic crisis and the political climate displayed the irony typical of students; the conversation only heated up when someone started talking about the latest occult scandal. When other subjects came up, tribal differences never played a role, but with the introduction of this topic they would suddenly start shouting about 'We Fang' or 'We Adouma'. All Ibinga's friends listened to a radio show on Afrique 1, where listeners could call in and talk about their own experiences with magic, and they told me not to bother going into offices or stores during the eleven o' clock broadcast; public life pretty much came to a standstill.

The Sunday before I left Gabon, Ibinga took me to a church service. She stepped out of the taxi in front of my hotel early that morning all dressed in white. She suggested that we go to the Evangelical Church; after all, my father had been a minister. Calling myself an unbeliever was something she could only see as a joke that had gotten out of hand: "You believe what your father believes."

A tepid wind was blowing and we decided to walk to church.

My hotel was in the Glass district, not far from where the dipsomaniacal King Glass had welcomed the English to Gabon. We passed the Hatton and Cookson warehouse, and even though that company currently deals in electrical equipment and televisions rather than ivory, tobacco, gunpowder and brandy, I found it just as strange as seeing a modern department store in Jakarta with a 'Dutch East India Company' sign above the door. When we walked past a bakery a bit later and I smelled the aroma of warm croissants, I knew for a fact that Gabon couldn't quite relinquish its colonial past.

We had to elbow our way into the church. It was as hot as an oven inside – members of the congregation kept fainting and being carried off. As soon as they came to in the shade of the mango tree, they would press a handkerchief soaked in eau de cologne to their noses and head back to their pews, eager to receive the good news once again. They were dressed as if for a wedding, the men in three-piece suits and the women in clouds of lace. They sang at the tops of their lungs, prayed with all their might and clapped their hands, while the preacher, with his lips up close to the microphone like an old-time performer, fanned his congregation's fire by calling out questions that required an answer.

He held no truck with the view that 'the old people' had denied the existence of a Supreme Being.

"Didn't one tribe call him *the Father Above*?"

"Oh yes, they did!"

"And didn't another tribe speak of *the Creator of Mankind*?"

"Oh, yea!"

But once, long ago, they had found that God too powerful and unapproachable to mention his name, and they had worshiped only the mediators between him and mankind, the ancestral spirits and deities, the god of the river, the god of rain, the god of the wind.

"But now we have seen the Light."

"The Light!"

"And now we are no longer afraid to turn directly to that God."

"Hosanna!"

The songs of the M'Pongwe, which were all in a minor key, were sung in six-part harmony; the rhythm seemed to have come from oarsmen, who bend down deep while struggling against the current and then pause for a moment when they straighten their backs. The last song began low and ended deliriously high; the final line spoke of wandering with no end in sight, with nothing but toil and slavery on the horizon:

"Heaven is our destination, oh yes, heaven is our destination."

Ibinga asked me what I'd heard in that song. I said: "A farewell." And for once I was right. A farewell to the jungle. Farewell to the primeval. Farewell to a civilization that had been forced to make way for another. Where was the justice in that?

The next day we took a taxi to the airport. The sun was hanging low in the sky above the estuary, and Ibinga told me that, in the *mvett*, the sun was called 'the face of the heavens'. Staring out of the window and without raising her voice, almost in a whisper, she began reciting:

> *The face of the heavens shines,*
> *The face of the heavens shines for all.*

Too bad some people are blind,
Blind people can't see the heavens' light.
Is life just?
Yes.
Is life just?
No!
Let us sing:
Yes and No!
Let us sing:
Yes and No!

We shook hands on the square in front of the airport. She wished me a safe journey, turned around and, just like in Massandé's village, with her shoulders hunched, she walked away.

SOURCES

Alexander, Caroline, *One Dry Season: In the Footsteps of Mary Kingsley*, London, 1990.

Arnaut, Robert, *Sur les traces de Stanley et Brazza*, Paris, 1989.

Balandier, Georges, *Afrique ambigüe*, Paris, 1957.

Balandier, Georges, *Sociologie actuelle de l'Afrique noire*, Paris, 1963.

Berman, Edgar, *In Africa with Schweitzer*, New York, 1986.

Bongo, El Hadj Omar, *Il était une fois . . . El Hadj Omar Bongo*, Paris, 1988.

Bosman, Willem, *Nauwkeurige beschryving van de Guinese Goud-, Tand- en Slavekust*, Utrecht, 1704.

Bouët-Willaumez, Edouard, *Commerce et traite des Noirs aux côtes occidentales d'Afrique*, Paris, 1848.

Bowdich, Thomas E., *Mission from Cape Coast Castle to Ashantee*, London, 1819.

Brazza, Pierre Savorgnan de, *Conférences et Lettres*, Paris, 1887.

Brazza, Pierre Savorgnan de, *Trois explorations dans l'Ouest Africain*, texte coordonné etc. par Nap. Ney, Paris, 1887.

Brazza, Pierre Savorgnan de, 'Voyages dans l'Ouest Africain', *Le Tour du Monde*, parts LIV and LVI, Paris, 1887, 1888.

Bresler, Fenton, *The Mystery of Georges Simenon: A Biography*, London, 1983.

Brisset, Claire, 'Le Gabon, une île du sous-peuplement', *Le Monde*, Paris, 2 April 1984.

Broc, Numa, 'Dictionnaire illustré des explorateurs et grands voyageurs français du XIXe siècle', Part I, *Afrique*, Paris, 1988.

Brodie, Fawn M., *The Devil Drives: A Life of Sir Richard Burton*, London, 1967.

Broecke, Pieter van den, *Korte historiael ende Journaelsche Aenteyckeninghe, van al 't gheen merck-waerdigh voorgevallen is, in de langhduerighe reysen, soo nae Cabo Verde, Angola etc.*, Haarlem, 1634, modern edition by K. Ratelband, The Hague, 1950.

Brunschwig, Henri, *Brazza explorateur, l'Ogooué*, Paris, 1966.

Brunschwig, Henri, *Brazza explorateur, Les traités Makoko*, Paris, 1973.

Burton, Richard F., *Two Trips to Gorilla-Land and the Cataracts of the Congo*, 2 volumes, London, 1876.

Burton, Richard F., *Wanderings in West Africa*, London, 1863.

Burton, Richard F., *Wit and Wisdom from West Africa, or, A Book of Proverbial Philosophy, Idioms, Enigmas, and Laconisms*, London, 1865.

Campbell, Olwen, *Mary Kingsley: A Victorian in the Jungle*, London, 1957.

Céline, Louis-Ferdinand, *Voyage au bout de la nuit*, Paris, l932.

Chaillu, Paul B. du, *The Country of the Dwarfs*, London, 1871, republished, 1928.

Chaillu, Paul B. du, *Explorations and Adventures in Equatorial Africa*, London, 1861.

Chaillu, Paul B. du, *A Journey to Ashango-Land and Further Penetration into Equatorial Africa*, London, 1867.

Chaillu, Paul B. du, *The Land of the Midnight Sun*, 2 volumes, London, 1888.

Chaillu, Paul B. du, *Stories of the Gorilla Country*, London, 1868.

Chambrun, Général de, *Brazza*, Paris, 1930.

Chastenet, Patrick and Philippe, *Simenon, Album de famille*, Paris, 1989.

Chavannes, Charles de, *Avec Brazza, Souvenirs de la Mission de l'Ouest Africain*, Paris, 1935.

Chavannes, Charles de, *Le Congo français, Ma collaboration avec Brazza, Nos relations jusqu'à sa mort*, Paris, 1937.

Cohen-Solal, Annie, *Sartre, 1905-1980*, including a detailed portrait of the Schweitzer family, Paris, 1985.

Compiègne, Marquis de, *l'Afrique Équatoriale*, 2 volumes, Paris, 1885.

Conrad, Joseph, *Heart of Darkness*, London, 1899.

Coquery-Vidrovitch, Catherine, *Brazza et la prise de possession du Congo*, Paris, 1969.

Cornevin, Robert, *Littératures d'Afrique noire de langue française*, Paris, 1976.

Dapper, Olfert, *Naukeurige Beschrijvinge der Afrikaensche gewesten van Egypten, Barbaryen, Libyen, Biledulgerid, Negroslant, Guinea, Ethiopïen, Abyssinië . . . Getrokken uit verscheyde hedendaegse Lantbeschrijvers en geschriften van bereisde ondersoeckers dier Landen*, Amsterdam, 1668.

Darlington, Charles F. and Alice B., *African Betrayal*, New York, 1968.

Dedet, Christian, *La mémoire du fleuve, l'Afrique aventureuse de Jean Michonet*, Paris, 1984.

Deschamps, Hubert, *Quinze ans de Gabon, Les débuts de l'établissement français, 1839-1853*, Paris, 1965.

Deschamps, Hubert, *Traditions orales et archives du Gabon*, Paris, 1962.

Fanon, F., *Peau noire, masques blancs*, Paris, 1952.

Fernandez, James W., 'Principles of Opposition and Vitality in Fang Aesthetics', *The Journal of Aesthetics and Art Criticism*, XXV, 1966.

Forshaw, Joseph M., *Parrots of the World*, London, 1989.

Fossey, Dian, *Gorillas in the Mist*, Boston, 1983.

Gardinier, David E., *Historical Dictionary of Gabon*, London, 1981.

Gaulme, François, *Le Gabon et son ombre*, Paris, 1988.

Gide, André, *Voyage au Congo*, Paris, 1927.

Glynn, Rosemary, *Mary Kingsley in Africa*, London, 1956.

Goulphin, Fred, *Les veillées de chasse d'Henri Guizard*, Paris, 1987.

Griffith, Nancy Snell, *Albert Schweitzer: An International Bibliography*, Boston, 1981.

Haltenorth, T., and Diller, H., *Mammifères d'Afrique*, Neuchâtel, Paris, 1985.

Horn, Alfred Aloysius, *Trader Horn, The Ivory Coast in the earlies, Written at the age of seventy-three, with such of the author's Philosophy as is the gift of Age and Experience, taken down and here edited by Ethelreda Lewis*, New York, 1928.

Howard, C., and Plumb, J. H., *West African Explorers*, Oxford, 1951.

Jones, Adam, 'Olfert Dapper et sa description de l'Afrique', *Objets interdits*, Paris, 1989.

Jonge, J. K. J. de, *De oorsprong van Neerland's bezittingen op de kust van Guinea*, The Hague, 1871.

Kalck, Pierre, *Histoire centrafricaine des origines à nos jours*, 4 volumes, Lille, 1973.

Kalck, Pierre, *P. Crampel, le centrafricain*, Paris, 1968.

Kingsley, George, *Notes on Sport and Travel*, London, 1900.

Kingsley, Mary, *The Story of West Africa*, London, 1900.

Kingsley, Mary, *Travels in West Africa*, London, 1897, republished, London, 1965 and 1982.

Kingsley, Mary, *West African Studies*, London, 1899, republished, London, 1964.

Lasserre, Guy, *Libreville et sa région*, Paris, 1958.

Lenz, Oskar, *Wanderungen in Afrika*, Vienna, 1895.

Levi-Strauss, Claude, *La Pensée Sauvage*, Paris, 1962.

Lind, Emil, *Albert Schweitzer, Leven en werk*, with a foreword by Stefan Zweig, Naarden, 1949.

Linschoten, Jan Huygen van, *Itinerario, Voyage ofte schipvaert van . . . naer Oost ofte Portugaels Indien, 1579-1592*, third volume, including *Beschrjvinghe van de gantsche custe van Guinea, Manicongo, etc.*, Amsterdam, 1596, modern edition by C. B. Burger Jr and F. W. T. Hunger, The Hague, 1934.

Livingstone, David, *Missionary Travels*, London, 1857.

Malo, H., *A l'enseigne de 'la Petite Vache'*, Paris, 1946.

Marche, Alfred, *Trois voyages dans l'Afrique occidentale*, Paris, 1879.

Marees, Pieter de, *Beschryvinghe ende historische verhael van het Gout Koninckrijck van Gunea*, Amsterdam, 1602, modern edition by S. P. L'Honoré Naber, The Hague, 1912.

Martin, Claude, *Die Regenwälder Westafrikas, Oekologie, Bedrohung, Schutz*, Basel, 1989.

Martin, Phyllis M., 'Du Loango', *Objets interdits*, Paris, 1989.

M'Ba, Léon, 'Essai de droit coutumier pahouin', *Bulletin de la Société des Recherches Congolaises*, June 1938.

M'Bokolo, Elikia, *Noirs et Blancs en Afrique Equatoriale, Les sociétés côtières et la pénétration française*, Paris, 1981.

M'Bokolo, Elikia, *Le Roi Denis*, Dakar, 1976.

M'Bot, Jean-Emile, *Un siècle d'histoire du Gabon raconté par l'iconographie*, Libreville, 1984.

McLynn, Frank, *Stanley: The Making of an African Explorer*, London, 1989.

Myer, Valerie Grosvenor, *A Victorian Lady in Africa: The Story of Mary Kingsley*, Southampton, 1989.

Nassau, Robert Hamill, *My Ogowé*, New York, 1914.

N'Dong N'Doutoume, Tsira, *Le Mvett, épopée fang*, Paris, 1970.

Nebout, Albert, 'La mission Crampel', *Le Tour du Monde*, 2nd trimester, Paris, 1892.

Nederveen Pieterse, Jan, *Wit over Zwart*, Amsterdam, 1990.

Neuhoff, H. O., *Le Gabon*, Bonn-Bad Godeberg, 1970.

N'Guema-Obam, Paulin, *Aspects de la religion Fang, essai d'interprétation de la formule de bénédiction*, Paris, 1983.

Nguéma, Zwè, *Un mvet*, transcribed by H. Pepper, published by P. and P. de Wolf, Paris, 1975.

Oosterwijk, Bram, *Vlucht na victorie, Lodewijk Pincoffs*, Rotterdam, 1979.

Paludanus (Ten Broecke), *Beschryvinghe van de Gantsche Custe van Guinea, Manicongo, Angola, etc.*, Amsterdam, 1596, republished in part as appendix to *Beschryvinghe van Pieter de Marees*, The Hague, 1912.

Péan, Pierre, *Affaires africaines*, Paris, 1983.

Perrois, Louis, *Art ancestral du Gabon*, Geneva, 1985.

Perrois, Louis, *Arts du Gabon, les arts plastiques du Bassin d'Ogooué*, Arnouville, 1979.

Rabut, Elisabeth, *Brazza, commissaire général: le Congo français, 1886-1897*, Paris, 1989.

Raponda-Walker, André, *Notes d'Histoire du Gabon*, Brazzaville, 1960.

Raponda-Walker, André, and Reynard, R., 'Anglais, Espagnols et Nord-Américains au Gabon aux XIX siècle', *Bulletin de l'Institut d'Etudes centrafricaines*, 1956.

Raponda-Walker, André, and Sillans, Roger, *Plantes utiles et inutiles du Gabon*, Paris, 1960.

Raponda-Walker, André, and Sillans, Roger, *Rites et croyances des peuples du Gabon*, Paris, 1962.

Ratanga-Atoz, Anges, *Histoire du Gabon*, Paris, 1985.

Ratelband, K., 'West-Afrika', *Nederland in de Vijf Werelddeelen*, Leiden, 1947.

Rémy, Mylène, *Le Gabon aujourd'hui*, Paris, 1987.

Ruiters, Dierick, *Toortse der Zee-vaert*, Amsterdam, 1623, modern edition by S. P. L'Honoré Naber, The Hague, 1913.

Schnapper, Bernard, *La politique et le commerce français dans le Golfe de Guinée de 1838 à 1871*, Paris, 1961.

Schweitzer, Albert, *Aan den zoom van het oerwoud*, Haarlem, 1928.

Schweitzer, Albert, *Bouwen in het oerwoud*, Haarlem, 1928.

Schweitzer, Albert, *From My African Notebook*, London, 1938.

Schweitzer, Albert, *Gesammelte Werke*, Munich, 1973.

Schweitzer, Albert, *Lambarene*, Haarlem, 1953.

Schweitzer, Albert, *Ma vie, ma pensée*, Paris, 1960.

Seaver, George, *David Livingstone, His Life and Letters*, London, 1957.

Serle, William, and Morel, Gérard J., *Les oiseaux de l'Ouest africain*, Neuchâtel, Paris, 1988.

Serval, Paul, 'Reconnaissance des routes qui mènent du Rhamboé à l'Ogowai', *Revue maritime et coloniale*, Paris 1863.

Sery, Patrick, 'Le noeud de vipères du Gabon', *l'Evénement du jeudi*, Paris, 17 April 1986.

Shoumatoff, Alex, *African Madness*, New York, 1988.

Simenon, Georges, *Le coup de lune*, Paris, 1933, republished, Paris, 1975.

Simenon, Georges, 'L'Heure du nègre', six reportages in the illustrated weekly *Voilà*, 1932, included in the collected reportages of Simenon found in *A la recherche de l'homme nu*, Paris, 1976.

Simenon, Georges, *Mémoires intimes*, Paris, 1981.

Sommer, Volker, *Die Affen*, Hamburg, 1989.

Stanley, Henry Morton, *Autobiography*, London, 1912.

Stanley, Henry Morton, *How I Found Livingstone*, New York, 1887.

Stanley, Henry Morton, *Stanley's Reizen, ontdekkingen en lotgevallen in Midden-Afrika*, 2 parts, 3 volumes, Amsterdam, 1886.

Stanley, Henry Morton, *Through the Dark Continent*, 2 volumes, London, 1878.

Stevenson, Catherine Barnes, *Victorian Women Travel Writers in Africa*, Boston, 1982.

Stoppelaar, J. H. de, *Balthasar de Moucheron*, The Hague, 1901.

Tessmann, G., *Die Pangwe*, 2 volumes, Berlin, 1913.

Trilles, R. P. H., *Les Pygmées dans la forêt équatoriale*, Paris, 1932.

Unger, W. S., *De oudste reizen van de Zeeuwen naar Oost-Indië*, The Hague, 1932.

Uzès, Duchesse d', *Le voyage de mon fils au Congo*, Paris, 1894.

Vassal, Joseph, 'La vie de François Rigail de Lastours', *La Géographie*, Paris, December 1931.

Vaucaire, Michel, *Paul du Chaillu*, New York, 1930.

Veistroffer, A., *Vingt ans dans la brousse, Souvenirs d'un ancien membre de la mission Savorgnan de Brazza dans l'Ouest africain*, Lille, 1931.

Viel, Hugues, 'Un chemin de fer pour le XXIe siècle', *Jeune Afrique*, Paris, 14 January 1987.

Vitoux, Frédéric, *Céline*, Paris, 1978.

Wassermann, Jakob, *Boela Matari, Het leven van Henry Morton Stanley*, Amsterdam, 1953.

Weinstein, Brian, *Gabon: Nation-Building on the Ogooué*, Massachusetts, 1966.

West, Richard, *Brazza of the Congo: European Exploration and Exploitation in French Equatorial Africa*, London, 1972.

Wilson, J. L., *Western Africa: Its History, Condition and Prospects*, London, 1856.

Yerkes, Robert and Ada, *The Great Apes*, Boston, 1929.

Zorzi, Elio, *Al Congo con Brazzà*, including the letters and diaries of Attalio Pecile, Rome, 1940.

LONELY PLANET JOURNEYS

JOURNEYS is a unique collection of travel writing – published by the company that understands travel better than anyone else.

It is a series for anyone who has ever experienced – or dreamed of – the magical moment when they encountered a strange culture or saw a place for the first time. They are tales to read while you're planning a trip, while you're on the road or while you're in an armchair, in front of a fire.

Lonely Planet guidebooks have always gone beyond providing simple nuts-and-bolts information, so it is a short step to JOURNEYS, a new series of outstanding titles that explore our planet through the eyes of a fascinating and diverse group of international travellers.

JOURNEYS books catch the spirit of a place, illuminate a culture, recount a crazy adventure, or introduce a fascinating way of life. They always entertain, and always enrich the experience of travel.

FULL CIRCLE

A South American Journey

Luis Sepúlveda (translated by Chris Andrews)

'A journey without a fixed itinerary' in the company of Chilean writer Luis Sepúlveda. Extravagant characters and extraordinary situations are memorably evoked: gauchos organising a tournament of lies, a scheming heiress on the lookout for a husband, a pilot with a corpse on board his plane . . . Part autobiography, part travel memoir, *Full Circle* brings us the distinctive voice of one of South America's most compelling writers.

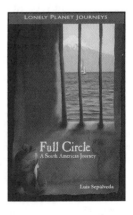

WINNER 1996 Astrolabe – Etonnants Voyageurs award for the best work of travel literature published in France.

THE GATES OF DAMASCUS
Lieve Joris (translated by Sam Garrett)

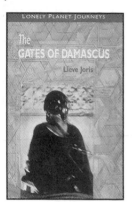

This best-selling book is a beautifully drawn portrait of day-to-day life in modern Syria. Through her intimate contact with local people, Lieve Joris draws us into the fascinating world that lies behind the gates of Damascus. Hala's husband is a political prisoner, jailed for his opposition to the Assad regime; through the author's friendship with Hala we see how Syrian politics impacts on the lives of ordinary people.

Written after the Gulf War, *The Gates of Damascus* offers a unique insight into the complexities of the Arab world.

IN RAJASTHAN
Royina Grewal

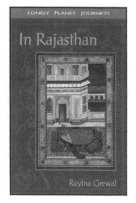

As she writes of her travels through Rajasthan, Indian writer Royina Grewal takes us behind the exotic facade of this fabled destination: here is an insider's perceptive account of India's most colourful state. *In Rajasthan* discusses folk music and architecture, feudal traditions and regional cuisine . . . Most of all, it focuses on people – from maharajas to camel trainers, from politicians to itinerant snake charmers – to convey the excitement and challenges of a region in transition.

ISLANDS IN THE CLOUDS
Travels in the Highlands of New Guinea
Isabella Tree

This is the fascinating account of a journey to the remote and beautiful Highlands of Papua New Guinea and Irian Jaya: one of the most extraordinary and dangerous regions on the planet. The author travels with a PNG Highlander who introduces her to his intriguing and complex world, which is changing rapidly as it collides with twentieth-century technology and the island's developing social and political systems. *Islands in the Clouds* is a thoughtful, moving book, full of insights into a region that is rarely noticed by the rest of the world.

KINGDOM OF THE FILM STARS
Journey into Jordan
Annie Caulfield

Kingdom of the Film Stars is a travel book and a love story. With honesty and humour, Annie Caulfield writes of travelling in Jordan and falling in love with a Bedouin with film-star looks.

The author offers fascinating insights into the country – from the tent life of traditional women to the hustle of downtown Amman. *Kingdom of the Film Stars* unpicks tight-woven Western myths about the Arab world, presenting cultural and political issues within the intimate framework of a compelling love story.

LOST JAPAN
Alex Kerr

Lost Japan draws on the author's personal experiences of Japan over thirty years. Alex Kerr takes his readers on a backstage tour, exploring different facets of his involvement with the country: friendships with Kabuki actors, buying and selling art, studying calligraphy, exploring rarely visited temples and shrines . . .

The Japanese edition of this book was awarded the 1994 Shincho Gakugei Literature Prize for the best work of non-fiction: the first time a foreigner has won this prestigious award.

SEAN & DAVID'S LONG DRIVE
Sean Condon

Sean and David are young townies who have rarely strayed beyond city limits. One day, for no good reason, they set out to discover their homeland, and what follows is a wildly entertaining adventure that covers half of Australia. Highlights include the weekly Hair Wax Report and a Croc-Spotting with Stew adventure.

Sean Condon has written a hilarious, offbeat road book that mixes sharp insights with deadpan humour and outright lies.

SHOPPING FOR BUDDHAS

Jeff Greenwald

Here in this distant, exotic land, we were compelled to raise the art of shopping to an experience that was, on the one hand, almost Zen – and, on the other hand, tinged with desperation like shopping at Macy's or Bloomingdale's during a one-day-only White Sale.

Shopping for Buddhas is Jeff Greenwald's story of his obsessive search for the perfect Buddha statue. In the backstreets of Kathmandu, he discovers more than he bargained for ... and his souvenir-hunting turns into an ironic metaphor for the clash between spiritual riches and material greed. Politics, religion and serious shopping collide in this witty account of an enlightening visit to Nepal.

SONGS TO AN AFRICAN SUNSET

A Zimbabwean Story

Sekai Nzenza-Shand

Songs to an African Sunset braids vividly personal stories into an intimate picture of contemporary Zimbabwe. Returning to her family's village after many years in the West, Sekai Nzenza-Shand discovers a world where ancestor worship, polygamy and witchcraft still govern the rhythms of daily life – and where drought, deforestation and AIDS have wrought devastating changes. With insight and affection, she explores a culture torn between respect for the old ways and the irresistible pull of the new.

RELATED TITLES FROM LONELY PLANET

Africa on a shoestring
This all-time classic guide to travel on this fascinating continent is packed with essential information every traveller needs before embarking on a trip from Marrakesh to Cape Town.

Central Africa
Journeying to Central Africa, the least visited area of Africa, requires a great deal of organisation and a reliable guide book. This guide is packed with hard-to-get information for a safe and enjoyable visit.

East Africa
East Africa's diverse landscape, exotic wildlife and fascinating people make for an unforgettable experience. This guide book has all the details an independent traveller needs.

North Africa
This is the most extensive guide to the Maghreb – Morocco, Algeria, Tunisia and Libya – and it's full of reliable travel information for every budget.

West Africa
West Africa is the vibrant heart of traditional African art, music and culture. Explore it easily with this comprehensive guide book, essential for every independent traveller, no matter what the budget.

Also available
Phrasebooks: Arabic (Egyptian) phrasebook, Arabic (Moroccan) phrasebook, Ethiopian (Amharic) phrasebook, Swahili phrasebook

Travel atlases: Egypt travel atlas, Kenya travel atlas, Zimbabwe, Botswana & Namibia travel atlas